MEDICINE AND PUBLIC HEALTH AT THE END OF EMPIRE

HOWARD WAITZKIN

Paradigm Publishers
Boulder • London

To the memory of my parents, Ed and Dorothy Waitzkin, who disagreed with me about nearly everything and therefore helped me clarify what I really wanted to say, and of Edmundo Granda, inspirational leader of Latin American social medicine.

Published in the United States by Paradigm Publishers, 2845 Wilderness Place, Suite 200, Boulder, CO 80301 USA.

Paradigm Publishers is the trade name of Birkenkamp & Company, LLC, Dean Birkenkamp, President and Publisher.

Library of Congress Cataloging-in-Publication Data

Waitzkin, Howard.
  Medicine and public health at the end of empire / Howard Waitzkin.
    p. ; cm.
  Includes bibliographical references.
  ISBN 978-1-59451-950-5 (hc : alk. paper) — ISBN 978-1-59451-951-2 (pb : alk. paper)
  1. Social medicine. 2. Imperialism—Health aspects. 3. Public health—Political aspects. I. Title.
  [DNLM: 1. Public Health—history. 2. Public Health—trends. 3. Health Services Accessibility—history. 4. Health Services Accessibility—trends. 5. History, 20th Century. 6. History, 21st Century. WA 11.1]
  RA418.W345 2011
  362.1—dc22
                                                                    2010036757

Printed and bound in the United States of America on acid-free paper that meets the standards of the American National Standard for Permanence of Paper for Printed Library Materials.

Designed and Typeset by Straight Creek Bookmakers.

15 14 13 12 11   1 2 3 4 5

CONTENTS

Preface

My work for this book sprang from activism and research, as a medical doctor and social scientist, in international health. During my years working as a primary care practitioner with the clinic system of the United Farm Workers (UFW) Union in the 1970s, I gradually became aware that one does not need to travel outside the United States to find the "Third World." Instead, areas quite close to home manifest problems and challenges that resemble those of countries usually labeled as economically less developed.

At about the same time, I learned that advances in Latin American social medicine, originating in countries considered less developed than the United States, offered illuminating insights into our own "more developed" country. My discovery contradicted the underlying assumptions in my prior education that superior research and intellectual work took place mainly in the United States and similar economically advanced nations.

Specifically, I discovered Latin American social medicine shortly after the military coup d'état that, on September 11, 1973, ended Chile's three-year, democratically elected, socialist government (called *Unidad Popular,* or Popular Unity), led by President Salvador Allende, a physician and leader in social medicine. In the UFW, organizers and members quickly began to talk about the dictatorship that followed and especially the deaths and political repression that the dictatorship perpetrated. Although I had hoped to spend part of the following year in Chile, contributing to the advances in medicine and public health that were occurring under the Unidad Popular government, the coup intervened. So instead of going to work in Chile, I became active in the international solidarity movement that tried to assist Chilean health workers and other citizens whom the military dictatorship had tortured, imprisoned, or otherwise threatened. Later, the solidarity movement extended to Argentina, Brazil, Uruguay, and several other countries in South and Central America—all of which were ruled during that period by dictatorships supported by the U.S. government and partly funded by the tax dollars of U.S. citizens.

As part of this solidarity effort, I collaborated with a colleague, Hilary Modell, who had worked during the previous two years with the *Unidad Popular* government in a community-based health program. After the coup, Hilary had escaped in one of the last Red Cross evacuation planes to leave Chile. Because North American health professionals knew little about the efforts of the *Unidad Popular* or the repression that followed the coup, we decided to write an article to spread knowledge about the situation in Chile. A Chilean colleague also collaborated on the article but chose to remain anonymous, due to the danger that he feared if his identity were to become known to the dictatorship. Eventually we were able to publish an influential article in the *New England Journal of Medicine,* which received worldwide attention.[1] Although the article mobilized further solidarity work in the United States, Canada, and Western Europe, our writing also incensed members of the Chilean dictatorship, which officially condemned Hilary and me. As a result, neither of us could travel to Chile for many years.

While carrying out research for this article in the Stanford University library, I made an astonishing discovery. In the library's card catalog I found a reference to a book written by Allende in 1939: *La Realidad Medico-Social Chilena* (The Chilean Medico-Social Reality).[2] I obtained a copy from the library of the Hoover Institute at Stanford, whose collection the U.S. Central Intelligence Agency funded as a resource for counterinsurgency research. As the Hoover Institute acknowledged, the intended purpose of this collection was to provide information useful for suppressing revolutionary movements in Latin America, Africa, and Asia.

Reading Allende's book was a transformative experience, in which I began to appreciate the importance and relevance of Latin American social medicine. Allende, who trained as a pathologist, wrote the book as minister of health for a newly elected popular-front government. Supported by his team at the ministry, Allende presented an analysis of the relationships among social structure, disease, and suffering. *La Realidad* conceptualized illness as a disturbance of the individual fostered by deprived social conditions. Breaking new ground in Latin America at the time, Allende described the "living conditions of the working classes" that generated illness. Allende emphasized the social conditions of underdevelopment, international dependency, and the effects of foreign debt and the work process. In *La Realidad,* Allende focused on several specific health problems, including maternal and infant mortality, tuberculosis, sexually transmitted and other communicable diseases, emotional disturbances, and occupational illnesses. Describing issues that had not been studied previously, he analyzed illegal abortion, the responsiveness of tuberculosis to economic advances rather than treatment innovations, the role of housing density in the causation of infectious diseases, and differences between generic and brand-name pricing in the pharmaceutical industry.

Seeing the relevance of Allende's book to many issues that we were facing in the United States, I began a long-term effort to study Latin American social medicine. Eventually this effort involved visits to several countries in Latin America where social medicine groups were working actively. During 1994–1995, I spent nine months in Latin America, fortunately sponsored by fellowships from the U.S. Fulbright Program and the Fogarty International Center of the U.S. National Institutes of Health, to conduct a more in-depth study of the field. This project allowed lengthy visits with social medicine groups in Chile, Argentina, Uruguay, Brazil, Mexico, Ecuador, and Cuba. In addition to providing me with further reading, colleagues generously shared their time with me for in-depth interviews.

Every two years, with rare exceptions, I also have attended the congresses of the Latin American Association of Social Medicine (*Asociación Latinoamericana de Medicina Social*, ALAMES). These meetings have helped me to keep up with current developments in Latin American social medicine and to maintain long-lasting friendships with Latin American colleagues. ALAMES congresses have facilitated my ongoing efforts to understand the changes in health services and public health policies spearheaded by colleagues who recently, with the advent of progressive governments in various countries (especially Brazil, Ecuador, Argentina, Uruguay, Chile, Venezuela, and Bolivia), have risen to prominent positions in those countries' ministries of health.

* * *

Guided by collaborations with Latin American colleagues, I began to study more deeply the overt and subtle relationships between health and empire. The examples of committed scholarship that Allende and more recent leaders of Latin American social medicine provided inspired a series of investigations into how health services and public health have intertwined with empire building, historically and in the present. These studies led to a perspective that public health and health services contributed not only to historical imperialism but also to the "neo-imperialist" patterns seen during more recent years. As military conquest and colonialism transformed into the somewhat more subtle forms of economic exploitation and political coercion (the latter always reinforced by the threat of military intervention), public health and health services have contributed to the maintenance of empire in new and sometimes surprising ways.

Yet, alongside worldwide economic crisis, resistance to empire has consolidated worldwide. Especially in Latin America, regimes that previously complied with the dictates and corporate interests of the United States and Western Europe have grown weak and have largely disappeared. Replacing these colonies and neo-colonies, new governments emerging through electoral, democratic procedures have resisted the historical patterns of empire. These new regimes increasingly have refused to accept the historical patterns of empire that fostered exploitation and poverty around the world. National and local leaders have entered into novel coalitions that have transformed previous patterns of political and economic dominance. Coinciding with a critical weakening of the international capitalist system during recurrent financial crises, the emergence of these new governments and coalitions during the early years of the twenty-first century has changed the fundamental nature of empire.

U.S. capitalism has become something different, with the socialization of wide sectors of the economy under government ownership, more and more resembling the "mixed" economic systems of Europe. Capitalism has not exactly ended, but it has become a system riddled with contradictions that no longer can sustain previous patterns of international domination. Now that U.S. capitalism as we have known it has ended, and empire in its previous form has ended as well, we need to understand more fully the relationships between empire and health and how these relationships are transforming.

*   *   *

The book's three parts focus on the past (referring to the period until approximately 1980), the present (including the more recent past, from 1980 to 2010), and the future. In explaining the historical patterns that have linked empire and health, Part 1 presents an overall conceptual approach that guides the analyses that follow. This framework places medicine and public health in the broader social context of capitalism and imperialism and argues that the transformations that have occurred in medicine and public health during the past two centuries gain clarity when this political-economic context receives close attention. In Chapter 1 I consider the key role that philanthropic organizations promoting public health have played in empire, the economic considerations that motivated the formation of our principal international health organizations, and how international trade agreements have linked public health to the strengthening of empire. The illness-generating conditions of historical capitalism and imperialism form the focus of Chapter 2, which clarifies the emergence of social epidemiology with its emphasis on the social determinants of illness and suffering. Chapter 3 details the international market for health products and services and the role this market has played in strengthening the worldwide operations of multinational corporations. In Chapter 4 I analyze some of the early resistance to imperialist domination that occurred in Chile and Cuba and how that resistance implied a transformation of public health and health services.

Part 2 addresses the relationships between empire and health during the current period of history, operationally defined as beginning in about 1980 and continuing until approximately 2010. Initially, this part of the book focuses on the broad policies during recent history that have strengthened empire and have weakened public health and health services. Chapter 5 explains the impact of neoliberal political-economic policies on public-sector health and mental health services, the process of privatizing these services, the emergence of a transnational capitalist class linked to the penetration of international markets for health products and insurance by multinational corporations, the impact of economic globalization on the nation state, and the resulting loss of nations' sovereignty in managing public health. In Chapter 6 I extend this analysis to the specific impacts of international trade agreements in public health and medicine, including the effects of trade rules and their enforcement, as well as the responses by health professionals and advocates. Chapter 7 untangles the relationships between macroeconomic policies and health, especially policies based on the assumption that enhancing health will lead to enhanced economic development through private investment.

The following chapters in Part 2 focus on the roles of multinational corporations and international financial institutions, as well as the ideologies and constructions of reality that provide a rationale for the actions of key stakeholders. Chapter 8 examines multinational managed care organizations and their attempts to export their for-profit operations from the United States to other countries, including countries whose national health programs aim to ensure universal access to care. International financial institutions and their efforts to foster "reforms" that encourage reduction of public-sector services and privatization of programs receive attention in Chapter 9; Mexico and Brazil serve as case examples. In Chapter 10, I examine the ideological underpinnings that justify such reforms, under the rubric of a new "common sense" that socially constructs a rationale for erosion of public services and expansion of the private sector. Chapter 11 explores in more detail the differing social constructions of key stakeholders in current struggles linking global trade, public health, and health services: government agencies, international financial institutions, international health organizations, multinational corporations, and advocacy groups. Militarism and ideologies supporting military intervention, which reinforce empire through actual or threatened intervention in countries that do not readily accede to the goals of the politically powerful and economically dominant, compose the theme of Chapter 12; the impact of war on the health and mental health of military personnel, as well as the emergence of civilian services for military personnel that aim to foster peace and a reduction in militarism, emerges as a key focus.

In Part 3, I examine the apparent end of empire as we have known it and the changes in medicine and public health that are occurring as empire slowly dies. Chapter 13 describes the flowering of social medicine in Latin America and argues that the accomplishments and insights of this field provide an inspirational model for future intellectual work and praxis in medicine and public health. In Chapter 14, which concludes the book, I present examples of key struggles toward more humane medical and public health systems that illustrate the conditions of the predictable future; based on path-breaking efforts in El Salvador, Bolivia, Mexico City, and Venezuela, I describe the contours of sociomedical activism in the post-empire era.

* * *

On the material front, colleagues and I have benefited from grants that have partially supported this work, from the National Library of Medicine (1G08 LM06688), the New Century Scholars Program of the U.S. Fulbright Commission, the John Simon Guggenheim Memorial Foundation, the Roothbert Fund, the U.S. Agency for Healthcare Research and Quality (1R03 HS13251), the National Institute of Mental Health (1R03 MH067012 and 1 R25 MH60288), the United Nations Research Institute for Social Development, RESIST, the Research Allocations Committee at the University of New Mexico, and the Robert Wood Johnson Foundation Center for Health Policy at the University of New Mexico. The views expressed in this book of course do not necessarily represent those of the funding agencies.

I feel indebted to many people for providing collegial input and moral support at several key junctures. This note provides inadequate acknowledgment, and I take full responsibility for any errors and problems in the manuscript. Rebeca Jasso-Aguilar made critical contributions to this work through collaboration over many years; she is a co-author of chapters 5 and 14 and provided assistance for several other chapters as well. Sofía Borges, my highly esteemed daughter, offered expert editorial advice and contributed with sensitivity to the book's design at a reasonable price. Jean Ellis-Sankari, Hilary Modell, Felipe Cabello, Lori Wallach, Carolyn Mountain, and Ron Voorhees provided helpful suggestions at several key points. I am very grateful to colleagues, comrades, and friends in Latin America—Jaime Breih, Arturo Campaña, Kenneth Camargo Jr., Alfredo Estrada, Celia Iriart, Silvia Lamadrid, Cristina Laurell, Francisco Mercado, Emerson Merhy, Jaime Sepúlveda, Mario Testa, Carolina Tetelbaum, Adriana Vega, and particularly Edmundo Granda, to whose memory I have dedicated the book. They and many other colleagues working in Latin American social medicine offered inspiring examples of committed intellectual work, praxis, and personal strength under sometimes quite severe adversity and danger. I acknowledge some other key contributions of colleagues and friends within the notes of the chapters that follow. Dean Birkenkamp provided very helpful guidance in his roles of editor and publisher, as he has done also in prior projects.

PART ONE

EMPIRE PAST

CHAPTER 1

EMPIRE'S HISTORICAL HEALTH COMPONENT

Although it is a complex, multifaceted phenomenon, I define "empire" in simple terms as expansion of economic activities—especially investment, sales, extraction of raw materials, and use of labor to produce commodities and services—beyond national boundaries, as well as the social, political, and economic effects of this expansion. Empire achieved many advantages for economically dominant countries. During the 1500s, a "world system" emerged in which a core group of nations came to control a worldwide network of economic exchange relationships.[1] For centuries, empire included military conquest and the maintenance of colonies under direct political control. The decline of colonialism in the twentieth century led to the emergence of political and economic "neocolonialism," by which poorer countries provided similar advantages to richer countries as they had under the earlier, more formal versions of colonialism.

Public health and health services played important roles in several phases of empire past. The connections among empire, public health, and health services operated through specific institutions, including philanthropic foundations, international financial institutions, organizations enforcing trade agreements, and international health organizations. Now I turn to each of these institutions and focus mainly on their early histories. Later in the book, I consider their more recent operations.

Philanthropic Foundations

Although notions about beneficent contributions by wealthy people to the needy date back in Western civilization to the Greek practice of "philanthropy," modern practices that included the formation of foundations with their own legal status began in the early twentieth century, largely through the efforts of Andrew Carnegie. After he amassed a fortune in the steel industry and initiated philanthropic ventures such as the Carnegie Libraries in towns throughout the United States, Carnegie offered his opinions about the social responsibilities of wealth in writings such as *The Gospel of Wealth*, published in 1901.[2]

Carnegie's book developed the principle that contributing to the needs of society was consistent with good business practices, partly to achieve favorable popular opinion about capitalist enterprises and individual entrepreneurs. By contributing intelligently to address social needs rather than squandering one's wealth, Carnegie argued, the businessperson also could ensure personal entry into the heavenly realm (thus, the framework of "gospel"). Among the book's other notable features, Carnegie distinguished between "imperialism" and the more virtuous "Americanism": "Imperialism implies naval and military force behind. Moral force, education, civilization are not the backbone of Imperialism. These are the moral forces which make for the higher civilization, for Americanism."[3] By creating interconnected philanthropic foundations, Carnegie acted to ensure that his beliefs achieved the fruits he preferred in the disposal of his earthly wealth and in his own heavenly future.

The most cogent early extension of philanthropic foundations to public health and health services involved John D. Rockefeller and the Rockefeller Foundation. With his fortune based in oil, Rockefeller emulated Carnegie's philanthropic activities, despite their conflicts in the realm of monopolistic business practices. However, Rockefeller and his associates moved more specifically to support public health activities and health services that would benefit the economic interests of Rockefeller-controlled corporations throughout the world.

In particular, the Rockefeller Foundation initiated international campaigns against infectious diseases such as hookworm, malaria, and yellow fever. Between 1913, the year of its founding, and 1920, the foundation supported the development of research institutes and disease eradication programs on every continent except Antarctica. Infectious diseases proved inconvenient for expanding capitalist enterprises due to several reasons, which became clear from the writings of Rockefeller and the managers of the Rockefeller Foundation.[4] First, these infections reduced the productivity of labor by diminishing the effort that workers could devote to the job (thus the designation of hookworm, for instance, as the "lazy disease"). Second, endemic infections in areas of the world designated for such efforts as mining, oil extraction, agriculture, and the opening of new markets for the sale of commodities made those areas unattractive for investors and for managerial personnel. Third, to the extent that corporations assumed responsibility for the care of workers, especially when workers were in short supply within remote geographical areas, the costs of care escalated when infectious diseases could not be prevented or easily treated.

To address these three problems—labor productivity, safety for investors and managers, and the costs of care—the Rockefeller Foundation's massive campaigns throughout the world fostered research and efficient delivery of services. These programs took on certain characteristics that persist to this day in some of Rockefeller's activities as well as in those of other foundations, international health organizations, and nongovernmental organizations. Rather than organizing "horizontal" programs to provide a full spectrum of preventive and curative health services, the foundation emphasized "vertical" programs initiated by the donor that focused on a small number of specific diseases, such as hookworm or malaria. In addition, rather than broad public health initiatives to improve economic and health conditions of disadvantaged populations, the foundation favored the development of vaccines and medications that could prevent and treat the infectious diseases designated as most problematic—an approach some referred to as the "magic bullet." Later in the book, I show how these orientations have persisted in even the most recent, large-scale efforts by foundations to address public health problems in less developed countries.[5]

International Financial Institutions and Trade Agreements

Although trade across nations and continents dates back centuries, the framework for modern international financial institutions and trade agreements began after World War II with the Bretton Woods accords. These accords, which gradually emerged as an important mechanism to protect the political-economic empires of the United States and Western European countries, grew from meetings in Bretton Woods, New Hampshire, that involved representatives of countries victorious in World War II. The agreements initially focused on the economic reconstruction of Europe. Between 1944 and 1947, the Bretton Woods negotiations led to the creation of the International Monetary Fund (IMF) and the World Bank, as well as the establishment of the General Agreement on Tariffs and Trade (GATT).[6]

By the 1960s, after the recovery of Europe, these institutions and agreements gradually expanded their focus to the less developed countries. The World Bank, for instance, adopted as its vision statement "our dream—a world without poverty."[7] However, because the IMF and World Bank provided most of their assistance through loans rather than grants, the debt burden of the poorer countries increased rapidly. By 1980, many less developed countries, including the poorest in the world, were spending on average about half their economic productivity, as measured by gross domestic product, on payment of their debts to international financial institutions, even though these institutions' goals usually emphasized the reduction of poverty. These international financial institutions during the early 1980s embraced a set of economic policies known as "the Washington consensus." Advocated primarily by the United States and the United Kingdom, these policies involved deregulation and privatization of public services, which added to the debt crisis by constraining even further the public health efforts and health services that less developed countries could provide.[8]

GATT initially aimed to reduce tariffs and quotas for trade among its twenty-three member nations. Its fairly simple principles included "most favored nation treatment" (according to which the same trade rules were applied to all participating nations) and "national treatment" (which required no discrimination in taxes and regulations between domestic and foreign goods).[9] GATT also established ongoing rounds of negotiations concerning trade agreements.

From their modest origins in GATT, international trade agreements eventually morphed into a massive structure of trade rules that would exert profound effects on public health and health services worldwide.[10] Although I consider recent trade agreements further in Chapter 6, the contours of the transition from GATT to what followed proved quite dramatic. As the pace of international economic transactions intensified, facilitated by technological advances in communications and transportation, the World Trade Organization (WTO) in 1994 replaced the loose collection of agreements subsumed under GATT. The WTO and regional trade agreements have sought to remove both tariff and nontariff barriers to trade.

Growing from the narrow scope of GATT, whose focus involved tariff barriers alone, the burgeoning array of international trade agreements encompassed under WTO expanded the purview of trade rules far beyond tariff barriers. Instead, the new trade agreements interpreted a variety of public health measures, such as environmental protection, occupational safety and health regulations, quality assurance for foods and drugs, intellectual property pertaining to patented medications and equipment, and even health services themselves as potential nontariff barriers to trade. As I argue later, this perspective in trade agreements transformed the sovereignty of governments to regulate public health and to provide health services.

International Health Organizations

The first approach to international public health organization evolved in Europe during the Middle Ages. At that time, some governments established local, national, and international *cordons sanitaires*—guarded boundaries that blocked people from leaving or entering geographical areas affected by epidemics of infectious diseases. In addition, governments imposed maritime quarantines that prevented ships from entering ports after visiting regions where epidemics were occurring. "Sanitary" authorities arose mostly on an ad hoc basis and remained active mainly when epidemics were present or anticipated.[11]

During the late nineteenth and early twentieth centuries, the rise of export economies and the expansion of economic interests worldwide triggered the demise of conventional maritime public health. Instead, the motivation for international cooperation in public health emerged largely from concerns about infectious diseases as detrimental to trade among nations that were participating in the expanding reach of capitalist enterprise. The need to protect ports, investments, and landholdings such as plantations from infectious diseases provided incentives for redesigning international public health.

The first formal international health organization arose in the Americas. Founded in Washington, D.C., during 1902, explicitly as a mechanism to protect trade and investments from the burden of disease, the International Sanitary Bureau focused on the prevention and control of epidemics.[12] Mosquito eradication campaigns and the implementation of a vaccine against yellow fever occupied public health professionals in this organization throughout the early twentieth century. During that period, plans proceeded for the construction of the Panama Canal, the development of agricultural enterprises in the "banana republics" of Central America and northern South America, and the extraction of mineral resources as raw materials for industrial production from such areas as southern Mexico, Venezuela, Colombia, and Brazil. Work in the tropics demanded public health initiatives against mosquito-borne diseases like yellow fever and malaria, parasitic illnesses like hookworm, and the more common viral and bacterial illnesses like endemic diarrhea.

As the first modern international health organization, the International Sanitary Bureau devoted much of its early activities to infectious disease surveillance, prevention, and treatment, largely to protect trade and economic activities throughout the Americas. Later, during the 1950s, the International Sanitary Bureau became the Regional Office for the Americas of the World Health Organization (WHO) and in 1958 changed its name to the Pan American Health Organization (PAHO). Subsequently, PAHO's public health mission broadened.[13] However, PAHO retained a focus on the protection of trade through the present day, and in general it supported the provisions of international trade agreements.

WHO emerged in 1948 as one of the component suborganizations of the United Nations (UN). Although prevention and control of infectious disease epidemics remained a key objective throughout its history, WHO did not frame its purpose in controlling infectious diseases as a way to protect trade and international economic transactions—as PAHO had done during its early history. Instead, during the 1970s, WHO prioritized the improved distribution of health services, especially primary health care. This orientation culminated in the famous WHO declaration on primary health care, issued at an international conference at Alma-Ata, USSR, in 1978, which provided guidelines for subsequent actions by WHO and its affiliated organizations.[14] As the principle of universal entitlement to primary care services throughout the world became one of WHO's priorities, the organization took a strong position of advocacy on behalf of programs to improve access to care, especially in the poorest countries.

During the late 1970s and early 1980s, however, WHO entered a chronic financial crisis produced largely because of the fragile financing provided for WHO's parent organization, the UN. Because of ideological opposition to several programs operated by component organizations of the UN, especially those of the United Nations Educational, Scientific, and Cultural Organization (UNESCO), the Reagan administration withheld from the UN large portions of the United States' annual dues. As a result, the UN began to experience increasing budgetary shortfalls, which it passed on to its component organizations, including WHO. Into this financial vacuum moved the World Bank, which began to contribute a large part of WHO's budget. (The precise proportion of WHO's budget dependent on the World Bank's financing remained shielded from public scrutiny.) As its financial base shifted more toward the World Bank and away from the UN, WHO's policies also transformed to an orientation that more closely resembled those of international financial institutions and trade agreements. The financial crisis that originated in the nonpayment of dues by the United States eventually led within WHO to a policy perspective regarding international trade that proved similar to PAHO's earlier orientation.

In these ways, the history of international health organizations manifested an ongoing collaboration with institutions that sought to protect commerce and trade. Constituted in the interest of trade, the organizational predecessor of PAHO devoted half a century of public health initiatives largely to the prevention and control of infections that threatened the viability of trade and investment. PAHO and eventually WHO sought improved health conditions in poor countries partly as a means to strengthen the economic positions of rich countries by facilitating activities that extracted raw materials and that opened new markets. The efforts of international health organizations on behalf of empire came to compose a major focus of the public health enterprise that these organizations fostered.

A Countervailing Viewpoint

I return to the above themes in Part 2, where I delve into the recent connections among empire, public health, and health services in more detail. How these more recent connections evolved, however, reflected in part the patterns established as empire emerged during the late nineteenth and early twentieth centuries and then flourished during the post–World War II era. The historical strands of empire already considered—extraction of raw materials and human capital, exploitation of a cheap labor force in less developed countries, the prominence of an international capitalist class, military conquest or the threat of conquest, the contributions of foundations to capitalist expansion abroad, the key positions of international financial organizations and trade agreements, and the major roles of international health organizations—become recurrent themes later in the book, as I account for the more recent ways that empire, public health, and health services have become closely linked.

Alongside the concepts and ideologies that provided rationales for the growth and maintenance of empire, a countervailing viewpoint emerged historically. The latter approach proved more critical of empire and uncovered troubling connections among capitalist enterprises, imperial expansion, ill health, and early death. This countervailing approach, which culminated in the current concern about the social determinants of illness, becomes the focus of the next chapter.

CHAPTER 2

ILLNESS-GENERATING CONDITIONS
OF CAPITALISM AND EMPIRE

Conditions of society that generate illness and mortality have become largely forgotten and rediscovered with each succeeding generation. Now, when disease-producing features of the environment and workplace threaten the survival of humanity and other life forms, it is not surprising that such problems would receive attention. But there is a long history of research and analysis about the relationships among political economic systems, the social determinants of health, and the health of populations that has been neglected, despite its relevance to our current situation.

How This Viewpoint Emerged

Three people—Friedrich Engels, Rudolf Virchow, and Salvador Allende—made major contributions to understanding the social origins of illness under capitalism and empire. Although other writers also have examined this topic,[1] the works of Engels, Virchow, and Allende are important in several respects. All three writers emphasized the importance of political economic systems as causes of illness-generating social conditions. Engels and Virchow provided analyses of the impact of political economic conditions[2] on health that essentially created the perspective of social medicine. Both men were active during the tumultuous years of the 1840s and both took decisive—though divergent—personal actions to correct the conditions they described through political economic change. Allende's key work appeared during a later historical period, the 1930s, and a different geopolitical context. While Engels and Virchow documented the impact of early capitalism, largely before the expansion of empire, Allende focused on empire and underdevelopment. Although little known in North America and Western Europe, Allende's studies in social medicine have influenced efforts to achieve political economic changes that improve health conditions in Latin America and elsewhere in the less developed world.

While Engels, Virchow, and Allende conveyed certain unifying themes that contribute to our understanding of the connections among health, capitalism, and empire, they also diverged in major ways, especially regarding the political economic structures of oppression that cause disease, the social contradictions that inhibit change, and directions of reform in political economic systems that would foster health rather than illness. A look backward to these prior works gives a historical perspective to issues that today gain even more urgency. Their works have influenced a new generation of researchers and activists, who also focus in large part on political economic systems as social determinants of health and illness.

Friedrich Engels

Engels wrote his first major book, *The Condition of the Working Class,* in England, under circumstances whose ironies now are well known.[3] Between 1842 and 1844, Engels was working in Manchester as a middle-level manager in a textile mill of which his father was co-owner. Engels carried out his managerial duties in a perfunctory manner while immersing himself in English working-class life. The richness of Engels's treatment of working-class existence has attracted much critical attention, both sympathetic and belligerent.[4] His analysis of the political economic origins of illness, though central to his account of working-class conditions, has received relatively little notice.

In this book Engels's theoretical position was unambiguous. For working-class people the roots of illness and early death lay in the organization of economic production and in the social environment.[5] British capitalism, Engels argued, forced working-class people to live and work under circumstances that inevitably caused sickness; this situation was not hidden but was well known to the capitalist class. The contradiction between profit and safety worsened health problems and stood in the way of necessary improvements.

Engels's theoretical perspective, however, focused on the profound impacts of political economic system and class structure, as well as the difficulties of change while the effects of social class under early industrial capitalism persisted. Considering the effects of environmental toxins, he claimed that the poorly planned housing in working-class districts did not permit adequate ventilation of toxic substances. Workers' apartments surrounded central courtyards without direct spatial communication to the street. Carbon-containing gases from combustion and human respiration gathered and lingered within living quarters. Because disposal systems did not exist for human and animal wastes, these materials left in courtyards, apartments, or the street resulted in severe air and water pollution. Such poor housing conditions led to an increase of infectious diseases, particularly tuberculosis. Engels noted that overcrowding and insufficient ventilation contributed to high mortality from tuberculosis in London and other industrial cities. Typhus, carried by lice, also spread due to inadequate sanitation and ventilation.

Turning to nutrition, Engels drew connections among social conditions, nutrition, and disease, emphasizing the expense and chronic shortages of food supplies for urban workers and their families. Lack of proper storage facilities at markets led to contamination and spoilage. Problems of malnutrition were especially acute for children. Engels discussed scrofula as a disease related to poor nutrition; this view antedated the discovery of bovine tuberculosis as the major cause of scrofula and pasteurization of milk as a preventive measure. He also described the skeletal deformities of rickets as a nutritional problem, long before the medical finding that dietary deficiency of vitamin D caused rickets.

Engels's analysis of alcoholism focused on the social forces that fostered excessive drinking. In Engels's view, alcoholism served as a response to the miseries of working-class life. Lacking alternative sources of emotional gratification, workers turned to alcohol. Individual workers could not be held responsible for alcohol abuse. Instead, alcoholism ultimately was the responsibility of the capitalist class:

> Liquor is their [workers'] only source of pleasure.... The working man ... must have something to make work worth his trouble, to make the prospect of the next day endurable.... Drunkenness has here ceased to be a vice, for which the vicious can be held responsible.... They who have degraded the working man to a mere object have the responsibility to bear.[6]

For Engels, because alcoholism was so firmly rooted in social structure, to attribute responsibility to the individual worker was misguided. If the experience of deprived social conditions caused alcoholism, the solution involved basic political economic change rather than treatment programs focusing on the individual.

Engels also analyzed structures of oppression within the social organization of medicine. He emphasized the maldistribution of medical personnel. According to Engels, working-class people coped with the "impossibility of employing skilled physicians in cases of illness."[7] Infirmaries that offered charitable services met only a small portion of people's needs for professional attention. Engels criticized the patent remedies containing opiates that apothecaries provided for childhood illnesses. High rates of infant mortality in working-class districts, Engels argued, were explainable partly by lack of medical care and partly by the promotion of inappropriate medications.

Engels next undertook an epidemiological investigation of mortality rates and social class, using demographic statistics compiled by public health officials. He showed that mortality rates were inversely related to social class, not only for entire cities but also within specific geographic districts of cities. He noted that in Manchester childhood mortality was substantially greater among working-class children than among children of the higher classes. In addition, Engels commented on the cumulative effects of class and urbanism on childhood mortality. He cited data that demonstrated higher death rates from epidemics of infectious diseases like smallpox, measles, scarlet fever, and whooping cough among working-class children. For Engels, crowding, poor housing, inadequate sanitation, and pollution—all standard features of urban life—combined with social class position in causing disease and early mortality.

In describing particular types of industrial work, Engels provided early accounts of occupational diseases that did not receive intensive study until well into the twentieth century. Many orthopedic disorders, in Engels's view, derived from the physical demands of industrialism. He discussed curvature of the spine, deformities of the lower extremities, flat feet, varicose veins, and leg ulcers as manifestations of work demands that required long periods of time in an upright posture. Engels commented on the health effects of posture, standing, and repetitive movements, noting that:

> All these affections are easily explained by the nature of factory work.... The operatives ... must stand the whole time. And one who sits down, say upon a window-ledge or a basket, is fined, and this perpetual upright position, this constant mechanical pressure of the upper portions of the body upon spinal column, hips, and legs, inevitably produces the results mentioned. This standing is not required by the work itself.[8]

The insight that chronic musculoskeletal disorders could result from unchanging posture or small, repetitive motions seems simple enough. Yet, this source of illness, which is quite different from a specific accident or exposure to a toxic substance, entered occupational medicine as a serious topic of concern only toward the end of the twentieth century.

Engels's discussions of occupational lung disease were detailed and far-reaching. His presentation of textile workers' pulmonary pathology antedated by many years the medical characterization of byssinosis, or brown lung:

In many rooms of the cotton and flax-spinning mills, the air is filled with fibrous dust, which produces chest affections, especially among workers in the carding and combing-rooms.... The most common effects of this breathing of dust are bloodspitting, hard, noisy breathing, pains in the chest, coughs, sleeplessness, in short, all the symptoms of asthma.[9]

Engels also offered a parallel description of "grinders' asthma," a respiratory disease caused by inhaling metal dust particles in the manufacture of knife blades and forks. The pathologic effects of cotton and metal dusts on the lung were similar; Engels noted the similarities of symptoms experienced by those two diverse groups of workers.

Engels analyzed the ravages of pulmonary disorder among coal miners. He reported that unventilated coal dust caused both acute and chronic pulmonary inflammation that frequently progressed to death. Engels observed that "black spittle"—the syndrome now called coal miners' pneumoconiosis, or black lung— was associated with other gastrointestinal, cardiac, and reproductive complications. By pointing out that this lung disease was preventable, Engels illustrated the contradiction between profit and safety as a political economic determinant of disease in capitalist industry:

Every case of this disease ends fatally.... In all the coal-mines which are properly ventilated this disease is unknown, while it frequently happens that miners who go from well to ill-ventilated mines are seized by it. The profit-greed of mine owners which prevents the use of ventilators is therefore responsible for the fact that this working-men's disease exists at all.[10]

After more than a century and a half, the same structural contradiction impedes the prevention of black lung.

Engels interspersed his remarks about disease with many other perceptions of class oppression. His argument implied that the solution to these health problems required basic political economic change; limited medical interventions would never yield the improvements that were most needed. Although Engels's early work on medical issues has eluded many later researchers and activists, his analysis exerted a major influence, both intellectual and political, on one of the founders of social medicine, Rudolf Virchow.

Rudolf Virchow

A nineteenth-century physician who made important contributions in social medicine, anthropology, cellular pathology, and parliamentary activity, Virchow developed a unified explanation of the physical and social forces that caused disease and human suffering. He used a dialectic approach to both biological and social problems, perceiving natural and social processes as a series of antitheses. In 1847, he anticipated the revolutions of 1848 by claiming that the apparent social tranquility would be "negated" through social conflict in order to reach a "higher synthesis."[11] Virchow used a similar dialectic analysis in tracing the process of scientific knowledge.[12]

Virchow manifested these orientations—of applied science, dialectics, and materialism—in his analyses of specific illnesses. He emphasized the concrete historical and material circumstances in which disease appeared, the contradictory political economic forces that impeded prevention, and researchers' role in advocating reform. In the analysis of multifactorial etiology, Virchow claimed that the most important causative factors were the material conditions of people's everyday lives. This view implied that an effective health-care system could not limit itself to treating the pathophysiological disturbances of individual patients.

Based on study of a typhus epidemic in Upper Silesia, a cholera epidemic in Berlin, and an outbreak of tuberculosis in Berlin during 1848 and 1849, Virchow developed a theory of epidemics that emphasized the political economic structures that fostered the spread of illness. He argued that defects of society were a necessary condition for the emergence of epidemics. Virchow classified certain disease entities as "crowd diseases" or "artificial diseases"; these included typhus, scurvy, tuberculosis, leprosy, cholera, relapsing fever, and some mental disorders. According to this analysis, inadequate social conditions increased the population's susceptibility to climate, infectious agents, and other specific causal factors—none of which alone was sufficient to produce an epidemic. For the prevention and eradication of epidemics, political economic change was as important as medical intervention, if not more so: "The improvement of medicine would eventually prolong human life, but improvement of social conditions could achieve this result even more rapidly and successfully."[13]

The social contradictions that Virchow most strongly emphasized were those of class structure. He described the deprivations that the working class endured and linked disease patterns to these deprivations. Virchow also noted that morbidity and mortality rates, especially for infants, were much higher in working-class districts of cities than in wealthier areas. As documentation, he used the statistics that Engels cited, as well as data that he himself gathered from German cities. Describing inadequate housing, nutrition, and clothing, Virchow criticized the apathy of government officials for ignoring these root causes of illness. Virchow expressed his outrage about class conditions most forcefully in his discussion of epidemics like the cholera outbreak in Berlin:

Is it not clear that our struggle is a social one, that our job is not to write instructions to upset the consumers of melons and salmon, of cakes and ice cream, in short, the comfortable bourgeoisie, but is to create institutions to protect the poor, who have no soft bread, no good meat, no warm clothing, and no bed, and who through their work cannot subsist on rice soup and camomile tea ... ? May the rich remember during the winter, when they sit in front of their hot stoves and give Christmas apples to their little ones, that the shiphands who brought the coal and the apples died from cholera. It is so sad that thousands always must die in misery, so that a few hundred may live well.[14]

For Virchow, the deprivations of working-class life created a susceptibility to disease. When infectious organisms, climatic changes, famine, or other causal factors were present, disease spread rapidly through the community.

Because he clarified the social origins of illness, Virchow advocated a broad scope for public health and the medical scientist. He attacked structures of oppression within medicine, particularly the policies of hospitals that required payment by the poor rather than assuming their care as a matter of social responsibility. Virchow envisioned the creation of a "public health service," an integrated system of publicly owned and operated health-care facilities, staffed by health workers employed by the state. Such a system would define health care as a constitutional right of citizenship. Included within this right were the political and economic conditions that contributed to health rather than to illness.[15]

Two other principles were central to Virchow's conception of public health: prevention and the state's responsibility to ensure material security for citizens. Virchow's focus on prevention derived primarily from his observation of epidemics, which he believed could be prevented by straightforward changes in social policies. He found a major cause in several poor potato harvests preceding the epidemics; government officials could have prevented malnutrition by distributing foodstuffs from other parts of the country. Virchow argued that prevention was largely a political economic problem: "Our politics were those of prophylaxis; our opponents preferred those of palliation."[16] Health workers could never accomplish disease prevention solely through activities within the medical sphere; material security also was essential. The state's responsibilities, Virchow argued, included providing work for "able-bodied" citizens. Only by conditions of economic production that guaranteed employment could workers obtain the economic security necessary for good health. Likewise, the physically disabled should enjoy the right of financial support by the state.[17]

Virchow's visions of the social origins of illness pointed out the wide scope of the medical task: the study of social conditions as part of clinical research and health workers' engagement in political action. Virchow frequently drew connections among medicine, social science, and politics: "Medicine is a social science, and politics is nothing more than medicine in larger scale."[18] Virchow's analysis of these issues faded from public discourse largely due to conservative political forces that shaped the course of scientific medicine during the late nineteenth and early twentieth centuries. His contributions set a standard for current attempts to understand and to challenge the political economic conditions that generate illness and suffering.

Salvador Allende

Although Allende's political endeavors remain better known than his medical career, his writings and efforts to reform medicine and public health served as one of several important influences on social medicine, especially in Latin America. Acknowledging intellectual debts to Engels, Virchow, and others who analyzed the social roots of illness in nineteenth-century Europe, Allende implemented a political economic model of medical problems in the context of empire and economic underdevelopment. This model emphasized societal characteristics that policy reform could modify.

Allende recognized that the health problems of Chilean people derived largely from the country's political and economic conditions. Writing in 1939 as minister of health for a popular-front government, Allende presented his analysis of the relationships among political economy, disease, and suffering in his book, *La Realidad Médico-Social Chilena*.[19] The book conceptualized illness as a disturbance of the individual that often was caused by deprived social conditions. The approach implied that social change was the only potentially therapeutic approach to many health problems. After an introduction on the connections between the political economic system and illness, Allende presented some geographic and demographic "antecedents" to contextualize specific health problems. Sharing a similar focus with Engels and Virchow, he focused on the "living conditions of the working classes."

In his account of working-class life, Allende emphasized capitalist imperialism, particularly the multinational corporations that extracted profit from Chilean natural resources and inexpensive labor. He claimed that to improve the health-care system, a popular-front government must change the nature of empire:

> For the capitalist enterprise it is of no concern that there is a population of workers who live in deplorable conditions, who risk being consumed by diseases or who vegetate in obscurity.... [Without] economic advancement ... it is impossible to accomplish anything serious from the viewpoints of hygiene or medicine ... because

it is impossible to give health and knowledge to a people who are malnourished, who wear rags, and who work at a level of unmerciful exploitation.[20]

His analytic tone and statistical tabulation thinly veiled Allende's outrage at the contradictions of class structure and underdevelopment that empire fostered.

Allende focused first on wages, which he viewed as a primary determinant of workers' health. Many of his political economic observations anticipated later concerns, including wage differentials for men and women, the impact of inflation, and the inadequacy of laws purporting to ensure subsistence-level income. He linked his exposition of wages directly to the problem of nutrition and presented comparative data on food availability, earning power, and economic development. Not only was the production of milk and other needed foodstuffs less efficient than in more developed countries, but Chilean workers' inferior earning power also made food less accessible. Reviewing the minimum requirement to ensure adequate nutrition, he found that the majority of Chilean workers could not obtain the elements of this diet on a regular basis. He argued that high infant mortality, skeletal deformities, tuberculosis, and other infectious diseases all had roots in inadequate nutrition; improvements depended on changed political and economic conditions.

With the same focus on concrete, material conditions, Allende then turned to clothing, housing, and sanitation facilities. He found that working people in Chile were inadequately clothed, largely because wages were low and the greatest proportion of income went for food and housing. The effects of insufficient clothing, Allende observed, were apparent in rates of upper respiratory infections, pneumonia, and tuberculosis, which were higher than in any economically developed country.

In his analysis of housing problems, Allende focused on population density, which largely reflected the geography of economic production. He noted that Chile had one of the highest rates of inhabitants per residential structure in the world; overcrowding fostered the spread of infectious diseases and poor hygiene. Again he cited comparative data that showed a correlation between population density and overall mortality. In a style similar to that of Engels and Virchow, Allende presented a concrete description of housing conditions, including details about insufficient beds, inadequate construction materials, and deficiencies in apartment buildings. He reviewed the provisions for private initiative in construction, found them unsatisfactory, and outlined the need for major public-sector investment in new housing. Allende then presented data on drinking water and sewerage systems for all provinces of Chile, noting that vast areas of the country lacked these rudimentary facilities.

His view of working-class conditions laid the groundwork for Allende's analysis of concrete medical problems. When he discussed specific diseases, he looked for their sources in the social and material environment. The medical problems that he considered included maternal and infant mortality, tuberculosis, sexually transmitted diseases, other infectious diseases, emotional disturbances, and occupational illnesses. He observed that maternal and infant mortality rates generally were far lower in developed than in less developed countries. After reviewing the major causes of death, he concluded that malnutrition and poor sanitation, both rooted in the political economy of underdevelopment, were major explanations for this excess mortality.

In the same section, Allende gave one of the first analyses of illegal abortion. He noted that a large proportion of deaths in gynecologic hospitals, about 30 percent, derived from abortions and their complications. Pointing out the high incidence of abortion complications among working-class women, he attributed this problem to economic deprivations of class structure. After a statistical account of complications, Allende allowed his outrage to surface:

> There are hundreds of working mothers who, because of anxiety about the inadequacy of their wages, induce abortion in order to prevent a new child from shrinking their already insignificant resources. Hundreds of working mothers lose their lives, impelled by the anxieties of economic reality.[21]

Allende designated tuberculosis as a "social disease" because its incidence differed so greatly among social classes. Writing before the antibiotic era, Allende reached conclusions similar to those of modern epidemiology—that is, the major decline in tuberculosis followed economic advances rather than therapeutic medical interventions. From statistics of the first three decades of the twentieth century, he noted that tuberculosis had decreased consistently in the economically developed countries of Western Europe and the United States. On the other hand, in economically less developed countries like Chile, little progress against the disease had occurred. Within the context of underdevelopment, tuberculosis exerted its most severe impact on the poor.

In his discussion of sexually transmitted diseases, Allende emphasized political economic conditions that favored the spread of syphilis and gonorrhea. He discussed deprivations of working-class life that encouraged prostitution. Citing the prevalence of prostitution in Santiago and other cities, as well as the early recruitment of women from poor families, he argued that social programs to eliminate prostitution through expansion of employment opportunities must precede significant improvements in sexually transmitted diseases.

Regarding other infectious diseases, Allende turned first to typhus, the same disease that shaped Virchow's views about the relationships between illness and the political economic system. Allende began his analysis with a straightforward statement: "Some [infectious diseases], like typhus, are an index of the state of pauperization of the masses."[22] Like Virchow in Upper Silesia, Allende found a disproportionate incidence of typhus in the Chilean working class. He then showed that bacillary and amebic dysentery and typhoid fever occurred because of inadequate drinking water and sanitation facilities in residential areas densely populated by working-class families. Similar problems fostered other infections, such as diphtheria, whooping cough, scarlet fever, measles, and trachoma.

Drug addiction troubled Allende deeply. In La *Realidad,* Allende analyzed the social and psychological problems that motivated people to use addictive drugs. Allende's political economic analysis of the causes of alcohol intoxication showed similarities to that of Engels:

> We see that one's wages, appreciably less than subsistence, are not enough to supply needed clothing, that one must inhabit inadequate housing ... [and that] one's food is not sufficient to produce the minimum of necessary caloric energy.... The worker reaches the conclusion that going to the tavern and intoxicating oneself is the apparent solution to all these problems. In the tavern one finds a lighted and heated place, and friends for distraction, making one forget the misery at home. In short, for the Chilean worker ... alcohol is not a stimulant but an anesthetic.[23]

Rooted in the social misery generated by conditions of capitalist production, alcoholism exerted a profound effect on health, an impact that Allende documented for a variety of illnesses, including gastrointestinal diseases, cirrhosis, delirium tremens, sexual dysfunction, birth defects, and tuberculosis. He also traced some of the more subtle societal outcomes of alcoholism, offering an early analysis of alcohol's impact on accidental deaths.

Allende analyzed monopoly capital and international expansion by the pharmaceutical industry, criticizing issues such as brand-name medications and pharmaceutical advertising. In perhaps the earliest discussion of its type, Allende compared the prices of brand-name drugs with their generic equivalents:

> Thus, for example, we find for a drug with important action on infectious diseases, sulfanilamide, these different names and prices: Prontosil $26.95, Gombardol $20.80, Septazina $21.60, Aseptil $18.00, Intersil $13.00, Acetilina $6.65. All these products, which in the eyes of the public appear with different names, correspond, in reality, to the same medication which is sold in a similar container and which contains 20 tablets of 0.50 grams of sulfanilamide.[24]

Beyond the issue of drug names, Allende also anticipated a later theme by criticizing pharmaceutical advertising: "Another problem in relation to the pharmaceutical specialties is . . . the excessive and charlatan propaganda attributing qualities and curative powers which are far from their real ones."[25] In connecting empire and health, Allende focused on such exploitation by multinational drug companies.

Allende concluded by proposing the policy position and plan for political action of the Ministry of Health within the popular-front government. In considering reform and its dilemmas, he reviewed the political economic origins of illness and the social structural remedies that were necessary. Allende refused to discuss specific health problems apart from macrolevel political economic issues. He introduced his policy proposals with a chapter titled "Considerations Regarding Human Capital." Analyzing the detrimental political economic impact of ill health among workers, he argued that a healthy population was a worthy goal both in its own right and also for the sake of national development. The country's productivity suffered because of workers' illness and early death, yet improving the health of workers was impossible without fundamental political economic changes in the society. These changes would include "an equitable distribution of the product of labor," state regulation of "production, distribution, and price of articles of food and clothing," a national housing program, and special attention to occupational health problems. The links between medicine and the broader political economy were inescapable: "All this means that the solution of the medico-social problems of the country would require precisely the solution of the economic problems that affect the proletarian classes."[26]

He then proposed specific reforms that he viewed as preconditions for an effective health system. These reforms called for profound changes in existing structures of power, finance, and economic production. First, he suggested modifications of wages, which if enacted would have led to a major redistribution of wealth. Regarding nutrition, he developed a plan to improve milk supplies, fishing, and refrigeration and suggested land reform provisions to enhance agricultural productivity. Recognizing the need for better housing, Allende proposed a concerted national effort in publicly supported construction as well as rent control in the private sector.

Allende did not emphasize programs of research or treatment for specific diseases; instead, he assumed that the greatest advances toward lowering morbidity and mortality would follow fundamental societal change. This orientation also pervaded his proposed "medico-social program." In this program, he suggested innovations including reorganization of the Ministry of Health, planning activities, control of pharmaceutical production and prices, occupational safety and health policies, measures supporting preventive medicine, and sanitation programs. Since the major social origins of illness included low wages, malnutrition, and poor housing, the first responsibility of the public health system, according to Allende, was to improve these conditions, some of which derived from the actions of multinational corporations. His vision implied that medical intervention without basic political economic change would remain ineffectual and, in a deep sense, misguided.

Capitalism, Empire, Illness, and Early Death

Engels, Virchow, and Allende developed divergent though complementary views about the social etiology of illness, which later generations have tended to forget and then to rediscover. Their work conceptualized unnecessary illness and premature death as inherent outcomes of capitalist production and the expansion of empire. The divergences reflected certain differences in theoretical orientation. For Engels, economic production was primary. Even in his early work, Engels emphasized the organization and process of production. Disease and early death, in his view, developed directly from exposure to dusts, chemicals, time pressures, bodily posture, visual demands, and related difficulties that workers faced in their jobs. Environmental pollution, bad housing, alcoholism, and malnutrition also contributed to the poor health of the working class, but these factors mainly reflected or exacerbated the structural contradictions of production itself.

While he shared Engels's view that the working class suffered disproportionately, Virchow focused on inequalities in the distribution and consumption of social resources. In Virchow's analysis, important sources of illness and early death included poverty, unemployment, malnutrition, cultural and educational deficits, political disenfranchisement, linguistic difficulties, inadequate medical facilities and personnel, and similar deficiencies that affected the working class. He believed that public officials could prevent epidemics by distributing food more efficiently. Disease and mortality, he argued, would improve if a "public health service" made medical care more available. Virchow did criticize profiteering by businessmen and the high fees of the private medical profession. But he did not emphasize the illness-generating conditions of production itself. Instead, he viewed unequal access to society's products as the principal problem of social medicine.

Allende also concerned himself with the impact of class structure but focused on the context of empire and underdevelopment. The deprivations that the working class experienced in countries like Chile reflected the exploitation of less developed countries by advanced capitalist nations. Allende attributed low wages, malnutrition, poor housing, and related problems directly to the extraction of wealth by international imperialism. He recognized that production itself could produce illness but, unlike Engels, devoted less attention to occupational illness per se. He did document distributional inequalities of goods and services that, as in Virchow's analysis, ravaged the working class. On the other hand, the most crucial political economic determinant of illness and death, in Allende's view, was the contradiction of development and underdevelopment. Economic advancement of the society as a whole, although impeded by empire, was the major precondition for meaningful improvements in medical care and individual health.

The contributions of Engels, Virchow, and Allende shared the framework of social causation. These writings conveyed a vision of multiple social structures and processes impinging on the individual. Disease was not the straightforward outcome of an infectious agent or pathophysiological disturbance. Instead, a variety of problems—including malnutrition, economic insecurity, occupational risks, bad housing, and lack of political power—created an underlying predisposition to disease and death. Although these writers differed in the specific factors they emphasized, they each saw illness as deeply embedded in the complexities of social reality. To the extent that social contradictions affected individual disease, therapeutic intervention that limited itself to the individual level proved both naive and futile. Social etiology implied social change as therapy, and the latter linked medical practice to political practice.

Another crucial divergence concerned policy, reform, and political strategy. Engels, Virchow, and Allende differed in their views of the strategies needed for change. They also held varying visions of the society in which these policies would take effect. Although their explanations of the social origins of illness complemented one another, the question of how to change illness-generating conditions evoked different strategic analyses.

Already present in his early work, Engels's strategy involved revolution, not reform. His documentation of the occupational and environmental conditions that caused illness and early death did not aim toward limited reform of those problems. Instead, he intended his data to serve, at least in part, as propaganda. The purpose was to provide a focus of political organizing among the working class. Notably, Engels did not advocate specific changes in the conditions he described. While he detailed the defects of housing, sanitation, occupational safety, maldistribution of medical personnel, and promotion of drugs, he did not explicitly seek reforms in any of these areas. The alternatives that he occasionally suggested, such as the cursory outlines of a public health service, were always speculations about how a more effective system might appear in a postrevolutionary society. The many deprivations of working-class life required fundamental change in the entire social order, rather than limited improvements in parts of society. The companion piece of *The Condition of the Working Class in England* was clearly *The Communist Manifesto*, with its aim to address problems such as unnecessary illness and early death through broad social revolution. The strategic implications of Engels's analysis of health problems were congruent with his role as a primary organizer of the First Internationale. From this perspective, reformism in health care made as little sense as any other piecemeal tinkering with capitalist society.

Taking a different approach to social change, Virchow favored policies of reform. Although he participated in the agitation of the late 1840s and doubted that the ruling circles would permit needed changes in response to peaceful challenges alone, he ultimately opted for reform rather than revolution. While the conditions he witnessed in the Upper Silesian typhus epidemic were horrifying, he believed that a series of reforms could correct the problem. The reforms he advocated transcended medicine to include rationalized food distribution, modifications in the educational system, political enfranchisement, and other changes at the level of social structure. He also adopted a broad view of the systematic reforms that were necessary in health care. An adequate health system, for example, demanded a public health service. In this service, health-care professionals would work as employees of the state and would act to correct maldistribution across class, geographical, and ethnic lines. As an overall political goal, Virchow favored a constitutional democracy that would reduce the power of the monarchy and nobility. He supported principles of socialism, particularly those that involved public ownership and rational organization of health and welfare facilities. However, Virchow argued against communism, mainly, he said, because of its naive view that a just society was feasible without a strong state apparatus. Virchow firmly believed that limited reforms within capitalist society were both appropriate and desirable, and he was optimistic that they would be effective.

Allende's conceptualization of political strategy was more complex than those of Engels or Virchow. In *La Realidad Medico-Social Chilena,* he unambiguously stated that the health problems of the working class were inherent in the contradictions of class structure, underdevelopment, and the oppressive international relations of empire. Without basic modification of these structural problems, he argued, limited medical reform would prove futile.

In Allende's view, revolutionary social change was necessary to achieve needed improvements in health services and outcomes. Throughout his life, Allende believed that progressive forces could achieve a socialist transformation of society through a sequence of peaceful actions within the framework of constitutional democracy. He and his coworkers based this position on a reading of prior socialist strategists, examples of other revolutions, and a detailed analysis of Chile's concrete historical and material reality. From this viewpoint, the most important health-related reforms transcended medicine. Allende called for improvements in housing, nutrition, employment, and other concrete manifestations of class oppression. Such reforms were preconditions for reduced morbidity and mortality; without them, changes in health-care services could not succeed. On the other hand, structural reforms in the social organization of medicine, including a public health service and a nationalized pharmaceutical and equipment industry, were desirable goals en route to a socialist society. Allende did not accurately anticipate the violence of national and international groups about to be dispossessed on the peaceful road to socialism. This grim result left the balance between reform and revolutionary alternatives incompletely resolved in strategies for change.

The social pathologies that distressed Engels, Virchow, and Allende continue to create suffering and early death. Public health generally has adopted the medical model of etiology. In this model, social conditions may increase susceptibility or exacerbate disease, but they are not primary causes like microbial agents or disturbances of normal physiology. Partly because research rarely has clarified the causes of illness within political economic systems, political strategy—both within and outside medicine—seldom has addressed the social roots of disease.

Inequalities of class, exploitation of workers, and conditions of capitalist production in the context of empire cause disease now as previously. The links between political economic conditions and disease become ever more urgent, as economic instability, unreliable food supplies, depletion of petroleum, nuclear and toxic chemical wastes, global warming, and related problems threaten the survival of humanity and other life forms. In Chapter 13, I present more recent perspectives on the social determinants of health, based largely on work in Latin American social medicine. As Engels, Virchow, and Allende argued and as more recent studies in social medicine have confirmed, efforts to improve the health of populations without addressing the social origins of illness ultimately will fail. Strategies that do address these social origins reveal the scope of reconstruction that is necessary for meaningful solutions, which I consider in the last part of the book.

*   *   *

The impacts of capitalism and empire, however, do not only operate as causes of illness and early death. Instead, illness and early death also provide a rationale for the development and marketing of new products. The promotion and sales of these products, usually involving technological advances, have further strengthened the capitalist system and have enhanced its ability to expand through empire. In the next chapter I present an important example of how new technologies, designed to improve health conditions but often without clear evidence of success in doing so, provided growing profitability for capitalist enterprises, as markets for these products expanded throughout the world.

CHAPTER 3

THE INTERNATIONAL MARKET
FOR HEALTH PRODUCTS AND SERVICES

In both advanced capitalist countries and less developed nations, the financial burden of health care became a major concern during what I refer to as empire past. Legislative and administrative maneuvers purportedly aimed for cost containment. Techniques in health services research entered into the evaluation of technology and clinical practices. The purposes of this chapter are to show the limitations of these approaches in light of medical technology's social history and to offer an alternative interpretation, which traces problems of costs to underlying social contradictions within the capitalist economy and the expansion of empire.

Methods to Address the Falling Rate of Profit

Health costs cannot be divorced from the structure of private profit, even though—surprisingly enough—the problem of profit often did not enter into analyses of the rapidly increasing costs of care during empire past. Many analyses of costs either ignored the contradictions of capitalism and empire, or accepted them as given. But the crisis of health costs intimately reflected the more general fiscal crisis that advanced capitalism faced worldwide. In analyses of costs, the connections between the health sector and the structure of the capitalist system received little attention. Limiting the level of analysis to a specific innovation or practice, while not perceiving the broader political economic context in which costly and ineffective procedures were introduced and promulgated, obscured potential solutions. Apparent irrationalities of health policy made sense when seen from the standpoint of capitalist profit structure; the overselling of numerous technological advances—including the computerized axial tomography, new laboratory techniques, fetal monitoring, many surgical procedures, and coronary care units for patients with heart attacks—reflected very similar structural problems.

One key theme that emerged from the history of technological advances in medicine involved corporate strategies to deal with the falling rate of profit. As Marx, in addition to Smith and Ricardo before him, pointed out, companies enjoyed a high rate of profit when they introduced a new product for the first time into a marketplace. However, as the new product saturated its market, the rate of profit almost always began to fall. To address this inherent problem, corporations developed strategies to maintain or to increase the rate of profit. Such strategies included raising the productivity of labor, diversifying into new product lines, and searching for new markets through international exports.[1] The social history of coronary care showed how the diffusion of technological advances with unproven effectiveness, which appeared quite irrational on the surface, played themselves out as inherent features of the capitalist economy and the expansion of empire.

The Political Economy of Coronary Care

Early History of Coronary Care Units

Intensive care for patients suffering heart attacks emerged rapidly during the 1960s, during empire past, with the development of coronary care units (CCUs). The rationale for the CCUs stemmed from findings in pathology and physiology about the nature of heart attacks. When a person has a heart attack, or myocardial infarction, a part of the heart muscle dies. For several days, this dying muscle acts as a source of electric instability that may cause serious irregularities in the heart's rhythm. If such an irregularity, or arrhythmia, occurs, the patient may die because the heart does not pump blood to vital organs. During the late 1950s and early 1960s, researchers in cardiology discovered techniques to control arrhythmias if caught in time. These techniques included intravenous drugs (such as lidocaine) and the application of electric shock to the chest wall (defibrillation).

The CCU's purpose was to provide continuous electronic monitoring of the heart's rhythm, through electrodes attached to the patient's chest and connected to electrocardiogram equipment. Through continuous monitoring, it was possible to begin treatment, by drugs or electric shock, immediately when an arrhythmia began. After a heart attack, a patient generally remained in a CCU during a critical period until the heart rhythm stabilized. Since the origin of

CCUs, medical practitioners have used them for other problems, including congestive heart failure or blood pressure abnormalities, which sometimes followed a heart attack. The CCU's major rationale, however, remained the monitoring and control of heart rhythm disturbances.

This rationale led to a reasonable hypothesis: that CCUs would reduce morbidity and mortality from heart attacks. As reasonable as this hypothesis appeared, however, it remained to be proved. A random controlled trial evaluating CCUs, in which patients would be randomly assigned to CCUs versus standard care and their comparative outcomes assessed, could have resolved such doubts. Nonetheless, CCUs proliferated throughout the United States and around the world during empire past without any definite documentation of their effectiveness. Clinicians and investigators did not try to perform random controlled trials regarding the outcomes of CCU care. Instead, they advocated the adoption of the intensive care approach, with the unproven assumption that CCUs would improve survival by controlling early heart rhythm disturbances. With an aura of scientific rigor, the promotion and acceptance of technology in coronary care bypassed the scientific demonstration of effectiveness. Early arguments for CCUs showed an optimism unrestrained by the requirements of hypothesis testing.

A controlled trial evaluating CCUs would have been important for several reasons. In the first place, one could imagine some possible ways in which intensive care could interfere with recovery after a heart attack. Iatrogenic disease may arise, for example, because of disturbances in body chemistry stemming from intravenous solutions. Life-threatening infections also are more likely to occur in the hospital. In addition, the intensive care setting can be a fear-provoking experience. Emotional upset can be life-threatening after a heart attack; for example, patients in CCUs have died suddenly after witnessing other patients' deaths. Such technical and psychological problems warranted assessment before concluding that CCUs were effective. Second, although CCUs might improve short-term mortality in the hospital, they may have little effect on longer-term outcomes during the weeks and months after patients leave the hospital. Properly evaluating intensive care would consider later survival and quality of life, beyond the acute period of hospitalization. Third, CCUs were enormously expensive. Capital expenditures for CCU equipment amounted to millions of dollars for a single hospital. The daily costs of care in CCUs were two to three times more expensive than for hospitalization without intensive care.

Despite the lack of controlled studies showing effectiveness, there were many calls for the expansion of CCUs to other hospitals and increased support from the U.S. government and private foundations. In 1968, the U.S. Department of Health, Education, and Welfare issued a set of Guidelines for CCUs.[2] Largely because of these recommendations, CCUs grew rapidly in the following years. Table 3-1 shows the expansion of CCUs in the United States between 1967 and

1974.[3] Although some regional variability was present, a large increase in the proportion and an even larger increase in the absolute number of hospitals with CCUs occurred during this period, still without demonstration of effectiveness.

Serious research on the effectiveness of CCUs did not begin until the 1970s. "Before-after" studies done during the 1960s could not lead to valid conclusions about effectiveness, since none of these studies used adequate control groups or randomization.[4] Later studies compared treatment of heart attack patients in hospital wards versus CCU settings.[5] Patients were "randomly" admitted to the CCU or the regular ward, simply based on the availability of CCU beds. Ward patients were the "control" group; CCU patients were the "experimental" group. From this research, it remained unclear whether CCUs improved in-hospital mortality.

Other research contrasted home versus hospital care.[6] In a prospective random controlled trial by Mather and colleagues in the United Kingdom, the one-year mortality was not different in the home and hospital groups, and there was no evidence that heart attack patients did better in the hospital. A second random controlled trial of home versus hospital treatment, conducted by Hill and colleagues also in the United Kingdom, tried to correct certain methodological difficulties of the Mather study by achieving a higher rate of randomization and strict criteria for the entry and exclusion of patients from the trial. This later study confirmed the earlier results; the researchers concluded that for the majority of patients with suspected heart attack, admission to a hospital "confers no clear advantage." A third study of the same problem in the United Kingdom used an epidemiological

Table 3-1 Growth of Coronary Care Units in the United States, by Region, 1967–1974

| | Coronary Care Units (% of Hospitals) | |
	1967	1974
United States	24.3	33.8
New England	29.0	36.8
Mid-Atlantic	33.8	44.2
East North Central	31.0	38.2
West North Central	17.0	25.3
South Atlantic	23.3	38.2
East South Central	13.4	30.1
West South Central	15.3	24.3
Mountain	21.4	29.3
Pacific	32.7	37.8

Source: see note 3.

approach. This investigation was not a random controlled trial but rather a twelve-month descriptive study of the incidence of heart attacks, how they were treated in practice, and the outcomes in terms of mortality. Both the crude and age-standardized mortality rates were better for patients treated at home.

These issues remained far from settled. The thrust of available research indicated that home care constituted a viable treatment alternative to hospital or CCU care for many patients with heart attacks. Early CCU investigations used unsound methods; more adequate studies did not confirm CCU effectiveness. One other question became clear: if intensive care was not demonstrably more effective than simple rest at home, how could we explain the tremendous proliferation of this very expensive form of treatment?

Explaining the Diffusion of Coronary Care Units

These events did not represent simply another uncritical acceptance of high technology in industrial society. Instead, one must search for the social conditions that fostered their growth and impeded their serious evaluation. Several elements played key roles in the political economy of coronary care during empire past: corporations, academic medical centers, private philanthropists, the state, and changes in the health-care labor force.

To survive, capitalist industries must produce and sell new products; expansion is a necessity for capitalist enterprises. The economic surplus must grow continually larger. Medical production also falls into this same category, although it is seldom viewed in this way. The economist Mandel emphasized the contradictions of the economic surplus: "For capitalist crises are incredible phenomena like nothing ever seen before. They are not crises of scarcity, like all pre-capitalist crises; they are crises of over-production."[7] This scenario also included the health-care system, where an overproduction of intensive care technology contrasted with the fact that many people lacked access to the simplest and most rudimentary medical services.

The Corporate Connection

Large profit-making corporations in the United States participated in essentially every phase of CCU research, development, promotion, and proliferation. Many companies involved themselves in the intensive care market. Here I consider the activities of two such firms: the Warner-Lambert Pharmaceutical Company and the Hewlett-Packard Company. I selected these corporations because information about their participation in coronary care was accessible, because they occupied prominent market positions, and because their worldwide expansion constituted an important phase of the international market in health-care products during empire past. However, many other firms, including at last eighty-five major companies, also participated in coronary care.

During the late 1970s, Warner-Lambert Pharmaceutical Company was a large multinational corporation, with $2.1 billion in assets and over $2.5 billion in sales annually. The corporation included a number of interrelated subsidiary companies. Warner-Chilcott Laboratories produced such drugs as Coly-Mycin, Gelusil, Anusol, Mandelamine, Peritrate, and Tedral. The Parke-Davis Company manufactured Caladryl lotion, medicated throat discs, influenza vaccines, Norlestrin contraceptives, Dilantin, Benadryl, Chloromycetin, and many other pharmaceuticals. Another division, Warner-Lambert Consumer Products, produced Listerine, Smith Brothers (cough drops), Bromo-Seltzer, Chiclets, DuBarry, Richard Hudnuts, Rolaids, Dentyne, Certs, Cool-ray Polaroid (sunglasses), and Oh! Henry (candy). Warner-Lambert International operated in more than forty countries.

Although several divisions of the Warner-Lambert conglomerate participated actively in the development and promotion of coronary care, the most prominent was the American Optical Company, which Warner-Lambert acquired during 1967. American Optical's research, development, and promotion of coronary care produced rapidly increasing profits after the mid-1960s.

After purchasing American Optical in 1967, Warner-Lambert maintained American Optical's emphasis on CCU technology and sought wider acceptance by health professionals and medical centers. Promotional materials contained the assumption, never proven, that the new technology was effective in reducing morbidity and mortality from heart disease. Early products and systems included the American Optical Cardiometer, a heart monitoring and resuscitation device; the Lown Cardioverter, the first direct-current defibrillator; and an Intensive Cardiac Care System that permitted simultaneous monitoring of sixteen patients by oscilloscopes, recording instruments, heart rate meters, and alarm systems.[8] In 1968 the company introduced a new line of monitoring instrumentation and implantable pacemakers. Regarding the monitoring systems, Warner-Lambert reported that "acceptance has far exceeded initial estimates" and that "to meet the increased demand for its products" the Medical Division was doubling the size of its plant in Bedford, Massachusetts.[9] By 1969, the company introduced another completely new line of Lown Cardioverters and Defibrillators and claimed that "this flexible line now meets the requirements of hospitals of all sizes."[10] The company continued to register expanding sales throughout the early 1970s.

Despite this growth, Warner-Lambert began to face a typical corporate problem: saturation of markets in the United States. Since coronary care technology was capital intensive, the number of hospitals in the United States that could buy coronary care systems, though large, was finite. Without other maneuvers, the demand for coronary care products eventually would decline. For this reason, Warner-Lambert began to implement new and predictable initiatives to ensure future growth.

First, the company expanded coronary care sales into foreign markets, especially in Latin America. Subsequently Warner-Lambert reported notable gains in sales in such countries as Argentina, Colombia, and Mexico, despite the fact that during the 1970s "political difficulties in southern Latin America slowed progress somewhat, particularly in Chile and Peru."[11] In short, the company dealt with market saturation in the United States partly by entering new markets within the U.S. sphere of influence during empire past.

In addition to the expansion of sales through empire, a second method to deal with market saturation involved further diversification in the coronary care field with products whose intent was to open new markets or to create obsolescence in existing systems. For example, in 1975 American Optical introduced two new instruments. The Pulsar 4, a lightweight portable defibrillator designed for local paramedic and emergency squads, created "an exceptionally strong sales demand." The Computer Assisted Monitoring System used a computer to anticipate and to control changes in cardiac patients' conditions and replaced many hospitals' CCU systems that American Optical had installed but that lacked computer capabilities. According to the 1975 annual report, these two instruments "helped contribute to record sales growth in 1975, following an equally successful performance in the previous year."[12] This strategy of diversification overlapped the first strategy of expansion through empire, because the corporation could promote these new products in less developed countries.

A third technique to ensure growth involved the modification of coronary care technology for new areas gaining public and professional attention. With an emphasis on preventive medicine, American Optical introduced a new line of electrocardiogram telemetry instruments, designed to provide early warning of heart attack or rhythm disturbance in ambulatory patients. In addition, American Optical began to apply similar monitoring technology to the field of occupational health and safety. In 1970 Warner-Lambert noted:

> Sales of safety products were lower in 1970 than in 1969 as a result of cutbacks in defense spending, the general business slowdown, and the lengthy automobile industry strike. The outlook for the future, however, is encouraging because of the increased industry and government concern with safety on the job, as evidenced by the passage of the Federal Occupational Safety and Health Act late in 1970.[13]

During each subsequent year, the sales of safety and health equipment, manufactured by the American Optical subsidiary and adopted partly from coronary care technology, continued to increase.

A second major corporation, the Hewlett-Packard Company, with more than $1.1 billion in assets and over $1.3 billion in sales at the time, followed a similar pattern in the coronary care marketplace. Hewlett-Packard was a less complex corporation than Warner-Lambert because it controlled fewer subsidiaries. On the other hand, Hewlett-Packard's growth led to enormous wealth for a relatively small number of stockholders. David Packard, chairman of the Hewlett-Packard board of directors and former assistant secretary of defense, as of 1978 owned Hewlett-Packard stock valued at approximately $562 million; the second-highest holdings by a corporate executive in his own company at the time were David Rockefeller's $13 million in shares of Chase Manhattan Bank.[14]

Since its founding in 1939, Hewlett-Packard grew from a small firm, manufacturing analytical and measuring instruments mainly for industry, to a leader in electronics. Until the early 1960s, its only major product designed for medical markets was a simple electrocardiogram machine. But during the 1960s, Hewlett-Packard introduced a series of innovations in coronary care that soon reached world markets.

Initially, Hewlett-Packard focused on the development of CCU technology, promoting equipment aggressively to hospitals with the consistent claim that cardiac monitors and related products were clearly effective in reducing mortality from heart attacks and rhythm disturbances. Hewlett-Packard's promotional literature made no reference to the problem of proving CCU effectiveness. Instead, such claims as the following remained unambiguous: "In the cardiac care unit pictured here at a Nevada hospital, for example, the system has alerted the staff to several emergencies that might otherwise have proved fatal, and the cardiac mortality rate has been cut in half."[15] Alternatively, "hundreds of lives are saved each year with the help of Hewlett-Packard patient monitoring systems installed in more than 1,000 hospitals throughout the world.... Pictured here is an HP system in the intensive care ward of a hospital in Montevideo, Uruguay."[16]

Fairly early in its involvement with coronary care, Hewlett-Packard emphasized the export of CCU technology to hospitals and practitioners abroad, anticipating the international sales that companies like Warner-Lambert already enjoyed during empire past. In 1966, the Hewlett-Packard annual report predicted that the effects of a slumping economy would be offset by "the great sales potential for our products, particularly medical instruments, in South American, Canadian, and Asian markets. These areas should support substantial gains in sales for a number of years."[17] Hewlett-Packard developed an elaborate promotional apparatus, including "mobile laboratories" that could be transported by airplane or bus, especially in less developed countries. By 1969, these exhibits had been "viewed by thousands of customers in Asia, Australia, Africa, and Latin America."[18] In materials prepared for potential investors, Hewlett-Packard made explicit statements about the advantages of international operations. For example, because Hewlett-Packard subsidiaries received "pioneer status" in Malaysia and Singapore, income generated in these countries remained essentially tax-free: "Had their income been taxed at the U.S. statutory rate of 48 percent in 1974, our net earnings would have been reduced by 37 cents a share."[19] By the mid-1970s, Hewlett-Packard's international medical equipment business, as measured by total orders, surpassed its domestic business. More than one hundred sales and service offices were operating in sixty-four countries.

Like Warner-Lambert, Hewlett-Packard also diversified its products to deal with the potential saturation of the coronary care market. During the late 1960s, the company introduced a series of complex computerized systems that were designed as an interface with electrocardiogram machines, monitoring devices, and other CCU products. Through the construction of computer-linked systems, as the company argued in its promotional activities, hospitals could achieve efficient data analysis for clinical decision making and CCU organization. A computerized system to analyze and interpret electrocardiograms led to the capability of processing up to five hundred electrocardiograms per eight-hour day.[20] Similar considerations of profitability motivated the development of telemetry systems for ambulatory patients with heart disease and battery-powered electrocardiogram machines designated for regions of less developed countries where electricity was not yet available for traditional machines.

From the corporate perspective, spiraling health-care expenditures, far from a problem to be solved, were the necessary fuel for desired profits. Corporations, however, were not the only organizations responsible for diffusing coronary care technology. Corporate profitability in coronary care and related fields would not have proved possible without the active support of clinicians and professionals who helped create new technology of unproven effectiveness and put it into use.

The Academic Medical Center Connection

Academic medical centers played a key role in the development and promotion of costly innovations like those in coronary care. These institutions composed a focus of monopoly capital in the health sector, yet they seldom attracted attention in critiques of technology. New approaches generally received their first clinical use in medical centers, before their adoption by practitioners in local communities and less developed countries. Both corporations considered here, Warner-Lambert and Hewlett-Packard, obtained important bases at medical centers located in geographic proximity to corporate headquarters. Academic cardiologists participated in the proliferation of CCU equipment; their work doubtless derived in part from a sincere belief that the new technologies would save lives and help patients, rather than greed or a desire for personal profit. Yet, their uncritical support for these innovations fostered CCUs' widespread acceptance without documented effectiveness.

Before its purchase by Warner-Lambert, American Optical—with headquarters in Southbridge, Massachusetts—established ties with the Peter Bent Brigham Hospital in Boston. The company worked with Bernard Lown, an eminent cardiologist, who served as an American Optical consultant, on the development of defibrillators and cardioverters. Lown pioneered the theoretical basis and clinical applications of these techniques, and American Optical engineers collaborated with Lown in the construction of working models. American Optical marketed and promoted several lines of defibrillators and cardioverters that bore Lown's name.

American Optical provided extensive support for technological innovation at the Peter Bent Brigham Hospital. The CCU developed in the mid-1960s received major grants from American Optical that Lown and his group acknowledged.[21] American Optical also used data and pictures from the Brigham's CCU in promotional literature distributed to the medical profession and potential investors. Lown and his group continued to influence the medical profession through a large number of publications, appearing in both the general medical and cardiology literature, that discussed CCU-linked diagnostic and therapeutic techniques. In these papers Lown emphasized the importance of automatic monitoring. He also advocated the widespread use of telemetry for ambulatory patients and computerized data-analysis systems, both areas into which American Optical diversified during the late 1960s and early 1970s. American Optical's relationship with Lown and his colleagues apparently proved beneficial for all concerned. The dynamics of heightened profits for American Optical and prestige for Lown did not provide optimal conditions for a detached, systematic appraisal of CCU effectiveness.

Hewlett-Packard's academic base was Stanford University Medical Center, located about one-half mile from corporate headquarters in Palo Alto, California. For many years William Hewlett, Hewlett-Packard's chief executive officer, served as a trustee of Stanford University. In addition, a private philanthropy established by Hewlett figured prominently among the university's financial benefactors.

More pertinent were Hewlett-Packard's links to the Division of Cardiology at Stanford. Donald Harrison, professor of medicine and chief of the Division of Cardiology, acted as Hewlett-Packard's primary consultant in the development of coronary care technology. Harrison and his colleagues at Stanford collaborated with Hewlett-Packard engineers in the design of CCU systems intended for marketing to both academic medical centers and community hospitals in the United States and abroad, including less developed countries. Hewlett-Packard helped construct working models of CCU components at Stanford University Hospital, under the direction of Harrison and other faculty members. Stanford physicians introduced these Hewlett-Packard systems into clinical use.

Innovations in the treatment of patients with heart disease exerted a profound impact on the costs of care at Stanford, setting a pattern for rising costs at hospitals throughout the world. As documented in a general study of the costs of treatment for several illnesses at Stanford, the effects of coronary care technology proved dramatic:

> Of the conditions covered by the 1964–1971 study, the changes in treatment in myocardial infarction had their most drastic effect on costs. This was due principally to the increased costs of intensive care units. In 1964, the Stanford Hospital had a relatively small Intensive Care Unit (ICU). It was used by only three of the 1964 coronary cases.... By 1971, the hospital had not only an ICU but also a Coronary Care Unit (CCU) and an intermediate CCU. Of the 1971 cases, only one did not receive at least some care in either the CCU or the intermediate CCU.[22]

Beyond the costs of coronary care beds, this study observed rapid increases in expensive inputs of care that derived from the intensive approach, such as laboratory tests, electrocardiograms, intravenous solutions, X-rays, inhalation therapy, and pharmaceuticals. As the investigators noted, these changes occurred even while doubt remained about the overall effectiveness of CCUs in reducing morbidity and mortality.

During the late 1960s and early 1970s, many articles from the Harrison group described new technological developments or discussed clinical issues tied to CCU care. Several papers acknowledged the use of Hewlett-Packard equipment and assistance. These academic clinicians also participated in continuing medical education programs on coronary care, both in the United States and abroad. The Stanford specialists played an important role in promoting technology in general and Hewlett-Packard products in particular.

Private Philanthropies

Philanthropic support also figured prominently in the growth of CCUs. The motivations for philanthropic spending included a complex mix of humanitarian goals and profit considerations (as they did in the early expansion of empire past, described in Chapter 1). These initiatives often emerged from the actions of corporate executives whose companies produced medical equipment or pharmaceuticals. Specific philanthropies enthusiastically supported the CCU approach.

Primary among the philanthropic proponents of CCUs was the American Heart Association, which sponsored research that led to the development of CCU products, especially monitoring systems. In addition, the association helped finance local hospitals establishing CCUs. The "underlying purpose" of these activities, according to an annual report of the association, was "to encourage and guide the formation of new [CCU] units in both large and small hospitals."[23]

Later in the 1960s the American Heart Association's annual number of estimated beneficiaries kept rising, again with undocumented claims of effectiveness. According to the 1968 annual report, doctors were helpless to deal with heart attacks until well into the twentieth century, the era that "Dr. Paul Dudley White characterized ... as 'B.C.'—Before Cardiology." Now, however,

> survival rates of hospitalized patients have been substantially increased by coronary care units.... Intensive coronary care units will be greatly expanded in hospitals treating acutely ill patients. At present, only about one third of hospitalized heart attack patients are fortunate enough to be placed in coronary care units. If all of them had the benefits of these monitoring and emergency service facilities, it is estimated that 50,000 more heart patients could be saved yearly.[24]

This unsubstantiated estimate persisted in American Heart Association literature into the early 1970s. During this same period the association cosponsored, with the U.S. Public Health Service and the American College of Cardiology, a series of national conferences on coronary care whose purpose was "the successful development of the CCU program" in all regions of the United States.

Other foundations also supported CCU proliferation. For example, the John A. Hartford Foundation gave generous support to several hospitals and medical centers during the early 1960s to develop monitoring capabilities. Recipients of Hartford wealth included Lown's group in Boston. The Hartford Foundation's public view of CCU effectiveness was unequivocal; the coronary care program "has demonstrated that a properly equipped and designed physical setting staffed with personnel trained to meet cardiac emergencies will provide prophylactic therapy which will materially enhance the survival of these patients and substantially reduce the mortality rates."[25] Another foundation that supported CCU growth, though somewhat less directly, was the W. R. Hewlett Foundation, founded by Hewlett-Packard's chief executive officer. The Hewlett Foundation earmarked large annual grants to Stanford University, which, after an undoubtedly fierce competitive evaluation of alternatives, chose Hewlett-Packard equipment for its CCU and other intensive care facilities.[26]

The commitment of private philanthropy to technological innovations emerged as a structural problem that transcended the personalities that controlled philanthropy at any specific time. The bequests that created philanthropies historically came largely from funds generated by North American industrial corporations oriented toward technological advances. Moreover, the investment portfolios of philanthropic organizations usually included stocks in a sizable number of industrial companies. Such structural conditions encouraged financial support for technological advances like those in coronary care. These same conditions tended to discourage philanthropic funding for new programs or organizational changes that would have modified the overall structure of the health-care system, which favored the position of corporations producing and selling high-technology products.

In addition, it is useful to ask which people made philanthropic decisions to fund CCU development. During the mid-1960s the American Heart Association's officers included eight physicians with primary commitments in cardiology, executives of two pharmaceutical companies, a metals company executive, a prominent banker, and several public officials (including Dwight Eisenhower). At the height of CCU promotion in 1968, the chairman of the American Heart Association's annual Heart Fund was a drug company executive. During the 1960s and early 1970s bankers and corporate executives also dominated the board at the Hartford Foundation. The Hewlett Foundation remained a family affair. Mr. and Mrs. W. R. Hewlett made the decisions about grants until the early 1970s, when R. W. Heyns—former chancellor of the University of California, Berkeley, and also a director of Norton Simon Inc., Kaiser Industries, and Levi-Strauss—assumed the foundation's presidency. It is not surprising that philanthropic policies supporting CCU proliferation showed a strong orientation toward the interests of major corporations.

The Role of the State

The state, in the form of governmental agencies, also played a key role in CCU growth. For instance, the U.S. Public Health Service provided substantial support to clinicians for CCU development during the early 1960s. An official of the U.S. Department of Health, Education, and Welfare provided an "estimate" of 50,000 potential lives saved annually by future CCUs[27]; without apparent basis in data, this figure became a slogan for CCU promotion. Conferences and publications by the Department of Health, Education, and Welfare during the late 1960s specified guidelines for adequate CCU equipment, even though the effectiveness of this approach remained unproven.

In these activities, three common functions of the state in capitalist societies became evident. First, in health policy the state used positive selection to support private enterprise by encouraging innovations that enhanced profits to major industrial corporations; the state did not enact policies that limited private profit in any serious way. Recognizing the high costs of CCU implementation, state agencies could have placed strict limitations on their number and distribution. For example, the Department of Health, Education, and Welfare might have called for the regionalization of CCU facilities and restrictions on their wider proliferation. Subsequently, studies of CCU mortality rates generally showed better outcomes in larger, busier centers and suggested the rationality of regionalized policies.[28] Policies of the Department of Health, Education, and Welfare fostered just the opposite development. By publishing guidelines that called for advanced CCU technology and by encouraging CCU proliferation to most community hospitals, the department ensured the profitability of corporate ventures in the coronary care field.

A second major function of the state involved legitimation of the capitalist system. State spending in coronary care enhanced the legitimacy of government and corporations when much of the public no longer held confidence in these institutions. The decade of the 1960s was a time of upheaval in the United States, as the civil rights movement questioned basic patterns of injustice. Opposition to the war in Indochina mobilized a large part of the population against government and corporate policies. Labor disputes arose frequently. Under such circumstances, when government and corporations faced large-scale crises of legitimacy, the state tended to intervene with health and welfare projects. Medical technology served as a "social capital expenditure" by which the state tried to counteract the recurrent legitimacy crises of the capitalist system.[29] Technologic innovations like CCUs became convenient legitimating expenditures, since they conveyed a message of deep concern for the public health while they also supported new sources of profit for large industrial firms.

Third, coinciding with the expansion of empire past, government agencies provided market research that guided domestic and foreign sales efforts. The Global Market Survey, published by the U.S. Department of Commerce, gave a detailed analysis of changes in medical facilities, hospital beds, and physicians throughout the world. This survey specified those countries that were prime targets for sales of biomedical equipment. For example, the 1973 survey pointed out that "major foreign markets for biomedical equipment are expected to grow at an average annual rate of 15 percent in the 1970s, nearly double the growth rate predicted for the U.S. domestic market."[30] The same report predicted that

West Germany (which would emphasize CCU construction), Japan, Brazil, Italy, and Israel would emerge as the largest short-term markets for products manufactured in the United States. According to the report, "market research studies identified specific equipment that present [*sic*] good to excellent U.S. sales opportunities in the 20 [international] markets"; "cardiologic-thoracic equipment" headed the list of products with high sales potential. Market research performed by state agencies encouraged the proliferation of CCUs and related innovations throughout the U.S. sphere of influence, as the capacity to generate profits overshadowed the issue of the technology's effectiveness.

Changes in the Health-Care Labor Force

Coronary care involved workers as well as equipment. Throughout the twentieth century, a process of deskilling occurred by which the skilled trades and professions became rationalized into simpler tasks that could be handled by less skilled and lower-paid workers.[31] For instance, in the construction industry, apprentices replaced skilled carpenters. Through deskilling of the health-care labor force, paraprofessionals took on rationalized tasks that could be specified by algorithms covering nearly all contingencies. During empire past, the deskilling process occurred not only in the United States but also worldwide, especially in less developed countries where corporations promoted CCU technology.

This deskilling process applied equally to CCUs and other intensive care facilities, where standard orders—often printed in advance—dealt with almost all situations that might arise. CCU work was glamorous, but as many health workers realized, much of this work could become quite routine. In some CCUs, the term "automatic pilot" appeared; this term referred to the preparation of routine intensive care orders, covering all anticipated possibilities, that subordinate health workers could follow. The term connoted the same process of deskilling that previously occurred in aeronautics.

The deskilling of the intensive care labor force was no accident. It occurred as part of a policy of manpower development that received support from professional, governmental, and corporate planners. During the late 1960s and early 1970s, the training of allied health personnel to deal with intensive care technology became a priority of educators and administrators. According to this view, it was important to train a "cadre of health workers capable of handling routine and purely functional duties."[32] The linkage between allied health workers and new technology became a clear assumption in this approach. There were limits on "the extent to which a markedly greater delegation of tasks can be achieved without the introduction of new technology" that compensates for aides' lack of "decisional training."[33] The availability of monitoring equipment in CCUs made this setting adaptable to staffing partly by technicians who could receive lower wages than doctors or nurses. Paramedical training programs, focusing on intensive care, became a goal of policy makers, even though they recognized the built-in obsolescence of monitoring equipment and the tendency of industrial corporations to "capitalize" in this field.[34]

Intensive care work, though portrayed as challenging and exciting, often was boring. In the face of its unproven effectiveness, coronary care technology still required workers throughout the world to care for costly machines and the patients to whom they were attached. Trained in routinized tasks, allied health technicians partially satisfied this need. Their deskilling, however, illustrated the same degradation of work that affected the labor force outside the health sector.

Technological Innovation and the International Capitalist System

The development, promotion, and proliferation of CCUs during empire past, first in the United States and then worldwide, represented a complex historical process. Similar processes occurred in the spread of many costly innovations and clinical practices. Tests of effectiveness seldom guided policy decisions fostering the diffusion of such technologies.

Although not exhaustive, an overview helps clarify the worldwide proliferation of CCUs and other medical "advances" during empire past (Figure 3-1). Corporate research and development led to the production of new technology, pharmaceuticals, and related innovations. The guiding motivation for corporations was profit. In this sense the commercialization of health care resembled that of nonmedical goods and services. Closely linked to corporations, philanthropies supported research and clinical practices that enhanced profits. Agencies of the state encouraged innovations by grants for investigation, financial assistance to medical centers adopting new technology, and advocacy of new clinical practices linked to the new technology. While state intervention benefited private enterprise, it also enhanced the faltering legitimacy of the capitalist political-economic system. Academic clinicians and investigators, based in teaching hospitals, helped develop technology and fostered its diffusion through professional publications and pronouncements in the public media. Corporate sales efforts cultivated markets in health institutions, both domestic and foreign, including those in less developed countries. Technologic change generated the need for allied health workers who were less skilled than professionals. The cyclical acceptance of technologic innovations by medical institutions involved capital expenditures that drove up the overall cost of health care worldwide.

Figure 3-1 Overview of the Development, Promotion, and Proliferation of Coronary Care Units and Similar Medical Advances

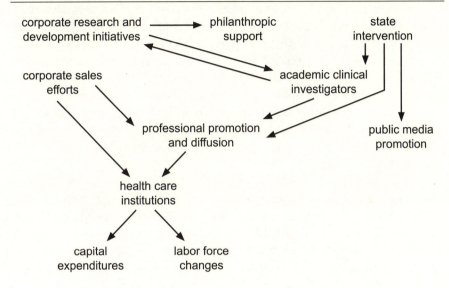

The belief that CCUs were effective in improving outcomes such as mortality and morbidity became so ingrained that even now professionals and patients rarely question whether the intensive care environment is the best place for patients to recuperate after heart attacks. One might hope that the unproved effectiveness of CCUs would have attracted more research during recent years, but that is not the case. For instance, when questions have arisen about the effectiveness of a particular procedure in the care of patients with heart attacks, random controlled trials have produced answers, but always with patients already admitted to CCUs.[35] From this perspective, researchers learned that prayer is relatively effective in improving outcomes among patients in CCUs after heart attacks.[36] On the other hand, investigators discovered that the Swan-Ganz catheter, which for many years measured patients' ventricular function in CCUs, proved not only ineffective but also possibly dangerous.[37] Showing again the persuasiveness of unproven but widely used practices, the American College of Cardiology—as part of its fiftieth anniversary celebration—republished an early article on CCUs as a landmark publication, even though the original article claimed to demonstrate CCUs' effectiveness without data from a random controlled trial.[38] Given the weight of such opinions, current committees monitoring research on human subjects probably would not approve an investigation that reexamined CCUs'

effectiveness by randomly assigning patients to CCU versus home treatment after heart attacks.

Meanwhile, in health care as in other areas, cost-effectiveness methodology restricted the level of analysis to the evaluation of specific innovations. Even when this approach did assess effectiveness of technology, as it actually did not do for coronary care technology, the cost-effectiveness approach obscured one fundamental source of high costs and ineffective practices: the profit motive. Apparent methodologic sophistication masked the analytic poverty of research that evaluated many different innovations while overlooking their common origins in the drive for profit. Because of this deficiency, cost-effectiveness analysis mystified the roots of expensive, ineffective practices in the very nature of the global capitalist system.

Defects of research, however, proved less dangerous than defects of policy. Cost containment in health care became a highly touted priority worldwide. Services whose effectiveness proved difficult to demonstrate by the new methodologies became prime candidates for cutbacks, including primary care and public health services. In both developed and less developed countries, poor people and minority groups, historically victimized, were the first to suffer from this purported rationalization of policy. (I analyze recent neoliberal policies leading to public-sector cutbacks in Part 2.) Meanwhile, private profit in health care, a major fuel for high costs, continued unabated. The promotion of high technology in medicine, which occurred in advanced capitalist countries and less developed countries of the periphery, may seem irrational when analyzed in terms of proven medical effectiveness. These trends appear considerably more rational when viewed from the needs of the international capitalist system.

*   *   *

Despite the wide impact that the diffusion of high medical technology exerted in service of corporate profits and the consolidation of economic empire, resistance to this approach arose in several areas of the world. This resistance usually took its conceptual bearings from social medicine and understanding the social determinants of illness and early death—for instance, from the work of Engels, Virchow, and Allende, as discussed in Chapter 2. The countervailing conceptual approach also lent itself to key historical struggles against the dominant model of capitalist medicine expanding through empire past. I now turn to two instructive examples of such struggles against the dominant model and on behalf of a different model, which confronted and tried to change the social conditions that caused illness and hastened early death.

CHAPTER 4

PATHS OF RESISTANCE TO EMPIRE IN PUBLIC HEALTH AND HEALTH SERVICES

The society in which medicine and public health are situated shapes the changes that occur within the medical sphere. In the context of empire past, Chile and Cuba took different paths, and their histories have much to teach about policy, strategy, and the nature of reform. Changes in health and public health systems paralleled transformations that were occurring throughout both societies. The countervailing conceptual approach of Engels, Virchow, and Allende influenced the social policies and health policies enacted in the two countries. This alternative model emphasized the importance of fundamental societal change as a route to improved health outcomes. Such a route involved modifying fundamentally the social determinants of illness and early death.

Until 1973, Chile enjoyed a long history of civilian government with strong traditions of social democracy and progressive programs of health and welfare. In Cuba prior to 1959, a dictatorship controlled the country, stark patterns of class privilege manifested themselves, and public health and welfare systems proved rudimentary at best. Both Latin American nations suffered from economic underdevelopment and dependency. After Chile and Cuba won political independence from Spanish and British imperialism, they both witnessed the exploitation and extraction of economic resources by North American corporations. In Chile, economic imperialism drained mineral resources like copper, and in Cuba, sugar and tourism provided rich sources of foreign profit. Poverty and imperialism constrained the effectiveness of health and welfare programs in both nations. When the *Unidad Popular* (UP, or Popular Unity) government headed by Salvador Allende took office during 1970, it aimed toward the nonviolent, gradual emergence of socialism. The military coup d'état of 1973 abruptly terminated Chile's widely watched "peaceful road" to a socialist society. On the other hand, Cuba's revolution was rapid, violent, and thorough in consolidating state power.

Both countries' histories demonstrate the linkages among medicine, public health, empire, and social change. The experiences of Chile and Cuba illustrate the limitations of major health-care reforms in the context of unresolved social contradictions and the advantages of health policies tied to broad, social structural change. In Chile, underlying contradictions impeded crucial reforms, both within and outside the health sector. Cuba's accomplishments—in reorganizing the health-care system, in adopting rationalized policies about medical technology, in restructuring community medicine, and in modifying doctor-patient relationships—grew organically from a wide-ranging social revolution.

The comparative histories of Chile and Cuba during empire past conveyed certain lessons that apply regardless of a society's level of development. First, health care is inextricably linked to a nation's political and economic systems. Second, problems within the health system emerge from and reinforce the larger contradictions in society. Third, incremental reforms in the health system exert little lasting impact without basic change in the social order. Such lessons of empire past also set a stage for the policies that shaped medicine and public health during empire present and empire future, to be considered later.

Chile: A Transformation Thwarted by Empire

In 1952, as a senator in the national congress, Salvador Allende proposed legislation that established a national health service (*Servicio Nacional de Salud,* SNS), a system that provided services to people who could not afford private practitioners. The SNS comprised a network of public hospitals and clinics. With the implementation of this program, health care became a right for all Chilean citizens.

The SNS, however, developed certain weaknesses, including physicians' tendency to use the system's facilities to provide private practice, which subsequently drained public resources. Because they could join the SNS voluntarily and could work on a part-time basis, doctors gained access to SNS hospitals and clinics, where they maintained offices to see both SNS and private patients. Although private practitioners were expected to work a fixed proportion of time for the SNS, these hours were not enforced by SNS officials. By the time the UP government took power in 1970, approximately 90 percent of Chilean physicians belonged to the SNS on a full- or part-time basis. In no sense, however, did this statistic represent a substantial commitment to public health.

Chile's national health insurance, National Medical Service of Employees (*SERvicio MEdico NAcional de Empleados*, SERMENA), established in 1968, added to the complexity and bureaucracy of the system, rather than improving and consolidating health care available for Chileans. SERMENA created still another health system in addition to the SNS and private practice. As a voluntary plan for health insurance similar to the Blue Cross–Blue Shield plans in the United States, SERMENA provided both hospitalization and ambulatory benefits for patients who decided to pay annual insurance premiums. In addition, SERMENA received public subsidies from government funds, which were used to pay doctors on a fee-for-service basis for seeing patients covered under the insurance plan.

A primary motivation for SERMENA was to provide continued support for fee-for-service private practice, and thus to subsidize the middle and upper classes who generally had utilized private practitioners. During the 1960s, Chile, like many other countries, faced rapid increases in the costs of medical care. Chile's middle class, who generally had used private practitioners rather than the SNS, felt these increases acutely. The medical profession became concerned that it would lose much of its private clientele. As a result, in 1968 the Christian Democratic Party presidential administration of Eduardo Frei Montalva established SERMENA, to provide nationally administered health insurance for the majority of professionals, owners of small businesses, and government employees. In this way, SERMENA directed even more of Chile's health resources into the private sector. Like the SNS, SERMENA provided important benefits to private practitioners while requiring no fundamental changes to improve the health care available for low-income Chileans.

The governments prior to Allende's UP administration had created a public health system but had not overcome the inequities of the private-public contradiction. Although most Chilean physicians worked part-time for the SNS, they also continued their own practices. Doctors received greater financial reward from their private patients and felt little motivation to devote energy to patients covered under public programs. Although the majority of Chilean citizens were "public" patients, overall health spending was considerably greater in the private sector than in the public sector. Per capita health expenditures were far higher for the small proportion of Chileans who obtained care from private practitioners than for those covered by SERMENA and the SNS. During 1969, for instance, fee-for-service private practice consumed approximately $100 per capita per year to serve 8 percent of the Chilean population; SERMENA used approximately $50 per capita per year to serve 22 percent of the population; and the SNS, serving 70 percent of Chile's population, received about $33 per capita per year.[1] These lopsided figures illustrated how the private sector created a drain on the financial resources and personnel available to serve people in the public sector.

With the enactment of SERMENA, Chile's medical care assumed the form of a three-class system, so that upper-, middle-, and lower-income people enjoyed access to different types of health care. The upper class maintained access to private practitioners and paid on a fee-for-service basis. Middle-class people usually obtained insurance coverage through SERMENA, which also paid doctors on a fee-for-service basis but with government subsidies financed by taxes. While low-income Chileans held a theoretical right to health care provided by the SNS, in practice Chile's problem of medical maldistribution still prevented low-income people from receiving adequate care.

The inequities of the multitiered system had become widely recognized, and several voices called for the adoption of a unified health service, or *Servicio Único*. *The Servicio Único* sought to abolish the private sector, either by banning the private practice of medicine or by heavily taxing private practice. If enacted, the *Servicio Único* theoretically would have provided services efficiently to people from all class backgrounds. The concept of *Servicio Único* clearly threatened the Chilean medical profession. Because this measure remained controversial, the UP coalition did not formally include it in the platform for the 1970 election.[2] The platform, which represented a compromise adopted jointly by several left-oriented parties, merely noted that health care was a basic right of all citizens.

Allende's UP administration favored a more equitable distribution of resources but never explicitly advocated the suppression of private practice, and it entered office without a clear policy directed toward eliminating the private-public duality. This government sought socialism through peaceful means. During its three years in office, it encouraged politicization in the health-care system and numerous other sectors. Although the UP assumed power over the executive branch of government through electoral processes, vast sectors of Chilean society remained autonomous. In particular, the UP did not gain control over the legislature, judiciary, and military. During its three years in office, while it encouraged politicization, the UP never came close to the consolidation of state power, as it initially anticipated. This weakness made the UP vulnerable to the armed overthrow, largely orchestrated by the United States, that Allende's devotion to nonviolent and constitutional processes could not prevent.

Opponents struggled to create a situation of shortages and economic chaos in an effort to undermine the UP, and the U.S. government (largely through the Central Intelligence Agency) supported and helped plan these destabilization efforts. Shortages of medications and equipment deeply affected the medical system. Since health care was closely linked to Chile's economic situation, the effects of empire and underdevelopment became clear during the UP period.

Economic policies that fostered the UP's downfall originated primarily in the United States, as multinational corporations viewed with dismay the prospect of a socialist government. Corporations such as International Telephone and Telegraph (ITT) actively conspired to prevent Allende from assuming the presidency after his election in 1970.[3] When the UP did take office, it moved to nationalize key industries dominated by North American interests. The most dramatic economic initiative occurred in 1971, when Chile nationalized its copper mines.

The financial establishments of the United States responded swiftly with an economic blockade against Chile, as the Nixon administration denied additional foreign aid, loans, or credit. U.S. representatives to international financial institutions (such as the International Monetary Fund, Export-Import Bank, World Bank, and Inter-American Development Bank), as well as large banks in the United States traditionally offering credit to foreign nations, withheld loans for nonmilitary purposes.

Due to Chile's dependence on loans for the purchase of imports, the country faced severe shortages of consumer goods. The dissatisfaction of middle-class Chilean consumers plunged the UP government into an increasingly untenable political position. ITT officials predicted the consequences of implementing a hard-line economic policy: "A more realistic hope among those who want to block Allende is that a swiftly deteriorating economy ... will touch off a wave of violence, resulting in a military coup."[4] While denying economic support in all civilian sectors, the U.S. government continued to provide financial and technical assistance to the Chilean military.[5]

Forces of empire, coupled with economic dependency, tempered Chile's ability to achieve lasting health-care reforms. The intertwining of medical underdevelopment and economic underdevelopment greatly limited health resources, hindering the UP's efforts. As the Chilean journalist Valenzuela observed, if Chile and similar countries spent the same proportion of their wealth for health care as did a developed country like the United States, the impact would be limited due to the less developed country's lower level of wealth. Valenzuela concluded: "Consequently every health policy should be narrowly united with the general policy regarding development of the country."[6]

Empire tempered Chile's ability to achieve lasting health-care reforms in other ways as well. Multinational corporations operating in less developed countries like Chile generally removed many times more profit than they invested. Products like medical instruments and drugs had been imported or manufactured in Chile by profitable subsidiaries of North American corporations (as described for coronary care technology in the last chapter). During the years prior to the UP government, foreign companies reaped approximately $9.8 billion in profits from

Chile.[7] This wealth, if not removed from the country, could have gone toward health and welfare, as well as general economic development.

In the health sector itself, resources also moved from less to more developed countries. Doctors trained in countries like Chile frequently migrated to developed nations like the United States, leading to a loss of human resources and capital for the poorer countries. Due to the flow of physicians to the United States, Latin America incurred an annual loss of more than $200 million, an amount roughly equivalent to the medical aid that the United States gave to Latin America for an entire decade.[8] When human and natural resources left the country in vast quantity, a less developed nation like Chile could not expect a substantial improvement in health care.

Medical professionals' class position also posed a problem for the UP's programs, as a majority of physicians held class interests that conflicted with progressive social change. The Chilean Medical Association consistently opposed the UP, for two primary reasons. First, as members of the upper middle class, physicians found that shortages of consumer goods became intolerable inconveniences for their customary lifestyles. Although these shortages, as well as price inflation affecting such products, resulted largely from economic sanctions imposed by the United States, most Chilean physicians blamed the UP government and Allende personally for Chile's difficulties. Second, Chilean doctors saw potential threats to their own professional dominance over the health-care system. The UP's support of consumer-worker councils in neighborhoods and hospitals (described below) implied an impending transformation of the health-care system in the direction of popular control.

The UP government established several public health programs designed to improve the distribution of resources throughout the country.[9] The UP's innovations emphasized nutrition, environmental health, and preventive care. Allende's analysis of the social origins of illness (as discussed in Chapter 2) and his view of needed social change as a precondition for progress in public health set the framework for the UP's primary reforms. The government provided a half liter per day of free milk to all children and pregnant or nursing mothers. Educational campaigns promoted better nutrition. The SNS developed a system of emergency care, whose purpose was to offer free services to all citizens for medical and surgical emergencies. To help reduce Chile's high rates of infant and perinatal mortality, the government set up a network of maternity clinics in small towns. Focusing also on occupational and environmental health, the UP tried to decrease the incidence of diseases like silicosis by requiring technical innovations in copper mining and industries that emitted mineral dusts in the processes of production. In addition, the government initiated programs to improve sanitation and housing, especially for low-income areas.

Attempting to correct maldistribution of health services that it inherited from previous administrations, the UP began to construct new hospitals and clinics and initiated financial incentives for practitioners willing to work in rural provinces. Such changes increased both ambulatory services and inpatient care in underserved areas. The UP also promoted short-term campaigns to focus attention on rural health problems. For instance, a "health train" sponsored by the government gave medical care to approximately 30,000 people during a tour of the southern provinces. These health reforms became highly visible and widely publicized.

Because the UP did not succeed in consolidating state power by gaining control over all branches of government, however, the executive branch could not employ compulsory mechanisms to achieve a thorough structural transformation of health care, and massive maldistribution of health personnel and facilities persisted. The UP could not nationalize the health system, and the government did not require doctors to serve in areas of the country that lacked adequate personnel. The UP also could not substantially expand the resources available for public health, since it was unable to impose any major restrictions on private practice. Regarding expensive medical technology, although the UP government made some initial efforts to regulate the sales of drugs and equipment, it failed to achieve a national formulary that limited private profits for multinational corporations. Broad social contradictions, including uneven development and the private-public duality, persisted as structural limitations to change.[10]

Regarding control and organization of the health-care system, the UP encouraged democratization and decentralization. These modifications signaled important shifts in financing and power. Generally the government supported increased worker and consumer control. In the industrial sector, this policy led to workers' administration of a number of factories, especially after several companies (including textiles, automotive repair industries, and metallurgical enterprises) were nationalized. In the health-care system, consumer-worker control gradually emerged at two levels: the community and the hospital.

Part of the UP program strove to decentralize medical care by placing greater emphasis on the neighborhood health centers. The goal of decentralization, together with efforts to democratize the health system and to encourage greater community participation, led to the enactment of *Decreto 602,* a government decree that provided a structure for active participation by health workers and community representatives. *Decreto 602* established four different councils, two on the neighborhood health center level and two on the level of the area hospital. Figure 4-1 presents a simplified diagram of the relations among these advisory councils, the neighborhood health centers, and the area hospitals.

Figure 4-1 Structure of Popular Participation
Under the Unidad Popular Government in Chile

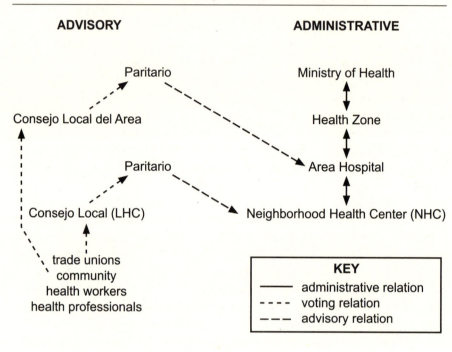

The UP initiated a Program of Sociocultural Development, one of whose goals was to integrate health teams and community members in identifying local needs. Cooperating with local organizations, the health teams offered health information and emphasized the importance of people's direct participation as knowledgeable community members. The health teams encouraged patients' assertive behavior with doctors. This activity pointed toward greater personal autonomy in health care and reduced professional dominance within doctor-patient relationships. In general, the health teams attempted to raise the level of medical and political consciousness and to encourage activism.

As community participation strengthened, many local health councils integrated themselves into other broad-based organizations concerned with food distribution, transportation, local security, and industrial production. When available health facilities appeared inadequate, local health council members took part in autonomous "committees to defend health." These groups became increasingly viable routes to achieve popular power. They also provided a basis for the massive efforts needed to maintain health care during later strikes and boycotts by the medical profession.

Paralleling these changes on the neighborhood level, comparable democratization of decision making occurred in many hospitals, especially those affiliated with medical schools. Within each specialty department, a governing council included elected representatives of professional and nonprofessional workers. The governing council made administrative and staffing decisions that formerly had fallen under the exclusive jurisdiction of high-ranking professionals. Influence of the departmental councils extended to the governance of the hospital as an institution. Departmental councils elected representatives—nonprofessional workers as well as physicians—to the council that made policy for the entire hospital. A restructuring of power relations in hospitals reflected a thrust toward democratization that occurred also in other Chilean institutions, including industrial enterprises and universities.

The effects of the coup on September 11, 1973, which the U.S. government helped plan and carry out, proved devastating to much of Chilean society and to its health-care system. Seizing power just six months after 44 percent of the Chilean people voted for the UP government in congressional elections, the military junta knew it needed to deal with its opponents and generally chose to execute them. During the first three months of dictatorship, approximately 10,000 people were killed, in a total Chilean population of 8 million.[11] The junta closed most neighborhood health centers that had operated in urban communities and rural areas. Decentralized medical services returned to the area hospitals, which members of the Chilean Medical Association again controlled. Community participation in health planning ended abruptly, and the local and area councils that influenced health policy under the UP disbanded. Within hospitals, the consumer-worker councils on the departmental and hospital levels were abolished. Private practitioners, under military scrutiny, regained control of the health system. The dictatorship also discontinued most of the UP government's preventive health programs or, as in the case of free milk distribution to children, private entrepreneurs took control of these programs. Low-income Chileans experienced even more severe difficulties in obtaining medical care than they faced prior to the UP period.

Health workers who supported the UP program suffered harsh reprisals, including work dismissal, imprisonment, and torture. Approximately two-thirds of the union of nonprofessional health workers were dismissed because of previous activities supporting the UP; one-third of members in the union of nonphysician health professionals also were fired. Rates of unemployment for both professional and nonprofessional health workers rose rapidly. Former directors of the neighborhood health centers were detained in the National Stadium with other political prisoners. At least thirty-five physicians were executed or died following torture. Medical school professors as well as general practitioners were imprisoned; torture was used routinely against doctors and other health workers. Some military physicians cooperated in administering torture, particularly by supervising the use of drugs during torture sessions.[12]

The Chilean experience proved deeply disturbing to those who upheld nonviolence and peaceful reform. Lacking state power and unwilling to arm the masses for military confrontation, the UP could not persuade the opposition to maintain legal and constitutional procedures. The brutality of Chile's dictatorship showed the harsh methods needed to withstand a widely supported movement toward progressive change.

Cuba: A Transformation Thwarting the Advance of Empire

Despite its problems, the health-care system that the UP government inherited in Chile was vastly superior to Cuba's prerevolutionary system. Cuba's medical services before 1959 were so limited that they require little discussion. The government operated a small number of clinics and public hospitals in Havana and a few other cities. These facilities were maldistributed and riddled by corruption. Private practitioners and clinics, located almost exclusively in the capital and large cities, served high-income Cubans on a fee-for-service basis. Insurance groups, or *mutualistas*, administered private insurance plans for descendants from specific geographic regions of Spain and for selected categories of industrial workers. The province of Havana contained 32 percent of the country's hospital beds and the only blood bank. There was not one public dental clinic. Cuba's only medical school, in Havana, trained doctors for private practice; most graduates remained in Havana, settled in other cities, or emigrated.

Before the revolution, low-income Cubans living in both urban and rural areas faced enormous obstacles to obtaining needed services.[13] More than 60 percent of the population had no regular access to medical care. Physicians, clinics, and hospitals in the private sector remained unavailable because of high fees and geographical maldistribution. Public sector medicine was rudimentary and usually inaccessible. Traditional healers (*curanderos*) and birth attendants (*comadronas*) provided services to Cuba's poor, but these practitioners could exert little impact on the diseases of underdevelopment. The infant mortality rate ranked among the world's worst. Cuba's people also suffered from a high incidence of such infectious diseases as tuberculosis, polio, malaria, intestinal parasites, acute diarrhea, diphtheria, and tetanus. Malnutrition heightened the risk of infection, and epidemics were frequent. In short, a coordinated public health system was nonexistent, expensive fees and maldistribution left much of the population without access to services, and patterns of disease and early death that were characteristic of underdevelopment ravaged the poor.

In Cuba, the revolution occurred swiftly and dramatically. After its military victory, the revolutionary government moved quickly to consolidate power, creating cooperative relationships that linked the mass organizations and the party's leadership. The new government controlled the armed forces and the executive branch. The legislature and judiciary ceased to exist in their prerevolutionary forms, and mass political organizations emerged throughout the country.[14] Previously clandestine local groups reconstituted themselves as Committees for the Defense of the Revolution (CDRs). Organized in local neighborhoods and workplaces, the CDRs initially concerned themselves with security and vigilance against counterrevolutionary activities. Later, the CDRs became the primary political structures for popular representation in policy decisions. Other major mass organizations included the Federation of Cuban Women, the association of small farmers, and the trade unions. All the mass organizations elected representatives at the local, regional, provincial, and national levels. The Cuban Communist Party, which came to hold ultimate responsibility for national policy decisions, assumed formal power after the mass organizations had established themselves. Cooperative relationships linked the mass organizations and the party's leadership. A new judicial system also emerged. Popularly elected people's courts generally decided disputes and made judgments about criminal actions at the local level. Regional, provincial, and national courts adjudicated weightier conflicts, including those that arose between labor unions and administrators of factories.

As in Chile, Cuban physicians occupied a privileged class position before the revolution; most maintained urban private practices that served high-income patients. The revolution's swiftness and largely military nature permitted little organized resistance by the medical profession. Also, because Cuba's public health system, hospitals, and clinics were already inadequate, strikes or other work stoppages by the profession could have had a much more limited impact than they did in Chile. Physicians found themselves in a radically different society whose future was unpredictable and difficult to control.

Cuba's revolutionary government took no measures to change the conditions of private medical practice. During the first years after the revolution, health professionals faced little objective change in their conditions of work. Doctors could continue their practices as before the revolution, with the same fee-for-service arrangement. In fact, the government offered financial incentives to physicians if they would work part-time in public hospitals and clinics. Doctors even received the option of office space and the use of technical facilities in public hospitals. Physicians and other citizens who owned homes and offices before the revolution retained their ownership rights.

Subjectively, however, many private practitioners perceived enormous threats. As one of its first priorities, the new government began planning for a reorganized public health system that would overcome previous inequities linked to poverty and geographic isolation. Physicians could participate in policy making, but other groups, including government leaders, mass organizations, and representatives of nonprofessional health workers, also would take part in health-care planning. As a result, doctors could anticipate a gradual loss of professional dominance and autonomy. In addition, creation of a nationally organized health-care system posed long-term financial dangers for private practitioners. The government proposed clinics and hospitals to provide publicly financed, high-quality services, which patients generally would receive free of charge. The availability of free care offered by the public sector would attract not only the poor and people without previous access to services, but also a part of practitioners' private clientele.

Private practitioners anticipated long-term changes in the conditions of practice and also a more general loss of class privilege. Although the new government permitted limited holdings in private property, it did restrict private investment in land and corporations. The government also sought a more equitable distribution of goods and services. Monitoring and rationing led to greater availability of products for people who previously faced hardship in obtaining the necessities of life. As legal and black-market prices outside the rationing system inflated rapidly, some products became harder to obtain for those accustomed to a degree of luxury.

Real or imagined, such threats proved intolerable for a large segment of the Cuban medical profession. By 1962, two years after the revolution, nearly half of Cuba's physicians had emigrated, mostly to the United States. At the country's sole medical school in Havana, whole departments simply ceased to function. During this period, physicians sympathetic to the revolution came from other countries to provide direct services and other assistance. Although these supporters offered a stopgap, the Cuban government faced a momentous crisis in the health-care system.

Forces of empire deepened this crisis still further, as the Kennedy administration initiated a series of interventions. This process led to a further breakdown of the health-care system. Primary among these ventures was the Bay of Pigs invasion of 1961. This unsuccessful military maneuver set the stage for an economic embargo that lasted even through the declining years of empire present.

Cuba's prerevolutionary economy was heavily dependent on the United States. In the medical sector, the United States generally was the sole supplier for equipment and pharmaceuticals; as an underdeveloped and dependent country, Cuba—like Chile—had paid a high price for medical products. Nevertheless, the United States had provided a regular source of needed equipment, supplies, and drugs. The economic embargo abruptly ended Cuba's ability to buy these goods, and severe shortages arose rapidly. For major radiologic and laboratory equipment, replacement parts became unavailable. In the long term, Cuba faced major decisions about the purchase of foreign technology, as opposed to the creation of new industries to manufacture medical products. The impact of empire, coupled with the prior class position of professionals, led to a further breakdown of the health-care system, as personnel left the country and supplies became difficult to obtain.

Yet, in contrast to Chile, the fact that the Cuban government had consolidated state power created the potential for basic change in medicine and public health. While Chile's incomplete revolution permitted policies that created limited reforms, the nature of Cuba's revolution encouraged more dramatic improvements that moved beyond reformism and toward a structurally different health-care system. The rapid transformation of Cuban society permitted a rapid reconstruction of its health-care system, and the consolidation of state power allowed for a remarkable series of reforms and structural modifications. The changes fostered the creation of a health-care system that, to a variety of observers, appeared the most responsive and effective in all of Latin America.[15]

Government policies rectified geographical maldistribution. In exchange for free education, graduates served a compulsory two-year period of practice in rural health centers and hospitals. Similar programs provided for a redistribution of nurses and allied health workers. Within a decade, each of Cuba's provinces contained a major regional hospital and an integrated system of clinics. More than half the new clinics were located in rural areas that previously had lacked such facilities.

The government also sought to change prior patterns of class structure and racism that limited the accessibility of health care. Even when doctors were within traveling distance, the high fees of private practice prevented low-income people from obtaining services. Racism compounded this problem of access, since the number of doctors and clients who were white was disproportionate to the ratio of whites to the general population. In postrevolutionary Cuba, health care became free to the patient at the point of delivery. Public financing assured that medical services, as well as most drugs and needed supplies, were available to patients, regardless of income. Patients received preventive, ambulatory, and inpatient services without charge. Afro-Cubans entered the profession of medicine in proportion to the population, and racism no longer hindered patients from seeking and obtaining care.

While the consolidation of state power permitted effective planning to overcome maldistribution and inaccessibility, the mass organizations took an active role in preventive medicine. The CDRs coordinated immunization campaigns in neighborhoods and workplaces and assisted people in obtaining early attention for medical problems. The Federation of Cuban Women helped coordinate prenatal, maternal, and infant care. Regarding occupational health, the association of small farmers and the trade unions monitored workplace safety, organizing educational campaigns to inform employees about work hazards. When national goals of high productivity interfered with safe working conditions, the trade unions intervened to protect workers. Coordinated central planning and activism by the mass organizations fostered prevention and accessible services.

After the early exodus of physicians, the private-public contradiction ceased to drain resources in any important way. Physicians who had engaged in private practice before 1959 could continue in the private sector on a full-time or part-time basis. New medical graduates, in exchange for free education, vowed not to engage in private practice but to remain in the public sector. Since primary and specialty services were available in public clinics and hospitals, patients saw little reason to consult private practitioners, unless they maintained relationships from before the revolution. The private sector withered, as older practitioners died or retired. By the late 1960s, the training of physicians after the revolution reversed the shortages that had resulted from the earlier exodus of practitioners. Especially in primary care, the ratios of physicians to population improved even in remote rural areas, so that the overall availability of medical practitioners reached or even surpassed that in economically advanced countries like the United States.

Physicians' social class allegiance also contributed to the successes of Cuban medicine. In contrast to Chile, where medical professionals consistently impeded the transition to socialism, Cuban physicians could do little in opposition other than leave the country. After the crisis of the early 1960s, the class origins of the new Cuban medical profession changed quickly. A large proportion of new graduates came from working-class or peasant families. For them, the revolution provided mobility into a satisfying and relatively prestigious field of work.

Although it might be expected that physicians trained after the revolution would enjoy certain privileges of higher class position, even critical observers of the Cuban health-care system found little evidence of such class privilege. This observation, however, did not imply that doctors lacked power. Doctors gained greater access to publicly owned automobiles for work-related travel and received somewhat higher salaries than other medical workers (the differential between highest and lowest incomes in the health-care system remained less than 20 percent of that in the United States), yet their housing and ability to buy consumer goods stayed approximately the same as that of other workers.[16] Commitment to public service, willingness to cooperate with the mass organizations, and tolerance for difficult conditions of practice reflected the medical profession's drastically different class origins and loyalties.

Professional dominance remained a source of tension and ambiguity, but this problem occurred within a framework of coordinated administration and democratic participation in decision making. The Ministry of Public Health organized the health-care system so that planning and administration could take place at the national, provincial, regional, and local levels. Figure 4-2 shows the structure of the system and the mechanisms for popular participation. At the local level, primary care practitioners' offices, polyclinics, municipal hospitals, and rural hospitals provided direct medical services. Mass organizations elected representatives to the local people's commissions on health, which helped implement such activities as immunization campaigns, control of infectious diseases, maternal and infant care, and occupational health monitoring. The local commissions also advised the administrative and clinical staffs about priorities and shortcomings. Following a reorganization in 1974, the municipal hospitals and polyclinics became directly accountable to elected municipal assemblies. The assemblies, which served as the formal structures of political representation known as "People's Power," held authority to request changes in the programs and personnel of the municipal hospitals and polyclinics when local needs warranted such changes or when dissatisfactions arose.

The organizational structure in Cuba permitted centralized planning and priority setting; it also encouraged decentralized implementation and flexibility. At each level of the system, medical professionals performed administrative and clinical tasks. To ensure responsiveness and accountability, however, the mass organizations, commissions on health, and assemblies took part in policy decisions. The principle of democratic centralism fostered participation by patients, community residents, and both professional and nonprofessional workers. Democratic participation balanced central planning and coordination, reducing bureaucratic rigidities.

The structure of the Cuban health-care system helped control the proliferation of costly medical technology, in contrast to the uncritical adoption of coronary care and related technologies in other less developed countries during empire past. At the national level, the Ministry of Public Health and the institutes of health evaluated the adoption of technical innovations, new equipment, and drugs. A national formulary of generic medications limited the drugs that physicians could prescribe. As in other industries, pharmaceutical production occurred within a nationalized and centrally planned enterprise (*empresa*), which manufactured

Figure 4-2 Structure of Popular Participation
in the Cuban Health-Care System

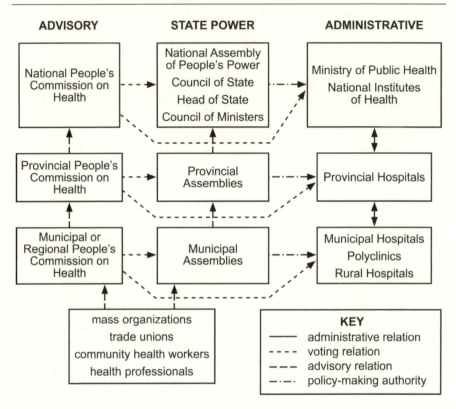

ADVISORY	STATE POWER	ADMINISTRATIVE

about 75 percent of the drugs and medical equipment used throughout the country. Beyond cutting costs, the Cuban pharmaceutical and equipment industry partly overcame the devastating effects of the economic embargo by the United States, which caused shortages of drugs and supplies.

In addition to structural transformations, the Ministry of Public Health devoted attention to nuances of the doctor-patient relationship. Staff turnover and an orientation toward specialty medicine led to widespread dissatisfaction among patients in local communities. As part of the programs in community and family medicine, research and teaching efforts emphasized the quality of professional-client interaction. Primary care teams, composed of doctors, nurses, and allied health workers, assumed responsibility for a designated panel of patients. Participation by psychologists, sanitary workers, epidemiologists, and social workers on these teams supported an integrated approach to each patient and family. Due to the prioritization on educating large numbers of physicians and other health workers, the primary care teams were able to provide services in neighborhoods of cities and in rural areas throughout the country.

The primary care teams did not medicalize problems that derived from social or psychological roots. Instead, team members facilitated change in patients' living or working conditions that interfered with health and well-being.[17] Educational campaigns in neighborhoods and workplaces encouraged citizens to express discontent and to suggest improvements, either to the primary care team directly or through the mass organizations.

Comparative Changes in the Context of Empire

In Chile, the health councils established to increase consumer-worker influence eventually took part in broader mass mobilization. This mobilization, however, seldom received direct support from the UP government. When mobilization occurred around health issues, it reflected a spontaneous movement by consumers and workers. The lack of explicit encouragement for mass political action was similar to the UP's hesitancy to promote mobilization in other areas of Chilean society. Critics of the UP questioned why the government—which appeared well aware of a planned military coup many months in advance—failed to arm the workers. Despite tactical explanations given at the time, this decision itself proved consistent with the government's restrained stance toward mass mobilization in health care and other sectors of the society. In the context of empire and with continuing attempts orchestrated by the United States to overthrow the UP government, this lack of strong support for mass mobilization helped explained why the forces of empire past prevailed in Chile.

Despite empire's interventions like the Bay of Pigs invasion, the economic embargo, and other attempts to destabilize the revolutionary government, Cuba transformed its rudimentary and crisis-ridden medical services into a rationalized and accessible system with startling accomplishments. The rapidity and comprehensiveness of these advances depended on revolutionary social change that consolidated state power and that claimed wide popular support. Mass mobilization in Cuba played a key role in the military success of the revolution, leading to a variety of achievements, of which a transformed health-care system was only one. Previously clandestine groups in neighborhoods and workplaces assigned themselves to the CDRs. The local groups became the primary organizations responsible for internal security but later took an active role in health-care activities. In addition to the CDRs, the Federation of Cuban Women, the association of small farmers, the trade unions, the commissions on health, and the assemblies of People's Power at the local, provincial, and national levels participated in policy making and implementation of health programs.

The persistence of the private-public contradiction in Chile reflected an overall failure to achieve state power. During the period of the UP government, no serious effort to nationalize the health-care system took place. During its height of popular support in 1971, the UP government missed a possible chance to gain control of several key institutions—legislature, judiciary, and military.[18] Many activists believed that the time had come to consolidate state power and that a successful coup would become much more likely if the UP did not seize this opportunity. However, Allende argued that attempts to control the military or other major institutions should proceed through standard electoral and administrative procedures that would allow a gradual transition toward a consolidation of power. Due to Allende's and the UP's reluctance to take stronger action, 1971 passed with most institutions outside the executive branch still controlled by powerful groups that opposed progress toward socialism and a unified health-care system.

Because the Cuban revolution resulted in a rapid consolidation of state power, the new government could move quickly to build a comprehensive approach to restructuring public health and medical services. Although the limited medical services that existed before the revolution temporarily declined with the exodus of Cuban physicians, the Ministry of Public Health was able to construct accessible facilities, to redistribute personnel, and to wage health campaigns in cooperation with the mass organizations. The government did not directly suppress private practice but instead recruited medical professionals committed to practice in the public sector. Availability of free and high-quality public services implied that over time the private sector would wither, as in fact occurred. The private-public contradiction did not undermine the accomplishments of Cuban medicine, and resolution of this contradiction depended largely on success in achieving state power.

The Chilean and Cuban experiences illustrated how, in the context of an empire hostile to progressive change, incremental reforms in health care could exert little lasting effect without basic change in society. One reason that meaningful reform proved so difficult when unaccompanied by broader social change involved the impact of class structure. In the prerevolutionary context, health professionals—either by birth or by occupational mobility—were members of the upper or upper-middle classes. As such, they held class interests that often impeded progress toward a more egalitarian distribution of goods and services. Doctors, like bankers and corporate managers, possessed economic advantages and customary lifestyles that they were unlikely to sacrifice on behalf of the poor. Besides economic interests, health professionals held dominant positions in the institutions where they worked. Because of their technical expertise, physicians usually believed that professional dominance over health policies was justified. From this vantage point, innovations that limited the profession's control over the conditions of practice were perceived as threatening.

In Chile, the medical profession worked against the UP government's attempts to bring equity and democratization to the health system, while the Cuban revolution led to a transformation of class structure, including the class position of the medical profession. When half the medical profession left the country, the Cuban government mandated active recruitment of students into the study of medicine. Young people from working-class and peasant families entered medical schools in unprecedented numbers, and their free education fostered a renewed commitment to public service. These graduates were less accustomed to the privileges of higher class position than their predecessors and were more willing to cooperate in decentralized and democratically controlled programs. Professional dominance remained a problem in Cuba, but resistance from the profession did not impede reorganization of the health-care system.

The comparative histories of Chile and Cuba revealed, in the context of empire past, the vulnerability of incremental reforms in the health-care system. Allende viewed his presidency as a transitional period in which a series of reforms would culminate in a socialist restructuring of society. To a limited extent, the government encouraged the establishment of local health councils, workers' organizations, and other new groupings whose eventual purpose was a thorough transformation of power relations in Chilean society. With occasional exceptions, however, these organizations did not achieve a redistribution of power. While such attempts at popular control contained a potential for more fundamental social change, they disintegrated in the face of armed attack in the military coup, supported by the international forces of empire. In Cuba, the mass organizations that initially formed as part of the revolutionary process later became a basis for popular participation in health policy that endured and deepened over time.

In particular, the Chilean experience demonstrated that dominant groups within a society, especially when allied with international supporters of empire, would not surrender power peacefully. In this light, societal transformation apparently became a precondition for popular control and lasting reform of health services. In Chile, where many perceived a potential for peaceful transition toward socialism and a democratized health system, Allende's hope that popular control could evolve by peaceful means proved an unrealizable dream.

*   *   *

The Chilean dictatorship also paved the way for a new set of political and economic policies that, during the last years of the twentieth century, facilitated a market-oriented transformation of medicine and public health not only in Chile but also in many other countries worldwide; I pursue this theme in Part 2 of this book. In addition, as I show in Part 3, these issues remain very much alive during the twenty-first century, as countries in Latin America and around the world try to free themselves from burdens of empire past and present.

During the early 1980s, partly in reaction to pressures exerted against empire in Cuba, Chile, Nicaragua, El Salvador, and elsewhere, new regimes in Washington, D.C., and in London began to develop and to implement policies that provided a transition from empire past to what I call empire present. The presidency of Ronald Reagan and the prime ministership of Margaret Thatcher consolidated a sophisticated approach to empire, involving economic and political policies that came to be known as neoliberalism and the Washington Consensus.

These policies exerted profound effects on medicine and public health worldwide. Operating through an emerging transnational ruling class, the forces of empire began to impose a different approach to domination. This approach involved such policies and processes as:

- privatization and dismantling of the public sector
- international trade agreements that restricted the sovereignty of nations to enact measures protecting public health
- macroeconomic policies that encouraged "investment in health" as a route to enhanced profits
- an expanded role for multinational corporations operating in health care
- predominance of international financial institutions in determining health policies, and
- an enlarged space for militarism as a mechanism to generate demand for corporatized medical and mental health services.

A unifying philosophy guided these policies and processes: neoliberalism. Such components of empire present become the focus of Part 2.

PART TWO

EMPIRE PRESENT

CHAPTER 5

NEOLIBERALISM AND HEALTH

With Rebeca Jasso-Aguilar[1]

Neoliberalism was a theory of political and economic practice that profoundly affected the relationships between health and empire present—the period of empire that extended approximately from 1980 until 2010. The theory of neoliberalism argued that market exchange maximized the social good and that human well-being could advance best by enhancing individual entrepreneurial activities within the framework of strong property rights, a free market, and free trade.[2] Neoliberalism claimed that economic growth was beneficial for everyone, at least in the long term. One of the theory's main assumptions was that economic development accompanied by regular growth of the economy constituted a necessary and sufficient condition to solve the problem of poverty.[3]

Beyond such economic considerations, neoliberalism also became a social, political, and cultural project.[4] Neoliberalism saw the role of the state as protecting market practices but opposed the state's roles in central planning and in the provision of public services, including medicine and public health. This opposition stemmed partly from a belief that central planning and the provision of public-sector services threatened the ability of businesspeople as well as ordinary citizens to achieve their purposes and to address social problems by exercising their personal freedom. In addition to a focus on the freedom of individuals, neoliberalism favored the free market principles of neoclassical economics, as elaborated during the second half of the nineteenth century by such figures as Alfred Marshall, William Stanley Jevons, and Leon Walras. These free market principles displaced those of the classical economic liberals who favored a relatively but not completely unregulated market, such as Adam Smith and David Ricardo; hence the term "neoliberal."[5]

One crucial difference between liberalism and neoliberalism involved the latter's preference for the socialization of risk, including the risk incurred by private corporations selling health products, services, and insurance. The socialization of risk facilitated investment in uncertain enterprises by protecting investments for the investors.[6] For instance, as in the economic crisis of the United States beginning in late 2008, the neoliberal state intervened to bail out private banks when their investments crashed. Several other terms also referred to neoliberalism: neoclassical, neoliberal, or libertarian economics; market capitalism; and market liberalism.[7] In addition, neoliberalism equated with the Washington Consensus, Reaganism, the new right agenda, corporate-led growth, and global restructuring.[8]

Neoliberalism and the Dismantling of the Public Sector

As David Harvey has shown, neoliberalism emerged as a specific project to restore power to the capitalist class. Economic policies during the decades after the Great Depression had affected the interests of the capitalist class adversely.[9] The Depression impacted not only the United States but also the global economy, leading economists worldwide to question the free market economic ideology that previously predominated. This questioning led to an exploration of alternative economic principles based on John Maynard Keynes's work, which assigned a more influential role to the state in economic development, as well as in the growth and expansion of capitalist enterprises.[10] Keynesian economics lay at the heart of New Deal policies in the United States, industrialization based on "import substitution" that reduced the dependency of less developed countries through the support of local industries, and a welfare state that protected citizens' well-being by intervening in the economy to prevent financial crises.[11] State management of the economy remained paramount until the 1970s.

At that point, however, critics perceived an exhaustion of Keynesian economic policies and argued that this orientation could not benefit capitalism further. This critique paved the way for an ideological shift in mainstream economics. Early leaders of neoliberalism—Friedrich von Hayek and Milton Friedman among others—founded the Mont Pelerin Society, which provided an international organization supporting the neoliberal orientation in economics.[12] Foundations and think tanks favoring these ideas, such as the Heritage Foundation in Washington and the Institute of Economic Affairs in London, gained prominent positions in influencing political and economic policies. The Nobel Prizes in economics awarded to Hayek in 1974 and to Friedman in 1976 signaled a change in intellectual climate and brought greater prestige to neoliberal theory, which began to expand its influence in a variety of fields, including medicine and public health.[13] During the administrations of Ronald Reagan and Margaret Thatcher, the work of Hayek and Friedman received serious attention both in the political world, where conservative governments took power in many countries, and in academia, where neoliberal economics gained unparalleled prestige as the leading social science.[14]

The apparent exhaustion of Keynesian economic policies, however, resulted from a deliberate and systematic dismantling of the public sector and/or deliberate practices that conveyed the perception of an exhausted public system; such dismantling took place very clearly in health-care and public health systems.[15] Schuld, for instance, documented intentional underspending in the public health system of El Salvador, leading to artificial shortages of doctors and medicines. Laurell and Iriart et al. found similar situations for the health-care and retirement pension systems in Mexico and Argentina. In these cases and others, shortages of financing and supplies accompanied a discourse highlighting the need for changes toward efficiency and modernization of the public system. This discourse underscored failures in the public sector and the superiority of the private sector in undertaking reforms. Shortages, accompanied by this discourse, helped shift public opinion in favor of privatization, which Iriart et al. referred to as the "common sense" of public-sector reform.[16] This dismantling of the public sector, as we will see, led to grave consequences for medicine and public health worldwide.

The Transnational Capitalist Class and Multinational Corporations

During the 1970s a transnational capitalist class refined its ability to act in concert. As William Robinson showed, this emerging class encompassed many countries throughout the world and included executives of transnational corporations, globalizing bureaucrats, politicians, professional groups, media executives, and officials of financial institutions.[17] Global class formation, from this perspective, also involved the emergence of a global proletariat. While the transnational capitalist class developed its own class consciousness, however, the transnational proletariat did not. In many countries, the transnational capitalist class pressed for legislation that favored its interests as a class rather than only as individuals seeking support for their own projects and purposes.[18] Such behavior helped explain the tremendous expansion of lobbying activities, the "revolving door" phenomenon by which lobbyists rotated in and out of government jobs, and the capture of regulatory agencies by special interest groups. This phenomenon occurred not only in the United States but also in many countries within the U.S. sphere of influence.

Multinational corporations became the major beneficiaries of the power restoration that the transnational capitalist class enjoyed. Corporate privileges dated back at least to those provided for merchants of the fifteenth and sixteenth centuries in England. A corporate charter bestowed by the Crown limited the investor's liability for corporate losses to the amount of the investment, a privilege not granted to individuals. Such a charter obliged a corporation to share profits with the Crown. During subsequent centuries, corporate interests continued to pressure governments to expand corporate rights and to diminish obligations. During the British colonization of North America, many new laws protected and extended corporate privileges. In 1897, President Rutherford Hayes declared that the government was no longer of, by, and for the people, but rather "of, by, and for corporations."[19]

Through the "revolving door," corporations gained power as elected officials and staff members of important legislative committees and administrative agencies moved among public-sector jobs and much higher paying positions with private, regulated industries. In this fashion, multinational insurance and pharmaceutical corporations attained powerful positions in key policy decisions affecting medicine and public health. About half of all lobbyists hired by pharmaceutical corporations, medical equipment firms, and managed care organizations previously worked for the federal government; some of them were former U.S. senators and representatives. For instance, the 2003 Medicare "reform" legislation set in motion an exodus from the executive branch, as top government officials negotiated jobs for themselves with affected industries while simultaneously leading negotiations to craft the bill. In addition, prominent drug industry and managed-care lobbyists moved into governmental positions. This two-way revolving door helped ensure profitability for major corporations operating in the health sector.[20]

In policy decisions, the interests of U.S.-based corporations and the U.S. government became substantially identical. The U.S. government frequently acted as a kind of sales representative, aggressively promoting U.S. corporations' interests at home and abroad. During various periods of empire present, the U.S. government applauded corporations' initiatives abroad, while corporations welcomed diplomatic and military efforts to protect empire. Corporate executives also engaged in "corporate diplomacy," helping other countries' governments in drafting legislation to regulate, for instance, foreign investment.[21] As described in the next chapter, corporate diplomacy reached a spectacular level during 1994, with the implementation of the World Trade Organization. Key international trade agreements affecting medicine and public health—for instance, those related to intellectual property rights and food safety—embraced input from affected industrial sectors, particularly multinational corporations dealing in pharmaceutical and agricultural products.[22]

Global corporations promoted loyalty to companies rather than to countries. Such corporations did not belong to or hold citizenship within specific nation-states, even though their headquarters physically existed in certain countries. In less developed countries, corporations attracted local managers and interested them in climbing the corporate ladder with incentives like international careers and positions abroad. This strategy increased managers' loyalty to the corporation and diminished their nationalist instincts, making them less critical and more tolerant of foreign economic penetration. But contrary to a commonly held view, corporations did not necessarily promote development in the countries where they established themselves.[23] In Latin America, governments tried to bring corporations into the most dynamic sectors of the economy, leaving the sluggish industries to local capital.[24] This tendency resulted in the host countries' neglect of research and development, leading to eventual disadvantages in available technology, medical equipment, and medications.

The Nation-State, Sovereignty, and Health

The rise of corporate power, the emergence of a transnational dominant class, and the ascendance of neoliberalism shaped the relationships between globalization and the nation-state, and these transitions reshaped medicine and public health worldwide. During what Robinson called the "third epoch of capitalism" (corresponding roughly to what this book calls "empire past") from the late nineteenth century through the 1970s, the nation-state emerged as an efficient and necessary system for organizing global capitalism.[25] Globalization, however, superseded the material circumstances that allowed the nation-state to emerge. As a result, the nation-state transformed into a transnational state. Rather than as an imposition from outside, this transformation occurred through an accommodation of actors both outside and inside the affected countries.

Globalization thus established the material conditions for the rise of a transnational capitalist class and a working class not restricted to national borders. The transnational capitalist class promoted trade policies and agreements concerning the environment, workplace safety, intellectual property, food, water, and professional licensing. In such efforts, the members of this class acted to reduce the capacity of governments to carry out their traditional functions in protecting public health and in providing health services.

The transnational class's institutional apparatuses—the Trilateral Commission, G-7 coalition of nations, European Union, Organisation for Economic Co-operation and Development, United Nations, International Monetary Fund, World Bank, and World Trade Organization—sought to perform the functions previously fulfilled by the dominant capitalist power, or "hegemon."[26] These apparatuses exercised transnational political and economic authority to reproduce class relations embedded in the global accumulation of capital, that is, to reproduce the transnational capitalist class. The site of this reproduction shifted from the nation-state to the transnational state, and the power of the dominant class became enhanced. New global relations between capital and labor, for instance, involved informalization of work procedures, flexibilization of work schedules, and an overall reduction in the earnings of labor.[27] In addition, the policy of "structural adjustment," which international financial institutions initiated as a condition of new or renegotiated loans to less developed countries, required a reduction and dismantling of services previously provided for the poor in the public sector (later chapters examine structural adjustment in greater depth). This overall transition led to the weakening of the working class as a collective actor. Organizations in civil society, with memberships composed mostly of volunteers, became the only actors capable of posing a meaningful challenge to corporations and neoliberalism.[28]

In line with Robinson's argument, Hardt and Negri suggested that a new type of sovereignty emerged in the global order, along with global markets and global circuits maintained by entrepreneurs.[29] Hardt and Negri referred to this new type of sovereignty as a transformed "Empire." From this viewpoint, Empire[30] differed from imperialism (which broadly characterized what we have called empire past) in how sovereignty was exercised. Sovereignty of the nation-state formed the cornerstone of historical imperialism and remained fundamental to colonialism and economic expansion. Under the new Empire, according to Negri and Hardt, the nation-state's sovereignty declined, along with its ability to regulate economic and cultural exchanges. As a result, even the most dominant nation-states could no longer remain supreme and sovereign authorities, within or outside their own borders.

Under Empire, with the loss of its sovereignty, the nation-state's ability to regulate public health and public life in general declined as well. The decline in the sovereignty of the nation-state, however, did not imply an overall decline in sovereignty. Rather, this change meant that sovereignty took a new form: a series of national and supranational institutions now exercised sovereignty, united under a single logic. This new form of sovereignty constituted Empire, "a form of governance without government."[31] The emerging national and supranational institutions, which Hardt and Negri called "organisms," paralleled the transnational state in Robinson's formulation.

From Hardt and Negri's perspective, Empire served as a basis for a new world order, which exerted power autonomously from nation-states, exercised regulatory authority, and, when necessary, employed coercion using legal instruments. A key feature of Empire involved its capacity "to present force as being in the service of right and peace."[32] In this new era, power operated through the "biopolitical production" of social life itself. Here, components of economic, political, and cultural life overlapped. Individuals came to be controlled not only through consciousness and ideology, but "in the body and with the body" through force exercised purportedly to enhance prospects for peace.[33]

Large transnational corporations constituted the connective fabric of the biopolitical world. Supranational organizations, such as the United Nations, International Monetary Fund, World Bank, and international trade agreements, did not maintain the legitimacy they had enjoyed during the prior world order composed of sovereign nation-states. Instead, their legitimacy depended on new functions that they could perform in the imperial order. One of these emerging functions involved the "formation and education of the administrative personnel of the imperial machine," who came to compose the dominant transnational capitalist class.[34]

In the era of Empire, a transformation of supranational law superseded the domestic laws of nation-states. Domestic law and supranational law operated in the terrain of recurrent international crises. This condition led to the emergence of a presumptive right to intervene, which became one prerogative of Empire.[35] Justified by an appeal to essential values of justice, such as resolving humanitarian problems, guaranteeing international accords, and imposing peace, dominant subjects in the world order achieved a right to intervene in the territory of nondominant subjects.

Under Empire, a variety of organizations, acting on the basis of moral imperatives, practiced a new form of moral intervention. These organizations proliferated outside formal government as nongovernmental organizations, which often intervened in public health and health services. Partly because governments did not run them directly, such organizations presumably acted on the basis of ethical and moral imperatives, identifying universal needs and defending human rights. Nongovernmental organizations, however, became some of the "most powerful, pacific weapons of the new world order."[36]

While Empire could wield enormous powers of oppression and destruction, it also offered new possibilities for forces of liberation.[37] Empire carried the seeds of a counter-Empire due to several factors: all humanity to some degree became subordinated to capital; the gap between rich and poor, and the number of people at these two poles, became more extreme; and lines of geographical and racial/ethnic exploitation increased. These conditions sustained Empire but also led to challenges that aimed to change Empire fundamentally. Struggles to contest, to subvert, and to construct a new alternative to Empire began to emerge. Among many other arenas, such struggles encompassed medicine and public health. Although Part 3 of this book explores such struggles for change, especially in the arena of health, as empire present transitions to empire future, we first need to understand in greater detail some key features of medicine and public health under empire present. That is the goal of Part 2.

*   *   *

Neoliberalism manifested its impact on health and health services nowhere more profoundly than through international trade agreements. As they emerged after 1980, these agreements modified fundamentally the sovereignty of the nation-state to protect the health of the public and the integrity of medical services. Arguably, during recent years of empire present, international trade agreements became the world's most important public health concern. Keenly promoted by the transnational capitalist class, such agreements became a central characteristic of international capitalism. These agreements impacted medicine and public health by modifying the ability of government to monitor and to protect the health of the population in such areas as the environment, the workplace, food, water, access to medications, and the control of health services themselves. The next chapter considers international trade agreements and their effects on health and health services as crucial components of empire present.

CHAPTER 6

INTERNATIONAL TRADE AGREEMENTS, MEDICINE, AND PUBLIC HEALTH

By the early twenty-first century, trade and international trade agreements transformed governments' ability to monitor and protect public health. Trade agreements restricted the capacity of government agencies to regulate occupational and environmental health conditions and food products and to ensure affordable access to medications and water. Such agreements covered a wide range of health services, health facilities, clinician licensing, and the distribution of tobacco and alcohol. To some extent, public health organizations began to grapple with trade-related threats to global health, including emerging infectious diseases and bioterrorism. However, these organizations did not consistently call attention to the potentially deleterious effects of trade agreements on public health and medical services.[1] Partly as a result, during the final years of what I have called empire present, trade agreements profoundly shaped policies that impacted health throughout the world.

Trade Rules

The World Trade Organization (WTO), as I describe in Chapter 1, emerged from the General Agreement on Tariffs and Trade (GATT) in 1994. Together with regional trade agreements initiated by the United States, WTO sought to remove both tariff and nontariff barriers to trade. The removal of nontariff barriers to trade affected the ability of national, state, and local governments to protect public health and medical services.

While *tariff barriers* to trade involved financial methods of protecting national industries from competition by foreign corporations, including import taxes, *nontariff barriers* referred to nonfinancial laws and regulations affecting trade, particularly those that governments used to ensure accountability and quality. In more than nine hundred pages of rules, the WTO set criteria for permissible or impermissible nontariff barriers, such as domestic policies governing environmental protection, food safety, and health services. The rules aimed to increase the volume of cross-border trade, with the assumption that increased trade would enhance wealth and well-being. While aiming to achieve "free" trade across borders, the rules in trade agreements limited governments' regulatory authority over trade while enhancing the authority of international financial institutions and trade organizations.[2]

WTO rules (under general exceptions of GATT, Article XX) permitted national and subnational "measures necessary to protect human, animal or plant life or health," but other provisions made this exception difficult to sustain in practice. For example, a country could be required to prove that its laws and regulations constituted the alternatives that were least restrictive to trade, and that they were not in fact disguised barriers to trade.[3] These rules also restricted public subsidies, particularly those designated for domestic health programs and institutions, as potentially "trade distortive." Requiring that such subsidies apply equally to domestic or foreign companies that provided services under public contracts preempted public policies that directed subsidies to domestic companies.

With particular relevance to public health, one WTO provision required "harmonization," which sought to reduce variation in nations' regulatory standards for goods and services. Proponents argued that harmonization would motivate some less developed countries to initiate labor and environmental standards where none previously existed.[4] Harmonization also could lead to erosion of existing standards, however, since it required uniform global standards at the level *least* restrictive to trade.[5] The WTO encouraged national governments to harmonize standards on issues as diverse as truck safety, pesticides, worker safety, community right-to-know laws about toxic hazards, consumer rights regarding essential services, banking and accounting standards, informational labeling of products, and pharmaceutical testing standards.

Trade Enforcement and National Sovereignty

WTO and regional agreements such as the North American Free Trade Agreement (NAFTA) superseded member countries' internal laws and regulations, including those governing health. Under these agreements, governments at all levels faced a loss of sovereignty in policy making pertinent to public health and health services. Technically, member nations applied voluntarily to join the WTO, yet most less developed countries perceived the potential threat of disadvantages in trade relations if they did not join.[6] Traditionally, government agencies at the federal, state, county, and municipal levels maintained responsibility for protecting public health by ensuring safe water supplies, controlling environmental threats, and monitoring industries for occupational health conditions. Trade agreements could reduce or eliminate such governmental activities, because WTO treated these activities as potential barriers to trade.

In cases of dispute, an appointed three-member WTO tribunal, rather than a local or national government, determined whether a challenged policy conformed to WTO rules. The tribunal included experts in trade but not necessarily in the subject matter of the cases, such as health or safety, or in the laws of the contesting countries.[7] Documents and hearings remained closed to the public, press, and state and local elected officials. Because the WTO treated federal governments as the sole members of the organization, only representatives of contesting countries could participate in the hearings, in addition to "experts" whose participation the tribunal requested.

When a tribunal found that a domestic law or regulation did not conform to WTO rules, the tribunal ordered that the contested transaction in question proceed. If a country failed to comply, the WTO could impose financial penalties and could authorize the "winning" country to apply trade sanctions against the "losing" country in whatever sector the winner chose until the other country complied. In challenges decided by WTO or NAFTA tribunals, corporations and investors caused governments to suffer financial consequences and trade sanctions from their efforts to pursue traditional public health functions (Table 6-1). Losing countries, grappling with imposed sanctions, usually succumbed to pressures for eliminating or changing the laws in question and not enacting similar laws in the future.

Trade Agreements and Health

International trade agreements under WTO applied to all 148 countries that belonged to the WTO. Such agreements pertinent to health included the General Agreement on Trade in Services (GATS), the Agreement on Trade-Related Aspects of Intellectual Property Rights (TRIPS), the Agreement on the Application of Sanitary and Phyto-Sanitary Standards (SPS), and the Agreement on Technical Barriers to Trade (TBT). In addition, regional agreements and

Table 6-1 Examples of Actions Under International Trade Agreements that Affect Public Health

Under Chapter 11 of the North American Free Trade Agreement (NAFTA), the Metalclad Corporation of the United States successfully sued the government of Mexico for damages after the state of San Luis Potosí prohibited Metalclad from reopening a toxic waste dump.

The Methanex Corporation of Canada sued the U.S. government in a challenge of environmental protections against a carcinogenic gasoline additive, methyl tertiary butyl ether (MTBE), banned by the State of California.

Acting on behalf of pharmaceutical corporations, the U.S. government invoked the Agreement on Trade-Related Aspects of Intellectual Property Rights (TRIPS) of the World Trade Organization (WTO) in working against attempts by South Africa, Thailand, Brazil, and India to produce low-cost anti-retroviral medications effective against AIDS.

Canada challenged France's ban on asbestos imports under WTO's Agreement on Technical Barriers to Trade (TBT). Although a WTO tribunal initially approved Canada's challenge, an appeals tribunal reversed the decision after international pressure.

On behalf of the beef and biotechnology industries, the United States successfully challenged the European Union's ban of beef treated with artificial hormones under the WTO Agreement on the Application of Sanitary and Phyto-Sanitary Standards (SPS).

The WTO General Agreement on Trade in Services (GATS) targeted the removal of restrictions on corporate involvement in public hospitals, water, and sanitation systems. GATS could affect state and national licensing requirements for professionals and could raise challenges to national health programs that limit participation by for-profit corporations.

nation-to-nation (bilateral) agreements proliferated, with provisions based on the WTO and NAFTA.

NAFTA

Initiated in 1994, NAFTA focused on expanding opportunities for new investments, acquisition of property, and opening services to competition by private corporations in the United States, Canada, and Mexico. Since its formation, NAFTA provisions incited numerous controversies, as U.S.-based manufacturing industries quickly moved their production operations to Mexico, where looser standards prevailed concerning environmental and occupational health, and most companies paid lower wages. Unemployment and cuts in benefits for workers remaining employed in the United States resulted in a growing number of un-insured workers and families.[8] Overall, NAFTA did not increase substantially the number of available jobs.[9]

In Mexico, NAFTA's impact proved very dramatic. Jobs lost in agriculture due to increased imports far outweighed the jobs created by export manufac-turing. Unemployment rose most significantly in rural areas. Between 1994 and 2003, the number of workers entering the labor market in Mexico totaled 9.3 million, while only 3 million new jobs were created. During this same pe-riod, due to price inflation, real wages lost approximately 20 percent of their purchasing power.[10] NAFTA also caused widespread environmental damage as agriculture shifted to large-scale, export-oriented farms that relied on water-polluting agro-chemicals and inefficient usage of water for irrigation. Chronic public health problems along the border between the United States and Mexico persisted or worsened.[11]

In a path-breaking provision concerning investments, Chapter 11 of NAFTA included a unique "investor's rights" mechanism by which individual foreign corporations (referred to as "investors") could directly sue any of the three participating national governments if the corporation encountered a barrier to trade that adversely affected its operations. Prior to NAFTA, trade agreements only permitted country-to-country enforcement by governments. NAFTA'S investor's rights provision allowed companies to sue for the loss of current or future profits, even if the loss was caused by a government agency's prohibiting the use of a toxic substance.[12]

Several landmark cases filed under Chapter 11 dealt with environmental health laws or regulations. For instance, a NAFTA tribunal awarded the U.S.-based Metalclad Company $16.7 million in its suit against Mexico. The Mexican state of San Luis Potosí refused permission for Metalclad to reopen a toxic waste dis-posal facility after a geological audit showed the facility would contaminate the local water supply, fueling community opposition to the reopening. Metalclad claimed that this local decision constituted an expropriation of its future potential profits and successfully sued Mexico.[13]

In addition, the Methanex Corporation of Canada initiated an approximately $1 billion suit against the United States after the State of California banned the use of methyl tertiary butyl ether (MTBE), a gasoline additive, because of its demonstrated tendency to cause cancer. Methanex produced methanol, a com-ponent of MTBE. Although a NAFTA trade tribunal eventually ruled against Methanex after intense pressure from environmental and public health groups, MTBE remained in use within California for more than four years until the final decision. This case exerted a chilling effect on environmental protections, as several other states deferred their planned bans on MTBE due to the threat imposed by the Methanex case.[14] Similar investors' rights provisions appeared in other regional and bilateral agreements.

Free Trade Area of the Americas (FTAA)

This regional trade agreement proposed to extend NAFTA to all thirty-one other nations in the Western Hemisphere except Cuba. Negotiations included efforts to introduce an investor's rights clause, similar to that of NAFTA, as well as features of GATS and other WTO agreements. The FTAA proposal fostered participation of multinational corporations in administering programs and institutions previously managed in the public sector, such as public hospitals and community health centers. U.S.-based insurance companies stated their interest in delivering services provided by public-sector social security systems throughout Latin America, as indicated in their testimony on the FTAA: "Public ownership of health care has made it difficult for U.S. private-sector health care providers to market in foreign countries.... Existing regulations ... present serious barriers ... , including restricting licensing of health care professionals, and excessive privacy and confidentiality regulations."[15]

Proponents of privatization emphasized inefficiencies and corruption in some countries' public-sector programs. In many countries, however, privatization and the participation of multinational corporations in public services had achieved problematic effects. Such changes in Latin America resulted in barriers to access due to copayments, private practitioners' refusal to see patients because of nonpayment, and bureaucratic confusion in the assignment of private providers. As I discuss in Chapter 8, public-sector expenditures increasingly paid for higher administrative costs and profits for investors, as clinical services decreased for the poor at public hospitals and health centers.[16] Similar trends occurred in Africa and Asia.[17]

Chapters of the FTAA proposal that directly related to public health covered trade in services, including health care, water, education, and energy; intellectual property, which addressed access to affordable medications; standards for the safety of plants and food; and rules about governments' allocation of subsidies and procurement of goods and services. The FTAA proposal additionally imposed the threat of a trade challenge against countries' decisions to maintain or to expand public services, as well as costly trade sanctions if privatized services were returned to the public sector. In addition, FTAA rules that affected public health appeared in chapters on financial investments, which contained language modeled on Chapter 11 of NAFTA, and the terms of trade in products, which aimed to enhance trade by restricting governments' regulation of product safety.

The FTAA proposal functioned in an entirely "top-down" fashion; all services were to be covered by all FTAA rules unless a country took action affirmatively to exclude specific services. This feature and others generated intense opposition throughout the Americas. Eventually Venezuela, Bolivia, Brazil, and Argentina— all opposing the FTAA in varying ways—united with other countries in Latin America to block further negotiations on the FTAA. As a result, FTAA itself did not go into effect. The principles of FTAA, however, were enacted through several regional agreements (such as the Dominican Republic–Central America Free Trade Agreement, DR-CAFTA) and bilateral agreements (such as the U.S.-Chile and U.S.-Peru Free Trade Agreements). Recognizing that it could not achieve the FTAA throughout the Americas, the United States therefore pressured countries in regions that were relatively weak politically, as in Central America, or that saw themselves as closely linked to U.S. policies, such as Chile and Peru. As a result, the United States hoped to consolidate trade agreements in the Americas through the mechanisms of regional and bilateral agreements, rather than an overarching FTAA that would have covered nearly the entire Western Hemisphere.

General Agreement on Trade in Services (GATS)

Recognizing the large and increasing proportion of economic activities devoted throughout the world to services as opposed to commodities, this WTO agreement encouraged private investment and deregulation in a wide spectrum of services, including many services in medicine and public health. The public sector previously provided a substantial portion of the latter services as part of a "safety net" that assisted people in need. Deregulation and privatization of such services raised serious threats to the viability and continuity of the public safety net. GATS treated human services such as health care, water and sanitation, energy, and education more or less equivalently as subject to trade rules.

Most GATS rules were "top-down" rules. That is, they already applied to services in WTO member countries and did not depend on additional ratification decisions by legislative bodies in the countries. For example, the Domestic Regulation rule required that government regulations regarding services, including health services, were "not more burdensome than necessary to ensure the quality of the service," and that certification procedures for service providers, technical standards, and licensing requirements did not become barriers to international trade in services.[18] When minimizing trade barriers conflicted with health standards, tribunals under WTO usually prioritized the former.[19] GATS rules restricting public subsidies for safety net services and governmental procurement of services for public programs, described below, also applied to all services.

Because many countries opposed expanding WTO rules to the service sector, GATS operated to some extent by a stepwise approach, in which governments could make sequential choices about nonrequired portions of the GATS proposals. Through a so-called bottom-up process, nations negotiated with each other to "commit" (or add to the list of) services covered by trade rules. One rule, "market access," prohibited governments from restricting the number or types of service providers. For instance, this rule could undermine local laws that limited the number of liquor stores on a block. A second rule, "national treatment," required a country to treat foreign companies in the same way as domestic companies.[20] Programs designed to achieve social goals, such as measures for ensuring accountability to national privacy regulations by restricting medical transcription services to domestic companies, violated this rule by "discriminating" against foreign corporations.

GATS specified four modes of services to which a country could commit:[21] (1) delivery of services based in one country to consumers based in another country; (2) delivery of services to foreign consumers within the provider's country; (3) investment in the services of another country; and (4) temporary migration by workers. When it committed to a specific range of services, a country had to include all those services under all GATS rules, and the rules made later reversal of commitments extremely difficult. Such provisions could restrict nations' or states' ability to limit foreign investments in their health-care systems, as well as affecting the probability of losing or attracting trained clinicians.

In GATS decisions about committing services, there was no formal process for public debate. Countries made confidential requests regarding services that they wanted other countries to commit, and the respondents could agree or not. Regarding public health, for instance, the European Union requested that the United States drop restrictions on private corporate involvement in water and sanitation systems, as well as in the retail distribution of alcohol products.[22] While the European Union announced that it would not commit further any of its own human services, the United States sought removal of barriers to trade that applied to health services, energy production and distribution, higher education, and environmental services.[23] Such negotiations continued with little public notice between 2000 and 2010.

Several countries submitted GATS requests with important implications for U.S. health services. For instance, India asked that the United States recognize foreign licensing and other certified qualifications of medical, nursing, and dental professionals when working in the United States. Mexico and Paraguay requested that the United States end limitations on foreign direct investment in hospitals and health facilities and eliminate the "restriction of federal and state reimbursement to licensed, certified facilities in the United States or a U.S. state," therefore permitting entry of corporations based outside the United States into these markets.[24]

Although the technical language of GATS generated controversy about its eventual impacts, the agreement affected public-sector health programs in several ways. GATS facilitated greater participation by private corporations within public health-care institutions. For instance, the United States included hospitals and health insurance (within GATS, the latter falls under financial services rather than health services) in its commitments. Under GATS rules on public subsidies and government procurement, subsidies to institutions for treatment of the underserved, graduate medical education, or research could be discontinued if challenged by other countries, or could be directed to foreign private corporations that offered competing services. Municipal and county governments that rejected bids or attempted to discontinue contracts with foreign companies could become liable to challenge. Although GATS proponents emphasized that countries' commitments remained voluntary, WTO rules permitted a variety of challenges to countries with national health programs, so that private, for-profit health-care corporations could receive public funding for their activities.[25]

Agreement on Trade-Related Aspects of Intellectual Property Rights (TRIPS)

The TRIPS agreement protected patents, copyrights, trademarks, and industrial designs across national borders. Based partly on the argument that such protections enhanced economic incentives for creativity and invention, this agreement covered patented medications and equipment, textbooks and journals, and engineering and architectural innovations for health institutions, as well as computer technologies.[26] TRIPS rules mandated that all WTO countries implement intellectual property protections that provided a twenty-year monopoly over patentable items. Entry into the WTO required that the United States extend patents from seventeen-year terms to the WTO's twenty-year standard.

TRIPS limited governments' ability to provide generic medications under publicly funded programs. For instance, federal and state government health programs such as Medicare and Medicaid paid substantially higher drug prices because of these patent extensions. Overall, TRIPS adversely impacted U.S. health-care cost containment efforts by extending the time period by which purchasers paid higher prices for medications covered by patent.[27]

This agreement especially affected access to medications for life-threatening conditions in low-income countries. TRIPS rules required most less developed countries to change their rules by 2001, while the "least developed countries" had to do so by 2016. One policy tool to deal with access to medications in low-income countries, permissible under TRIPS rules, involved "compulsory licensing." Under this provision, a country could require that a pharmaceutical company receive a government license to market a needed medication under patent at a lower price than the company could charge under usual market conditions. The U.S. government supported efforts under TRIPS to prevent the governments of South Africa, Thailand, Brazil, and India from initiating compulsory licenses for production of generic alternatives for AIDS medications under patent.[28]

Due to concerns among professionals, legislators, and advocates, the Doha round of negotiations in 2001 proposed to relax some of TRIPS's most severe rules about patent protection for medications useful in treating AIDS. Partly by threatening to impose compulsory licensing, Brazil's government obtained low prices from pharmaceutical companies; this change facilitated improvements in the country's AIDS morbidity and mortality outcomes.[29] In 2003, the U.S. pharmaceutical industry abandoned its insistence that the relaxed rules apply only to medications for AIDS, tuberculosis, and malaria.[30] The resulting agreement gave the WTO control over a complex process for approving lowered medication prices under limited circumstances and left the issue of accessible medications in the less developed countries unresolved.[31]

Overview of International Trade Agreements and Health

Table 6-2 shows the immense scope under which trade agreements impacted public health and health services. The table includes the above agreements and others, such as those pertaining to food safety and environmental health.

Actions by Health Professionals and Advocates

During empire present, concern about trade policies that generated adverse effects on public health increased worldwide.[32] Specific examples showed that organized resistance could block or reverse such policies. For instance, the coordinated international efforts to expand availability of AIDS medications in Africa despite TRIPS restrictions led to changes in trade policies that made these medications much more accessible. Partly by threatening to impose compulsory licensing, Brazil's government obtained low medication prices that helped improve local AIDS outcomes.[33] In similar acts of resistance, communities in Bolivia succeeded in reversing the privatization of water supplies. Through a series of protests, a coalition of health professionals, nonprofessional health workers, and patients who used public hospitals in El Salvador repeatedly blocked the privatization of those institutions. These efforts set in motion patterns of resistance that

Table 6-2 Summary of Key International Trade Agreements Pertinent to Public Health

Treaty, Organization, or Law	Focus	Ratification or Negotiation Status	Examples of Cases Relevant to Public Health
General Agreement on Trade and Tariffs (GATT)	Part of Bretton Woods accords at end of World War II; reduced tariffs as financial barrier to trade.	Applied to all 148 nations that now participate in WTO.	Venezuela won a challenge to U.S. Clean Air Act of 1990, weakening regulation of gasoline contaminants that contribute to pollution.
World Trade Organization (WTO)	Emerged in 1994 from the Uruguay round of GATT negotiations. Created a stable organization with staff. Aimed to remove tariff and nontariff barriers to trade.	Included all WTO member nations.	See below under separate trade agreements.
Trade Promotion Authority ("Fast Track")	U.S. Congress delegated authority for negotiation of trade agreements to the president; permitted only approval or disapproval without amendment by Congress.	Fast Track legislation passed periodically.	The U.S. government used Fast Track to negotiate NAFTA.
North American Free Trade Agreement (NAFTA)*	Removed most restrictions on trade among the United States, Canada, and Mexico.	Implemented, 1994.	Under Chapter 11, the U.S. Metalclad Corporation successfully sued Mexico on toxic waste restrictions. The Methanex Corporation of Canada challenged the United States because of California's ban on a cancer-causing gasoline additive.

Table 6-2 continues on next page

Table 6-2 continued

Treaty, Organization, or Law	Focus	Ratification or Negotiation Status	Examples of Cases Relevant to Public Health
Free Trade Area of the Americas (FTAA)*	Would have extended NAFTA to all countries of the Western Hemisphere except Cuba.	Blocked by several countries in Latin America.	This agreement would have opened public-sector health-care services and institutions to corporate participation. Such a provision remained a part of regional and binational agreements negotiated with the United States.
General Agreement on Trade in Services (GATS)**	Attempted to open public-sector health services, national health programs, public hospitals and clinics, professional licensure, water, and sanitation systems to participation by private corporations.	Applied to WTO member nations; commitments by countries varied depending on negotiations.	Countries' requests targeted professional licensing requirements and restrictions on corporate involvement in drinking water and wastewater systems.
Agreement on Trade-Related Aspects of Intellectual Property Rights (TRIPS)**	Protected patents, copyrights, trademarks, and industrial designs across national boundaries; limited governments' ability to introduce medication programs and to restrict the availability and reimbursement of medications under publicly funded programs.	Applied to WTO member nations; rules concerning medications for conditions such as AIDS remained under negotiation.	On behalf of pharmaceutical corporations, the United States challenged attempts by South Africa, Thailand, Brazil, and India to produce low-cost antiretroviral medications effective against AIDS.

Table 6-2 continues on next page

Table 6-2 continued

Treaty, Organization, or Law	Focus	Ratification or Negotiation Status	Examples of Cases Relevant to Public Health
Agreement on Technical Barriers to Trade (TBT)**	Reduced barriers to trade that derived from technical standards and regulations applying to the safety and quality of products; covered tobacco and alcohol, toxic substances and waste, pharmaceuticals, biological agents, foodstuffs, and manufactured goods.	Applied to WTO member nations.	In its challenge of France's ban on asbestos imports, Canada argued that international standards required the "least trade-restrictive" regulations; a WTO tribunal approved the challenge, although an appeals tribunal rejected Canada's claim after international pressure.

On behalf of the beef and biotechnology industries, the United States successfully challenged the European Union's ban of beef treated with artificial hormones. |

Notes. *Regional trade agreements (apply only to signatory nations).
**WTO trade agreements (apply to all WTO member nations).

eventually stopped or muted the impact of international trade agreements on medicine and public health.

Chapter 14 provides further details about resistance and alternative projects, including struggles against privatization of public hospitals and public water supplies. Such efforts occurred in the context of a growing international network of organizations that emphasized a strengthened public sector, that critically assessed corporatization in health care encouraged by international trade agreements, and that expressed concern about the impact of global trade on public health, health services, and democracy.

*   *   *

International trade agreements exerted their effects within a context of more general "macroeconomic" policies that reinforced patterns of empire in medicine and public health. These policies replicated the historical patterns that emerged in the early twentieth century (discussed in Chapter 1), as foundations, international financial organizations, and international health organizations collaborated to foster health policies that promoted trade and the interests of multinational corporations. The recent cycle of macroeconomic policies likewise encouraged "investment in health" through initiatives that facilitated a corporatized and privatized approach to medicine and public health in less developed countries. In the next chapter I examine these policies as they emerged during empire present.

CHAPTER 7

MACROECONOMICS AND HEALTH

The conceptualization of illness as a cause of poverty and underdevelopment, rather than poverty and underdevelopment as causes of illness, has reappeared cyclically since the late 1800s. As I note in Chapter 1, such a perspective characterized the early efforts of organizations like the Rockefeller Foundation and Pan American Health Organization in their attempts to reduce the economic impacts of such infections as yellow fever and malaria. One rationale for these programs given publicly at the time emphasized the importance of controlling such infections as part of a strategy to improve living conditions and health among the world's poverty-stricken and underdeveloped populations. But that was not the only rationale.

Enhancing Empire by Enhancing Health

Parallel to this humanitarian rationale, these organizations' leaders also sought to make large areas of the world, then ravaged by debilitating and potentially fatal diseases, safe for such activities as commercial travel, construction projects, extractive enterprises such as mining and agriculture, and industrial production. Philanthropic and public-health leaders promoted efforts to control endemic infections partly in collaboration with corporations whose international operations would benefit from safe conditions and a healthy labor force.

This "vertical" approach to health policy, which favored the provision of specific vaccines and medications for specific bothersome diseases, contrasted with a "horizontal" approach, which encouraged the formation of a strong public health and primary care infrastructure in less developed countries. Advocates of the horizontal vision argued that a broad system of public health and primary care services could address major public health problems like endemic infections more effectively than particular "magic bullets," such as vaccines or antibiotics. Partly influenced by the primary health-care movement within the World Health Organization (WHO) during the 1970s and 1980s, the horizontal vision gained substantial support worldwide, at least for a brief time.

During the 1990s, the middle phase of what I call "empire present," the pendulum swung back toward the preference for vertical interventions. This renewed stance emphasized macroeconomic policies that involved national and international economic relationships (rather than the microeconomic policies pertinent to markets for specific goods and services), as well as the roles of public health and health services in these broad economic relationships. The orientation emerged largely from the efforts of the World Bank and affiliated international financial institutions, as well as key private foundations. Again attention turned to vaccines and medications as technological solutions to the health problems of the underdeveloped world. And again this orientation facilitated the financial operations of multinational corporations in less developed countries.

The World Bank's controversial *World Development Report* of 1993, titled "Investing in Health," became a path-breaking guidebook that encouraged public health and primary care interventions as a route to prosperity.[1] This book's content, like its title, conveyed a double meaning—investing to improve health, economic productivity, and poverty; and investing capital, especially private capital, as a route to private profit in the health sector. Beyond its potential contribution to economic development, the report advocated health interventions to improve opportunities for international investors in countries with high disease burdens that interfered with a productive labor force. As observers in Latin America, India, and Africa noted, the World Bank's 1993 report opened avenues for private investment, especially through programs formerly managed in the public sector.[2]

An Influential Example of "Investing in Health": The Report on Macroeconomics and Health

The *Report of the Commission on Macroeconomics and Health: Investing in Health for Economic Development* (hereafter, *Report*),[3] published by WHO in 2001, proved a particularly influential document that claimed to define the relationships between health and the economy during the late years of empire present. This *Report* led to a series of WHO projects on economic issues in health policy, health services, and public health. The *Report*'s orientation partly reflected a marked reduction in funding for WHO from the United Nations, its parent organization, and a major increase in funding of WHO activities by the World Bank (a shift that Chapter 1 explores). Many of the *Report*'s conceptual and methodological approaches mirrored the World Bank's orientation to health and economic development. Partly for that reason, the *Report* gave a revealing picture of the dominant ideology that shaped international health policies as empire present was drawing to a close.

Most of the commissioners responsible for the *Report* held extensive experience with the World Bank, International Monetary Fund (IMF), or other international financial institutions. The commissioners showed little background in collaborating with other types of social organizations (Table 7-1). Notably absent among the commissioners were representatives of nongovernmental organizations, political parties, unions, professional organizations in medicine and public health, organizations of indigenous or ethnic/racial minorities, activists in occupational and environmental health, and members of the worldwide movement targeting economic globalization.

The Meanings of "Investing in Health"

The *Report* emphasized its central theme at the beginning: "Improving the health and longevity of the poor is, in one sense, an end in itself, a fundamental goal of economic development. But it is also a *means* to achieving the other development goals relating to poverty reduction."[4] Therefore, the goal of improving health conditions of the poor became a key element of economic development strategies. From this viewpoint, reducing the burden of the endemic infections that plagued the poorest countries—AIDS, tuberculosis, and malaria—would increase workforce productivity, facilitate investment, and enhance economic development.

A policy emphasis on "investing in health" (the *Report*'s subtitle) echoed the influential and controversial *World Development Report, Investing in Health*, published in 1993 by the World Bank.[5] As already noted, the terminology of the title conveyed a double meaning—investing in health to improve health and productivity, and investing capital as a route to private profit in the health sector. These two meanings of investment, complementary but distinct, pervaded the macroeconomic *Report*. As Jeffrey Sachs, the commission's chair, stated in an address about the *Report*'s public health implications at the American Public Health Association's annual meeting in 2001, "What investor would invest his capital in a malarial country?"[6]

The *Report*'s "key" recommendation was "that the world's low- and middle-income countries, in partnership with high-income countries, should scale up

Table 7-1 Commissioners of the Report
on Macroeconomics and Health*

• J. Sachs (USA): chair, former professor of international trade at Harvard University, then professor of economics at Columbia University, extensive consulting in Eastern Europe and Latin America on governmental reforms tied to economic development and privatization policies.

• I. J. Ahluwalia (India): economist, expert on India's economic reforms and development.

• K. Y. Amoako (Ghana): economist, United Nations; previously with the World Bank.

• E. Aninat (Chile): economist, deputy managing director of the IMF.

• D. Cohen (France): economist, long-term consultant to the World Bank.

• Z. Diabre (Burkina Faso): businessman (Burkina Brewery Corporation), recently associate administrator of the UN Development Program.

• E. Doryan (Costa Rica): previously vice president of the World Bank, then special representative of the World Bank to the UN in New York.

• R. G. A. Feachem (UK): director, Institute for Global Health, University of California, San Francisco and Berkeley; formerly director of health, nutrition, and population at the World Bank, and dean of the London School of Hygiene and Tropical Medicine; editor-in-chief, Bulletin of the World Health Organization.

• R. W. Fogel (USA): professor of business and economics, University of Chicago; Nobel laureate on long-term business cycles; more recent work on nutrition and mortality.

• D. T. Jamison (USA): professor and director of Program on Global Health and Education, University of California, Los Angeles; previously senior economist at the World Bank.

• T. Kato (Japan): adviser to the president, Bank of Tokyo-Mitsubishi; prior G-7 deputy representing Japan, and executive director of the Asian Development Bank.

• N. Lustig (Mexico): president, Universidad de las Américas–Puebla; previously senior adviser and chief of the poverty and inequality unit at the Inter-American Development Bank; codirector of World Bank's World Development Report 2000/2001: Attacking Poverty.

• A. Mills (UK): professor of health economics and policy, London School of Hygiene and Tropical Medicine; adviser to "many multilateral and bilateral agencies."

• T. Moe (Norway): deputy secretary-general of the Organisation for Economic Co-operation and Development (OECD); formerly chief economic adviser, Finance Ministry of Norway.

• M. Singh (India): opposition leader, Parliament; formerly finance minister and governor of the Reserve Bank of India.

• H. E. Supachai Panitchpakdi (Thailand): director-general designate, World Trade Organization; formerly minister of commerce, Thailand, president of Thai Military Bank, and chairman of Nava Finance and Securities.

• L. Tyson (USA): dean, School of Business, University of California, Berkeley, and dean-designate, London School of Business; formerly chair of White House Council of Economic Advisors.

• H. Varmus (USA): president and chief executive officer, Memorial Sloan-Kettering Cancer Center; former director of U.S. National Institutes of Health, Nobel Laureate in Physiology or Medicine; consultant to pharmaceutical and biotechnology firms.

* Affiliations approximately at the time of the Report.

the access of the world's poor to essential health services, including a focus on specific interventions." To accomplish this recommendation, the "high-income countries" would "commit vastly increased financial assistance, in the form of grants."[7] By its emphasis on grants rather than loans, the *Report* broke with the historical traditions of the World Bank and IMF by implicitly recognizing the deleterious debt burden (to which the *Report* referred as the "overhang" of debt), imposed by prior policies of lending agencies.[8] In this sense, the *Report* reflected a growing orientation within the World Bank, and in opposition to the policies of the IMF, that grants should replace loans as a major funding strategy, especially for the poorest countries. The *Report* also recommended widening the World Bank's sphere of influence in health and public health organizations. Specifically, the *Report* called for markedly increased grants by the World Bank to WHO programs.[9]

In asserting that disease was a major determinant of poverty, the *Report* argued that investments to improve health constituted a key strategy toward economic development, distancing itself from prior interpretations of poverty as a cause of disease. Instead, the *Report* emphasized various data on the "channels of influence from disease to economic development."[10] The *Report* deemphasized social determinants of disease, such as class hierarchies, inequalities of income and wealth, and racial discrimination. Although the *Report* referred to health as "an end in itself," the focus on economic productivity diminished the importance of health itself as a fundamental human right.

Financing Versus Reform

According to the *Report,* governmental reform in less developed countries had to accompany new financial contributions from wealthy donor nations. Such reform involved "streamlining" the public sector, privatization, public funding of private services, and the introduction of market principles based on competition. Although these elements of reform resembled structural adjustment, previously required by the World Bank and IMF for new or renegotiated loans, the *Report* argued that both external financing and reforms had to occur simultaneously. Reforms would involve an increase in less developed countries' capacity to plan, implement, and assess the proposed health intervention programs that the *Report* was suggesting. The *Report* argued against structural adjustment policies that required cutbacks in public-sector expenditures and against loans requiring increased indebtedness. Instead, the report argued that public spending should increase and largely should support the private sector. Public subsidization underpinned the *Report*'s recommendation for "public-private partnerships."[11]

A proposal of guaranteed public funding for private providers, including for-profit providers, made explicit a public subsidization of the private sector. Such a proposal was consistent with World Trade Organization (WTO) trade agreements. For instance, as discussed in the previous chapter, multinational corporations' ability to sell publicly funded health services, which emerged in the General Agreement on Trade in Services (GATS), proved consistent with the *Report*'s recommendations.[12]

"Close-to-Client" Systems: Public Funding for Private Providers

The *Report* argued for interventions that involved health centers, small health "posts," and outreach services. The "close-to-client" system "would involve a mix of state and non-state health service providers, with financing guaranteed by the state."[13] In this model the government could own and operate service units, or it could "contract for services with for-profit and not-for-profit providers." A varied spectrum of providers would create "competition and a safety valve in case of failure of the public system." The competitive, private-public system would increase efficiency, while public financing would offer stability and predictability.

In this way, a mixed, private-public model with public financing emerged as the favored policy approach to public health and medical services in the targeted countries. This model had appeared with clarity in the World Bank's 1993 Report, *Investing in Health*.[14] The same model also gained expression in WHO's *World Health Report 2000*,[15] which tried to rank the health systems of all countries throughout the world. "Responsiveness," one of the main criteria used in the ranking, was defined in large part by patients' choice, which in practice meant a choice among private and public options for care. Nations with unified public systems by definition ranked low on this criterion.

The *Report*'s proposal of guaranteed public funding for private providers, including for-profit providers, attracted notice for several reasons. This proposal made explicit a public subsidization of the private sector that remained largely implicit in prior policy documents. As already noted, such a proposal also was consistent with trade agreements under the WTO, such as GATS. While it did not criticize structural adjustment policies of international financial institutions that required cutbacks in public-sector expenditures, the *Report* argued for a somewhat different policy: "public-sector spending on health is needed to provide critical public goods (such as epidemic disease control) and to ensure enough resources for the poor to gain access to health services."[16] From this viewpoint, public expenditures would increase and would largely support the private sector.

Consistent with World Bank policies, the *Report* advocated public expenditures for a limited package of "essential" services for the poor, while people with higher incomes would purchase more extensive services in the private sector.[17] This orientation did not reference the Alma-Ata declaration, which (as discussed in Chapter 1) advocated primary health care for all. According to the *Report,* experts would assess the cost-effectiveness of specific services and the experts' recommendation would determine which "essential" services would warrant financial support from government. This approach distinguished between the rights of the poor and the nonpoor, rather than favoring the ethical and economic underpinnings of national health programs based on solidarity, where the system's success depended on participation by all groups in the society.

The Meanings of Prepayment

To target public spending for the poor, the *Report* called for "prepaid community financing schemes," which to some extent would replace personal, out-of-pocket spending.[18] Prior WHO publications coordinated with the World Bank, such as WHO's *World Health Report 2000,*[19] favored prepayment as a way to increase the fairness of financing health-care systems. From this viewpoint, the rationale for prepayment held that out-of-pocket payments disproportionately burdened the poor and therefore became an economically regressive financial structure.

Prepayment, however, could lead to less beneficial effects. In economically developed countries, prepaid managed care often exerted adverse impacts on the accessibility and outcomes of care for the poor.[20] Prepayment proposals also opened markets for multinational managed care and insurance corporations. For these corporations, as I discuss further in the next chapter, public financing of private managed care programs permitted the use of social security trust funds as an investment strategy.

One motivation for the expansion of for-profit managed care organizations from the United States to Latin America, Africa, and Asia involved access to these public or quasi-public social security trust funds. In most middle-income and some low-income countries, these trust funds covered health-care and retirement benefits for workers and sometimes their families. Even in the context of underdevelopment, the social security funds became large enough to provide a substantial new source of finance capital. For instance, as for-profit managed care organizations entered markets in Latin America, they targeted the social security funds as large reservoirs for capitation payments.[21] Capitation refers to prepayment of a negotiated sum of money to the managed care organization by an employer, public agency, family, or individual per covered person per unit of time, typically a month. Policies favoring prepaid capitations and public support for private providers therefore offered new sources of capital for short-term investment. As in the United States, the lag period between receipt of capitations and provision of services permitted high rates of profit that derived in part from short-term investments that the prepayment structure encouraged.

The meaning of prepayment shifted historically during empire present, and the *Report*'s proposals reinforced this shift. In the nonprofit context, managed care organizations (previously called "health maintenance organizations") emphasized preventive services, because the fixed capitations motivated these organizations to prevent costly episodes of illness. Since more expensive services reduced the earnings of the prepaid system, the emphasis on prevention guided efforts to reduce hospitalization, surgery, and costly procedures.

Within the for-profit context, however, the prepayment of premiums for "covered lives" served a second purpose: the ability to make short-term investments that increased earnings for executives and shareholders. In the United States, for-profit managed care organizations entered Medicaid and Medicare markets to serve low-income and elderly people. The same organizations often left these markets after several years, when the rate of profit began to fall because the organizations had to provide more services. As they left U.S. markets, some of these managed care organizations entered Latin American markets.[22] Predictably, the guaranty of public financing for prepaid services, as advocated in the *Report*, reinforced the investment practices of multinational managed care and insurance corporations.

Donor Financing: Unspoken Options

In a "war against disease," the *Report* argued, "massive, donor-supported scaling up of health interventions in the low-income world" had to occur.[23] To achieve increased financing of interventions targeting endemic infections (especially AIDS, tuberculosis, and malaria), the *Report* called for annual contributions from high-income countries totaling about "0.1 percent of donor GNP [gross national product]." In calculating these expenditures, the *Report* assumed vertical implementation of new interventions to combat endemic infections and directed attention away from the horizontal development of integrated national health programs. The *Report* did not specify a clear voluntary or mandatory policy by which the high-income countries would accomplish this financial transfer. Further, the *Report* offered a skeptical vision of the likelihood that its recommendations would achieve compliance: "These financial targets are a vision of what should be done, rather than a prediction of what will happen." With the benefit of hindsight, this skepticism proved justified because, as empire present drew to a close, the high-income countries came nowhere close to such contributions, even though the *Report* set the bar very low.

The *Report* stayed silent on two key issues: (1) mandatory policies to achieve the interventions proposed, and (2) more fundamental policies to achieve an overall redistribution of wealth from rich nations to poor nations. Specific redistributional policies that would have implemented financing by wealthy countries to combat poverty, and the diseases associated with poverty, remained unstated. This lapse appeared despite the *Report*'s call for high-income countries to ensure that lack of donor funds would not impede the provision of health services to the "world's poorest peoples." The political challenges of redistributing wealth through taxation and/or budgetary reallocation remained too prickly to tackle.

In particular, one important policy proposal did not appear at all in the *Report*: the so-called Tobin tax, proposed initially by James Tobin, a Nobel laureate in economics.[24] This proposal would impose a very small tax on international financial transactions, including electronic transfers. One goal of the Tobin tax was to moderate short-term international speculation in currencies that adversely affected the economies of low-income countries. Later versions of the Tobin tax, proposed by other advocates, argued that proceeds from the tax could be used to reduce poverty in low-income countries affected by international currency transfers, as well as to prevent volatility and collapse of stock markets.[25] At the time of the *Report*, and even as empire present was drawing to a close, the more than $1 trillion transferred daily in such transactions remained almost entirely untaxed. If a tax of approximately 0.5 percent were levied on these financial transfers, and if the tax revenues were given to low-income countries affected by the specific transactions, analyses indicated that the proceeds from the tax— conservatively estimated at $150 billion to $300 billion annually—soon would eliminate the crushing burdens of poverty and debt that the recipient countries faced. In contrast, the *Report* called for total annual donor spending of $27 billion by 2007 and $38 billion by 2015.[26] If part of the proceeds of a Tobin tax were used to finance the interventions proposed in the *Report*, the viability of the interventions would have become realistic rather than ephemeral, as in the unspecified, voluntary donor contributions that the *Report* recommended. Although very small, a Tobin tax would have led to a dramatic transfer of wealth from rich to poor countries. Given the tax's simplicity and massive implications for reducing poverty and disease, the *Report*'s silence about such a tax on international financial transactions became rather deafening.

The Value of Life: Disability-Adjusted Life Years (DALYs)

A quantitative methodology with important ideological implications guided economic analyses in the *Report*. The authors justified their recommendations based partly on quantitative estimates concerning years of life saved from infectious diseases and nutritional deficiencies. From this viewpoint, DALYs "add together the increased years of life and reduced years of living with disabilities."[27] Since people without disability could work more productively, the *Report* projected "tens or hundreds of billions of dollars more per year through increased per capita incomes." Accompanying tables and background papers provided the basis for this projection, which offered a macroeconomic rationale for interventions to reduce endemic infections.

The methodology of DALYs received wide and trenchant criticism.[28] Such a methodological approach appeared in multiple publications and influential policy reports, many stemming from the World Bank and WHO. Critics of the method focused on its ideological assumption that defined human life in terms of economic productivity. With the DALY method, arguments for public health interventions therefore gained credence from the interventions' capacity to increase years of productive work.

This economic valuation of life also diminished the value of life lived with disability. A measure that attached more value to life without disability than to life with disability implicitly devalued the lives of disabled people. Although the *Report* tipped its hat to "the importance of health in its own right," it emphasized: "the wisdom of every culture also teaches that 'health is wealth' in a more instrumental sense as well."[29] However, the instrumental ideology underlying the analysis of health mainly as a means toward economic productivity, as opposed to a fundamental human right, was receiving challenges during the waning days of empire present, despite the mathematics of DALYs.

Trade Agreements Versus Corporate Responsibility

The *Report* called on the pharmaceutical industry to act responsibly in the "war" on endemic infections. In addition to price discounts and donated medications, the *Report* mandated pharmaceutical corporations to "ensure that low-income countries (and the donors on their behalf) have access to essential medicines at near-production cost (sometimes termed the *lowest viable commercial price*) rather than the much higher prices that are typical of high-income markets."[30] Yet, implying doubts about the pharmaceutical industry's voluntary acquiescence to these recommendations, the commissioners invoked sanctions of international trade rules: "If industry cooperation is not enough or not forthcoming on a general and reliable basis, the rules of international trade should be applied in a manner that insures the same results."

Paradoxically, the commissioners also expressed the tensions of applying sanctions that interfered with patent laws and trade agreements: "At the same time, it is vital to ensure that increased access for the poor does not undermine the stimulus to future innovation that derives from the system of intellectual property rights."[31] The *Report* analyzed the challenges in providing medications for the poor and recommended that international trade agreements, such as the Agreement on Trade-Related Intellectual Property Rights (TRIPS), "should be applied in a manner that gives priority to the health needs of the poor."[32]

The contradictions of favoring free trade agreements that protected patent rights, while ensuring maximum access to effective medications for endemic infections, pervaded the *Report*. As I describe in the previous chapter, issues of corporate greed manifested themselves perhaps nowhere more clearly than in the struggles about disseminating new generations of medications effective against AIDS, tuberculosis, malaria, and other endemic infections. When corporations reduced prices and/or donated medications for these infections, such apparently voluntary actions followed massive and widely publicized struggles by organized professionals, nonprofessional health workers, activists, and governmental bodies in the nations most affected by the infections.

Trade agreements like TRIPS, implemented through the WTO and the closely affiliated World Intellectual Property Organization (WIPO), protected the intellectual property rights that historically limited access to the most needed medications under patent. In the pharmaceutical industry, generally the most profitable of capitalist industries, humanitarian motivations to reduce the rate of profit through voluntary price reductions to the "lowest viable commercial price" remained pitted against the interests of executives and stockholders. Trade agreements privileged these corporate interests. Even the drug donation programs cited favorably by the *Report* came with huge tax advantages for the pharmaceutical corporations producing the needed medications. Despite arguments by commission staff members that patents did not impede access to AIDS treatment,[33] the adverse impact of patents on medication availability led to outrage throughout the world, as well as explicit recommendations from such groups as the United Kingdom's Commission on Intellectual Property Rights for changes in WTO and WIPO patent procedures.[34] When it recommended voluntarism from the pharmaceutical industry, the *Report* reinforced skepticism about how its vision would impact endemic infections that urgently required effective drug treatment. Such contradictions permeated international health policies at the end of empire present.

Recycling Public Health Interventions to Facilitate Investment

Throughout the twentieth century, as I discuss in Chapter 1, the Rockefeller Foundation sponsored "vertical" campaigns against endemic infections:

hookworm, yellow fever, tuberculosis, schistosomiasis, and malaria, among others. Rockefeller campaigns interpreted these infections as impediments to labor productivity, investment, and economic development. Rockefeller-funded programs also recognized that endemic infections blocked key infrastructure projects that would enhance the ability of enterprises based in the United States and Western Europe to extract raw materials and to transport products and workers throughout the world. The history of yellow fever and the Panama Canal, for instance, provided justification for Rockefeller-initiated interventions in many countries. Such campaigns did not foster a broader, "horizontal" infrastructure that could provide integrated public health and primary care services. Following the example of yellow fever and the Panama Canal, these interventions instead aimed to improve the economic circumstances of enterprises in the imperial countries by improving the health of the imperialized.

The *Report on Macroeconomics and Health* updated this earlier Rockefellerism. Like this unacknowledged predecessor in macroeconomic thought, the *Report* called for investment to reduce poverty in poor countries—while enhancing the economic prospects of the rich in both rich and poor countries alike. This approach also revived a vertical approach to the "categorical" eradication of specific diseases, rather than encouraging the development of integrated health-care systems. Health as a fundamental human value, worthy of investment for its own sake, slipped from consciousness, as did the vision of redistributing wealth as a worthy goal in macroeconomic policy.

More recent efforts by WHO, the Gates Foundation, the International Fund for AIDS, the World Bank, and other agencies focusing on global health replicated the failed policies of earlier eras.[35] Such influential programs that linked public health, health services, and economic development generally emphasized vertical interventions that focused on technological fixes to address specific diseases, rather than the horizontal enhancement of public health infrastructure. As empire present was concluding, this old ideologic wine produced a familiar euphoria as it appeared in new bottles. The enduring inequalities of health and wealth that the *Report* acknowledged nonetheless demanded a less inebriated struggle for enduring macroeconomic change than the *Report*'s highly placed commissioners were willing to concede.

*   *   *

Aside from such macroeconomic issues, contradictions linked late capitalism with medicine and public health also in the microeconomic territory of specific industries. For instance, just as health-care corporations faced a falling rate of profit in the United States and Western Europe and for that reason marketed coronary care technology throughout the world during empire past, as I discuss in Chapter 3, corporations that marketed services rather than commodities needed to deal with similar structural problems during empire present. The constraint of a falling rate of profit and the motivation to open new markets internationally became very clear in the realm of managed care. Like their corporate predecessors that marketed high-technology commodities, corporations that sold managed care services turned from domestic to international markets as a way to address the contradictions they faced. This social history becomes the focus of the next chapter.

CHAPTER **8**

THE EXPORTATION OF MANAGED CARE

In December 1999, near the end of empire present, Archbishop Desmond Tutu, Nobel Peace Prize winner from South Africa, gave the keynote address for an important conference in Miami Beach: the International Summit of Managed Care. The price for attending this conference, excluding travel, room, and meals, was $1,395. Sponsored by the American Association of Health Plans and the Academy for International Health Studies, the conference targeted "chief executive officers, presidents, board chairs, chief financial officers, directors of marketing, and business development officers."

Although it received far less attention than the massive protests against the World Trade Organization in Seattle one week earlier, the Miami Beach summit manifested the same issues to which protesters had objected in Seattle. The World Bank, International Monetary Fund, and U.S. Agency for International Development used the summit to promote an expanded role for multinational managed care corporations in health care throughout the world. Representatives of these international financial institutions emphasized the privatization of public health systems and social security funds in Latin America, Africa, and Asia. Participants from the World Health Organization and the Pan American Health Organization played prominent roles. Also participating were officials from Mexico, Brazil, Argentina, Chile, Colombia, Uruguay, Paraguay, India, Nepal, Thailand, Indonesia, Philippines, Singapore, Nigeria, Zimbabwe, South Africa, Cameroon, Oman, United Arab Emirates, Romania, Canada, Germany, the Netherlands, Switzerland, and Australia. Little dissent emerged about policies that called for public-sector cutbacks, privatization, and greatly expanded activities for multinational managed care organizations throughout the less developed world.

Economic Conditions That Fostered Exportation

Managed care refers to health-care services under the administrative control of large, private organizations, with prepaid, "capitated" financing. (Chapter 6 gives a definition of capitated payment.) Beyond the capitation fee, people covered under managed care almost always pay additional copayments when they actually receive services. By the mid-1990s, most insured persons in the United States and many other countries came to be covered by managed care organizations.

As managed care plans expanded during the mid-1990s, the rate of profit began to fall, and the market became increasingly saturated.[1] This decreasing rate of profit resembled that experienced with most other goods and services over time, as had occurred, for instance, in the case of coronary care technology two decades earlier, which Chapter 3 describes. Under these circumstances, corporations sought new markets abroad. In 1996, the president of the Association of Latin American Pre-Paid Health Plans noted the relationship between market saturation and exportation: "By the year 2000, it is estimated [that] 80 percent of the total U.S. population will be insured by some sort of MCO [managed care organization]. Since 70 percent of all American MCOs are for-profit enterprises, new markets are needed to sustain growth and return on investment."[2]

Facing a declining rate of profit, the U.S. managed care industry was struggling with higher costs of services provided to patients, insufficient premiums, and an increasingly competitive market. Under these circumstances, mergers of managed care organizations sought to enhance their bargaining positions, but the industry's problems persisted. By 1998, managed care organizations began to raise premiums several points above the 2.5 percent inflation rate, citing an inability to control medical costs as much as predicted. This increase proved dramatic when compared to the premium increases of 1 percent or less offered in the mid-1990s.[3] Fluctuations in the stock market reflected the financial difficulties of the managed care industry. From 1990 to 1995, managed care organization stocks surged an average of 33 percent a year, far ahead of the overall market. By 1997, these organizations' worsening stock market values disappointed analysts and investors.[4] This weaker stock market position persisted for the next several years.

In the United States by that time, for-profit managed care organizations entered the public-sector programs of Medicare and Medicaid. However, these programs proved less amenable to managed care than industry officials had anticipated. The initial profits from Medicare had been large because federal payments for Medicare managed care organization members had risen as much as 10.5 percent per year. But in 1997, Congress limited future years' premium increases to 2 percent. Concern grew about managed care organizations' ability to manage costs within these stipulated premium increases. In the Medicaid market, many states also ratcheted down their payments to these organizations.[5]

To address these problems, managed care organizations exited from Medicare and Medicaid programs in multiple geographic areas. In some areas, these organizations dismantled their programs after three or four years, having made extensive short-term profits from capitated patients. Managed care organizations generated profits by keeping costs, especially to pay for services to patients, as low as possible. Rapid entry into and exit from public markets left patients and their public insurance programs vulnerable and searching for new, publicly funded alternatives. The American Association of Health Plans (AAHP) estimated that managed care organizations' withdrawals from providing services affected at least 711,000 Medicare beneficiaries. According to these estimates, Aetna's pullout affected 355,000 members in eleven states, while CIGNA's exit impacted 104,000 members in thirteen states.[6] By the end of 2001, Aetna's exit from numerous Medicare markets affected an additional 105,000 members—a number equivalent to 38 percent of its Medicare membership. Several other companies, including PacifiCare Health Systems and Health Net, also were exiting Medicare plans across the country, leaving approximately 500,000 subscribers to seek new medical coverage.[7] According to various estimates, the total number of beneficiaries who lost their plans during 1999–2001 rose to more than 1.7 million.[8]

According to the U.S. Health Care Financing Administration, managed care organizations received more than enough federal payments to provide basic Medicare benefits. However, these payments did not cover the extra benefits offered by the organizations, without adversely impacting profits. Managed care organizations also complained that the Balanced Budget Act of 1997 capped reimbursement increases at 2 percent annually, a rate that did not keep pace with rising medical costs.[9] Organizations like Aetna tried to address their high costs by increasing premiums when renewing contracts and by evaluating markets and products with the intention of exiting when financial or strategic purposes were not met.

Managed care in the United States during the 1990s therefore evolved with an initial cycle of tremendous expansion and then a notable contraction. As the domestic market became more contentious and less attractive, a transition from national to multinational managed care occurred. U.S. and European multinational corporations, including pharmaceutical companies, long-term care corporations, and managed care organizations, turned to international markets in seeking alternative sources of profit.[10] Corporations exported managed care as the main organizational format, as opposed to other forms of commercial insurance, because managed care had become the dominant form of health-care organization in the United States and had emerged as the most profitable framework for commercial organizations to provide health insurance.

In Latin America, the health-care market presented lucrative opportunities.[11] Still relatively untouched by the privatization wave that had swept the region in previous years, the health-care sector was about to undergo reforms that would open the door to private capital. After implementation of reforms, favorable economic conditions under this scenario would fuel a long-term boom for investors. Latin America had become ripe for multinational corporations' investments and operations in health care.[12]

The Managed Care Market and Social Security Funds in Latin America

As managed care organizations set their sights on foreign markets, Europe initially looked promising. Reforms in several European national health programs introduced principles of managed care, market competition, and the privatization of public services.[13] These reforms, as components of neoliberalism, received strong support from the Thatcher government in Britain, as well as varying degrees of enthusiasm from conservative parties in other countries. Alain Enthoven and his disciples, who orchestrated the managed care proposals that shaped the Clinton administration's ill-fated efforts for a national health program, served as consultants for European governments undertaking these reforms.[14] The popularity of public-sector programs in Europe, however, proved powerful disincentives to privatization. After the mid-1990s, especially as managed care became increasingly unpopular in the United States, European countries such as the United Kingdom, the Netherlands, and Sweden reversed many policies that attempted to privatize their national health programs.[15] Although debates about privatization and "marketization" of the European national health programs continued during the later years of empire present, such debates in general did not lead to fundamental changes in the systems' fundamentally public character.[16]

With managed care saturation taking place domestically and with limited prospects in Europe, U.S.-based managed care organizations turned to less developed countries, especially in Latin America. In the tradition of tobacco and pesticides, U.S. corporations exported, in the form of managed care, products and practices that had come under heavy criticism domestically. The exportation of managed care received enthusiastic support from the World Bank, other international financial institutions, and multinational corporations. On the receiving end, less developed countries experienced strong pressure to accept managed care as the organizational framework for privatization of their health and social security systems. Managed care organizations and investment funds rapidly entered the Latin American market, and this experience served as a model for the exportation of managed care to Africa and Asia.

In a study of managed care in Latin America, colleagues and I focused on its exportation from the United States and its impact on health-care delivery and public health services.[17] The research considered the exportation of managed care by investor-owned, for-profit corporations that passed on financial risk to physicians, hospitals, and clinics, as opposed to those that simply sold commercial indemnity insurance. Our results showed that the health-care and social security funds of less developed countries became a major source of new capital and high rates of profit for these corporations, especially through the investment of prepaid capitation payments. We found that the rhetoric for these policy changes emphasized an ideology of the private market as a route to more efficient and accessible services (a rhetoric that, by the way, became quite seductive for progressive leaders like Archbishop Tutu, who received sizable honoraria and consulting fees). However, the evidence that such market reforms actually would improve problems of inefficiency, costs, and access remained slim indeed within the United States and virtually nonexistent elsewhere. The rhetoric easily gained acceptance by leaders in less developed countries. As public systems were dismantled and privatized under the auspices of managed care, multinational corporations entered the field, reaped large profits, and exited within several years. Then the countries that these multinational corporations had invaded faced even more challenging prospects in reconstructing their public systems.

Corporations that entered the managed care market in Latin America reported substantial revenues relative to expenditures. During the mid-1990s, Sul America Seguros, a corporation in Brazil whose extensive managed care operations were half-owned by Aetna, generated single-year revenues of more than $1.2 billion.[18] Annual managed care revenues in Brazil during this period were estimated at $2.99 billion.[19] Targeting the somewhat smaller market in Argentina, Galeno Life TIM, a managed care organization controlled by the EXXEL Group, a multinational investment fund, posted annual revenues of $181 million.

Executives responsible for the exportation of managed care emphasized the financial rewards of international markets. They rarely referred to preventive care or quality control, goals that historically some managed care organizations in the United States had valued. Support for education and research also failed to emerge as an explicit goal.

In explaining their financial motivations for entering the Latin American marketplace, managed care executives consistently referred to the importance of access to the social security funds of these countries. In contrast to the United States, most Latin American countries had organized social security systems that included health-care benefits as well as retirement benefits for many employed workers in large private or public enterprises. Employers and workers contributed to these social security funds. For workers who were not covered by social security, and for unemployed people, most Latin American countries also had established public-sector health-care institutions, including public hospitals and clinics.

Throughout Latin America, the social security systems held large trust funds, managed by governmental or publicly regulated agencies. U.S. executives perceived these funds as a significant new source of finance capital. For instance, a managed care executive whom the EXXEL Group recruited from Indianapolis noted: "It's a very lucrative market.... The real opportunity here for an investor-owned company is to develop tools in the *prepagas* [prepaid] market in anticipation of the *obras sociales* [social security] market."[20] From this perspective, managed care organizations' penetration of the private market became a stepping stone to the potentially more profitable public market based in social security trust funds.

Privatization of government health programs and social security systems permitted major capital expansion for managed care organizations and investment funds. Public-sector programs in such countries as Colombia and Argentina suffered from inefficiency, escalating costs, and corruption, which fueled arguments for privatization.[21] As an early model for change, the Chilean constitution of 1980, initiated by the Pinochet dictatorship, permitted the diversion of government health-care and social security funds to privatized managed care institutions (*Instituciones de Salud Previsional*, ISAPRE), which then could be bought by multinational insurance companies.[22] Access to privatized social security funds—termed "the mañana pension bonanza" in a trade journal[23]— created multibillion-dollar capital pools available for reinvestment by participating multinational corporations.

An expanding Latin American upper middle class constituted a potential new market for managed care.[24] This expansion produced a larger number of families with incomes high enough to purchase private health insurance. Executives anticipated that managed care would attract wealthier consumers, due to the advantages of a regular primary care provider, continuity of care, and the management of costly subspecialty services and advanced technology. Payment for managed care premiums would come from a combination of employer contributions, patient copayments, and social security funds. Investors also showed enthusiasm about strong economic growth rates (for instance, 7 percent annually in Chile and 5.5 percent in Argentina) and the low proportion of population already covered by private insurers.[25]

The Rising Trajectory of Managed Care in Latin America

The World Bank and other international financial institutions favored the privatization of public services and the entry of managed care corporations into Latin American markets. As noted in previous chapters, these institutions' structural adjustment policies required privatization, reduced public-sector expenditures, and repayment of prior loans. During the mid-1990s, annual payments on foreign debts ranged from 21.3 percent of gross domestic product in Guatemala to 360.3 percent in Guyana, with an average of 42.4 percent for Latin America as a whole.[26] If countries failed to implement structural adjustment, international financial institutions threatened them with cutting off or drastically reducing loans, credit to buy essential imports, and food aid. Within Latin American governments and corporations, politicians and managers collaborated with the international financial institutions in the implementation of structural adjustment policies.

In the widely debated *1993 World Development Report,* "Investing in Health," the World Bank argued that inefficiencies in public-sector programs hindered the delivery of services as well as reduction of poverty.[27] As I discussed in the previous chapter, this report advocated incentives for private insurance, privatization of public services, promotion of market competition, and emphasis on primary care and prevention. Through this document and subsequent policies, the World Bank promulgated an ideology that "health is a private matter and health care a private good,"[28] which encouraged the entry of private, for-profit managed care organizations into countries that accepted loans from the World Bank.

Other international financial institutions participated in the same reform strategies. The Inter-American Development Bank offered lines of credit for changes in organizational structure and physical facilities of hospitals and clinics consistent with privatization. In Argentina, this bank collaborated with the World Bank in supporting the conversion of public hospitals to become "hospitals of self-management" (*hospitales de auto-gestión*), where managed care principles required the hospitals to compete with private hospitals in the market for patients covered under social security programs.[29] International financial institutions' support of public hospital reform in Colombia proceeded along similar lines.[30] The International Monetary Fund (IMF) made new loans conditional on macroeconomic indicators of public-sector cutbacks, privatization, and the introduction of managed care, partly to reduce public expenditures and national budget deficits.[31] Pressures exerted by the IMF encouraged private management of services and social security funds previously managed in the public sector.

Multinational corporations used several strategies to enhance the exportation of managed care. The most important involved joint ventures with companies based outside the United States that provided an established clientele and helped multinational corporations circumvent national laws that restricted foreign ownership.[32] Most managed care joint ventures did not replicate the "staff-model" principles that some U.S.-based managed care organizations maintained, such as providing salaries to physicians to reduce financial risk on a year-to-year basis.[33] Instead, the Latin American ventures involved several elements: investor ownership; for-profit status; a designated, enrolled population; prepayment for services; and a contracted physician panel that assumed financial risk in providing primary and specialty care. These arrangements also included some degree of social security financing and the introduction of private management or ownership in public programs.

The second expansion strategy involved a trade show approach, through which corporations organized conventions or presentations at professional meetings to expand interest in managed care principles.[34] Attendees at such meetings included Latin American health-care leaders who received financial assistance from corporations, the World Bank, or both. The World Bank justified this support as consistent with its policies requiring reforms that favored the privatization of health services in less developed countries, benefiting corporations based mainly in the United States and Europe.[35] International health organizations, including the Pan American Health Organization and World Health Organization, also supported and helped to legitimate these privatization efforts.[36]

A third strategy that favored managed care expansion in international markets involved the use of governments to influence international trade organizations, especially the World Trade Organization. Governments exerted this influence by setting agendas at trade organizations' meetings and ensuring commitments from other countries that benefited managed care organizations based in the United States and Europe.[37] Previous trade barriers fell as international trade agreements negotiated through the World Trade Organization or on a regional basis (such as the North American Free Trade Agreement, NAFTA) facilitated managed care organizations' entry into national markets. (Chapter 6 presents the contours of these trade agreements.) The global operations of multinational corporations also led them to seek managed care benefits for employees based abroad. For example, after the initiation of NAFTA, corporations with Mexico City operations, including IBM, Johnson & Johnson, Bristol-Myers Squibb, and Hewlett-Packard, formed a consortium to enhance managed care efforts.[38]

Aided by these strategies, several multinational managed care organizations expanded rapidly in Latin America during the mid-1990s. Between 1996 and 2000, Aetna entered into joint ventures with domestic companies in Mexico, Brazil, Venezuela, Argentina, and Colombia. These efforts encompassed not only expanding into but also exiting from certain markets that became inconsistent with the company's focus on the high growth potential of the world's emerging markets.[39] Aetna's reports for investors and government regulators during this period emphasized intentions to invest in markets outside the United States that showed the potential for favorable long-term returns. With a $300 million investment, Aetna acquired 49 percent interest in Sul America Seguros, the largest insurance company of Brazil, with 1.6 million managed care enrollees.[40] Through its Chilean subsidiaries, the corporation covered 60,000 members. Aetna purchased interests in the ISAPREs, the publicly subsidized managed care organizations introduced during the Chilean dictatorship. Aetna's managed care operations also expanded rapidly in Peru and Mexico; the Mexican venture (Méximed) provided services along the U.S.–Mexico border.[41]

Although CIGNA's main international operations focused on Japan, during the late 1990s it initiated managed care operations throughout Latin America.[42] In Brazil, CIGNA managed 2.5 million enrollees through a joint venture with a large bank and a prepaid health plan. This CIGNA venture served enrollees through a network of more than 1,400 hospitals, 3,800 clinics, and 10,500 physicians.[43] CIGNA Salud ISAPRE in Chile provided managed care coverage for about 100,000 lives. In Guatemala, CIGNA covered 40,000 lives through its managed care system.[44] During the same period, CIGNA also expanded rapidly in Argentina and Mexico.

Among its far-flung financial interests, the American International Group (AIG) also opened a Latin American operation in managed care. AIG obtained a 49 percent partnership with a major Brazilian insurance company diversifying into managed care activities. By gaining the right to administer public and private pension funds in Mexico, Chile, Argentina, Peru, and Colombia, AIG obtained additional capital to finance managed care expansion. Because many Latin American countries linked retirement pension plans to health-care benefits, this corporation's activities advanced the overall trend toward privatization of public social security trust funds.[45]

The EXXEL Group, a multinational investment fund, pursued managed care operations in several Latin American countries. In Argentina, EXXEL purchased three older prepaid health plans to form the country's largest managed care organization, whose enrollment soon tripled. EXXEL recruited several U.S. managed care executives to administer its Argentine operations. Among its consultants, EXXEL listed two former U.S. ambassadors to Argentina. EXXEL also made inroads into managed care markets in Brazil, Chile, and Uruguay.[46] In other markets, EXXEL held controlling interests in restaurants, supermarkets, credit card services, music stores, former public utilities, a private mail service, duty-free shops, and tax collecting agencies at airports.[47]

EXXEL manifested a new development in international managed care, since it redirected U.S. investments into Latin American markets without traditional reporting requirements or regulatory controls. By incorporating in the Cayman Islands, the EXXEL Group circumvented mandatory reporting of bank accounts, additional assets, and taxation required by the Securities and Exchange Commission and other U.S. regulatory agencies. In promotional materials, EXXEL listed major U.S. investors, including Brown University, Massachusetts Institute of Technology, Columbia University, Princeton University, and the Ford Foundation.[48] However, in their annual reports and in our interviews with their investment officers, these U.S. institutions did not report investments in EXXEL. The investments that EXXEL claimed apparently represented shares that the U.S. institutions purchased in mutual funds, of which the institutions' investment officers were not aware.

The Falling Trajectory That Followed

As they previously had done in the Medicare and Medicaid markets, most U.S.-based managed care organizations exited from the Latin American managed care markets when the rate of profit began to fall there as well. By 1999 Aetna was experiencing problems of corporate instability and declining stock value. Although its reports to the U.S. Securities and Exchange Commission showed international operations as marginally profitable, Aetna began selling its joint ventures. In December 2000 the company sold Aetna International and Global Financial Services to Amsterdam-based ING Group NV. Aetna's officers emphasized that the sale aimed at consolidating the corporation's activities in the U.S. health-care market, which had become relatively inefficient and unprofitable, and at enhancing stockholders' confidence and stock value. Substantial additional assets resulted from the sale of Aetna's foreign subsidiaries.[49]

Also in 1999, CIGNA began its departure from the Latin American managed care market.[50] CIGNA's rate of profit in Brazil's private health-care markets predictably decreased. In January 2003, citing growth potential below the company's long-term expectations, CIGNA sold its remaining health-care operations to a Brazilian company, Amil, after extracting major profits initially from prepaid capitation fees.

The behavior of these corporations, which rapidly entered and then exited foreign markets, attracted wide notice in Latin America. Declining profitability clearly contributed to these corporate decisions. The wealth in Latin American social security funds derived from contributions by government, employers, and employees during decades of job growth and economic expansion. Privatization in Latin America led to widespread unemployment, which drastically reduced contributions to public social security funds. Cutbacks in government support for health care, which resulted from the structural adjustment poli- cies imposed by the World Bank and International Monetary Fund under the framework of "reform," further diminished these public-sector contributions. From this perspective, the social security funds represented an initially lucra- tive opportunity; later Latin America did not remain "the gold mine that it looked like it would be during the heady days of policy reforms at the begin- ning of the 1990s."[51]

The domestic U.S. market also played a role in managed care organizations' withdrawal from Latin American markets. In the case of Aetna, stockholder pressure directed the company to focus its attention on the U.S. market, partly in consideration of new profits to be generated due to anticipated expansion of Medicare. As Medicare "reform" went into effect at the end of 2003, the advan- tages for the private health insurance industry became clear. Within one year, the modification of Medicare generated more than $50 billion in additional revenue for managed care organizations, in part through higher government payments to attract seniors into private health plans that supplemented Medicare coverage.[52] Annual return on investment reached 10 percent, the level at which managed care earned its highest rates of profit during the early and mid-1990s. Not surpris- ingly, insurance corporations strongly advocated Medicare reform, which became another massive public subsidization of the private sector in health care.

Challenges to Public Health and Medical Services

As in the United States, concern in Latin America about managed care focused on restricted access for vulnerable patients and on reduced spending for clinical services as a result of administrative costs and the need to pay dividends to inves- tors. Copayments required under managed care plans introduced barriers to access and increased strain on public hospitals and clinics. In Chile, approximately 24 percent of patients covered by the ISAPRE managed care organizations received services in public clinics and hospitals because they could not afford copayments averaging 8.6 percent of the ISAPREs' overall collections.[53] Self-management (*auto-gestión*) policies in Argentina's and Brazil's public hospitals fostered com- petition for capitation payments from social security funds and private insurance companies, as well as copayments from patients. To apply for free care at these public institutions, indigent patients underwent lengthy means testing that re- quired documentation of impoverishment; at some hospitals, the rejection rate for such applications averaged between 30 percent and 40 percent.[54]

Public hospitals in Argentina that had not yet converted to managed care faced an influx of patients covered by privatized social security funds. Such public hospitals in Buenos Aires reported approximately 1.25 million outpatient visits annually by patients who were covered by the privately administered social security fund for retired persons. Before turning to public hospitals, these elderly patients had encountered barriers to access due to copayments, private practitioners' refusal to see them because of nonpayment by the social security fund, and bureaucratic confusion in the assignment of providers.[55]

As for-profit managed care organizations took over public institutions, increased administrative costs diverted funds from clinical services. In Argentina, after the EXXEL Group obtained contracts to manage the nineteen public hospitals in the province of San Luis, administrators sought to reduce the proportion of uninsured patients. To attract patients with private insurance and social security plans, Buenos Aires's public hospitals hired management firms that received a fixed percentage of billings.[56] Administrative and promotional costs accounted for 19 percent of the Chilean ISAPREs' annual expenditures, reducing the proportion of the budget available to pay for actual services to patients.[57]

Managed care organizations in Latin America attracted healthier patients, whereas sicker patients gravitated to the public sector. In Chile, the ISAPREs captured capitations for younger workers without chronic medical conditions. As a result, only 3.2 percent of patients covered by the ISAPREs were more than sixty years old, in comparison to 8.9 percent of the general population and 12 percent of patients seen at public hospitals and clinics.[58] Even though the privatized ISAPREs received government subsidies, the small proportion of the oldest and sickest patients for which they provided care, in contrast to the proportion cared for in public health-care institutions, contributed to the public sector's chronic financial crisis.

Resistance to Managed Care and the Emergence of Alternative Proposals

The exportation of managed care encountered opposition, which varied among countries but generally included coalitions of unions, professional associations, educators, and indigenous and community-based organizations. In Ecuador, such a coalition resisted the introduction of private managed care within public hospitals and clinics.[59] During 1995, this coalition organized voters in preparation for a national plebiscite that elicited the population's preferences concerning the privatization of eleven sectors of the economy, including health care, petroleum, transportation, and public utilities. For all eleven propositions in the plebiscite, approximately two-thirds of Ecuadorian voters opposed privatization. After the plebiscite, the coalition continued to resist privatization and organized educational campaigns concerning managed care as a component of initiatives to privatize public-sector services.

In Brazil, physicians and public health activists resisted the introduction of managed care.[60] For instance, activists affiliated with the Brazilian national Workers Party (*Partido dos Trabalhadores*) opposed privatization of public services under managed care organizations. Government officials representing this party and elected in Brasilia, Santos, Rio de Janeiro, and other cities worked to oppose privatization policies and successfully implemented alternative proposals that strengthened public services at the municipal level. Members of the Workers Party and other political activists emphasized that the revised Brazilian constitution of 1988 guaranteed access to health care as a right of citizenship, to be provided through a "unified health service." Organizing in the national and state legislatures called attention to the contradiction between the constitution's mandates and privatization policies that encouraged the introduction of managed care under for-profit corporations. Physicians' associations challenged managed care principles and worked together to enhance their power in bargaining collectively with managed care organizations. One example involved UNIMED, a cooperative that included thousands of physician practitioners. UNIMED succeeded in limiting managed care organizations' control over the conditions of medical practice and helped block initiatives to privatize public-sector services under the auspices of managed care.

Managed care organizations encountered less resistance in other countries, such as Argentina, Chile, and Colombia, where prior dictatorships or authoritarian governments facilitated the privatization of public services. On the other hand, professional associations and unions organized campaigns against the entry of managed care organizations into public systems. In Chile, the national medical association (*Colegio Médico*) resisted the expansion of the ISAPREs through the use of the public national health fund (*Fondo Nacional de Salud*, FONASA). In Argentina, health professionals collaborated with a national organization of labor unions (*Central de Trabajadores Argentinos*, CTA) in educational efforts to encourage debate concerning privatization and managed care. As result of these efforts, an intense social movement, especially in the province of Córdoba, impeded the privatization of public health and social security services. An international coalition of unions representing public-sector workers, Public Services International, also helped organize opposition to managed care in several countries.

* * *

Struggles against managed care as one manifestation of neoliberal policies continued throughout the last years of empire present. Such efforts receive more attention in the last chapter of this book, which focuses on the contours of change during the brief future of empire that remains. Meanwhile, to understand more clearly how policies of "reform" generated suffering and anger during empire present, I now turn to the collaboration of multinational corporations and international financial institutions in Latin America's two most populous countries. In these countries, furious efforts to impose the neoliberal model eventually failed. Such efforts and failures generated concern and resistance not only there but also, through example, in many other countries of the less developed world.

CHAPTER 9

CORPORATIONS, INTERNATIONAL FINANCIAL
INSTITUTIONS, AND HEALTH SERVICES

Globalization raised some big problems for health care and public health during empire present. In this chapter I examine how "health reform," guided not too gently by multinational corporations and international financial institutions, took place in the two most populous countries of Latin America—Mexico and Brazil.[1] Although I delve into components of these problems in prior chapters, a brief summary will give a context for the events in Mexico and Brazil that I then consider.

Influenced by public policy makers in the United States, such organizations as the World Bank, International Monetary Fund, and World Trade Organization advocated policies that encouraged reduction and privatization of health care and public health services previously provided in the public sector.[2] These international financial institutions intervened in social policy by requiring major health-care and social security reforms. Loan conditions and renegotiations of debt payments constituted the major tools of political leverage used by international financial institutions. Such policies also affected the orientation of international health organizations, especially the World Health Organization and the Pan American Health Organization. The latter organizations accepted funding from the World Bank and initiated programs influenced by the Bank's policies. These programs favored a large role for private, multinational corporations in international public health efforts and in the provision of direct health services.

Such changes took place as multinational corporations were expanding world-wide. Corporations' flight to foreign sites with lower labor costs and fewer environmental regulations led to unemployment and loss of health insurance benefits for U.S. workers.[3] As I discuss in the previous chapter, insurance corporations and managed care organizations faced declining rates of profit in U.S. markets and entered foreign markets, usually seeking access to public social security funds designated for health-care and retirement benefits.[4] When managed care organizations shifted their focus to foreign public trust funds as a source of new capital, they tended to withdraw from U.S. Medicare and Medicaid markets. Older and low-income patients, many with complex and challenging medical conditions, needed to contend with a disruption of the services they needed.

The governments of the United States and countries in Western Europe, influenced by multinational corporations, exerted power to achieve disproportionate effects on the World Trade Organization's policies, as well as those of regional trade agreements. Through effects on health policy, this collaboration involving the world's wealthiest nations inevitably affected the direction that public health efforts and medical care would take in less developed countries. According to analysts who viewed these phenomena from the perspective of the United Kingdom, "When the U.S. and the EC [European Community] can agree on which direction global regulatory change should take, that is usually the direction it does take."[5] Less developed countries did not exert similar influence, which meant that their preferences generally did not reach the forefront of trade negotiations.

"Reform" in Mexico

Beginning in 1995, the Mexican government began to implement major reforms of health and social security policies, with financial support from the International Monetary Fund and World Bank. The previous structure of the Mexican health system became the target for reforms that followed. Mexico's health system was divided into two subsystems, the social security system and the Ministry of Health, each serving a different population.

Social security coverage was mandatory for workers in the formal labor sector, who generally were employees of large companies or government agencies. Such workers benefited from the principles of "integrity, solidarity, redistribution, and public administration" that guided the national social security system; that is, participants paid according to income but received services according to need.[6] Social security consisted of two parallel "institutes": the Mexican Institute of Social Security (*Instituto Mexicano de Seguridad Social,* IMSS) covered workers in the private sector, while the Institute of Security and Social Services for Workers of the State (*Instituto de Seguridad y Servicios Sociales para Trabajadores del Estado,* ISSSTE) provided insurance for workers in the public sector. Family members in addition to workers themselves usually received at least some coverage under these two institutes. Social security increased coverage steadily during the 1980s and early 1990s and eventually incorporated previously unprotected groups, such as university students, taxi drivers, and bus drivers.[7]

In principle, the Ministry of Health was responsible for the health care of the "uninsurable" or "open" population. Public hospitals and clinics provided most services for the Ministry of Health, with funding from the national and (to a lesser extent) the state governments' tax revenues. Although the ministry traditionally provided a variety of services, comprehensive health care did not reach the entire eligible population, partly because public hospitals and clinics did not exist in many rural areas. During the early 1990s, before "reform," about 10 million Mexicans lacked access to any type of health care.

The Mexican government presented the basic characteristics of the reform to the World Bank before presenting it to Mexico's Congress. A 1995 World Bank document where this information appeared[8] mentioned three proposals for possible reforms in the operation of Mexico's social security system: to change from progressive, mandatory, employee-employer contribution rates to flat rates; to allow employers to opt out of the social security system, with a requirement that the employers provide access to private managed care organizations for their employees; and to permit uninsured people with regular incomes to buy into social security.[9] The document also listed several government strategies as part of the health-care reform, which included: to guarantee a "basic package" of preventive and primary care services; to decentralize responsibilities and budgetary authority for services; and to reorient the role of the central Ministry of Health to a more normative one, emphasizing stewardship of the system rather than direct service delivery. The final goal of the reform was "to have the public Social Security institutions finance but not provide services."[10] This same document referred to the reform as "complex and risky," with potentially "dramatic financial consequences."[11]

Under pressure from the World Bank, Mexico's Congress approved the reform in 1995, despite protests, criticisms, mobilizations, and alternative proposals, and the reform went into effect in July 1997. By transitioning from public financing and services to private administration and service provision, the new social security law opened numerous doors to private investment. Private managed care organizations then could compete for IMSS-insured clients, receive funds from the Social Security Health Fund, and purchase services from IMSS specialty hospitals or the public National Health Institutes.[12] Social security reform left the system open to private investment while simultaneously transferring resources from the public to the private sector.

"Reform" in Brazil

In Brazil, after pressure from international financial institutions and particularly the International Monetary Fund, the government reduced social spending substantially, with serious results for health services. A broad package of controversial measures included the 1999 reduction of the health budget by $854 million.[13] In letters of intent to the International Monetary Fund, the government committed itself to seeking alternatives that permitted multinational corporations to gain access to public social security funds.[14]

Before "reform" began, the Brazilian health system functioned as a mixed public-private system. The public system operated in two ways: (1) services were both financed by and provided in the public system, using public resources and facilities; and (2) services were provided in the private sector where no public services and/or facilities were available but were financed by the public sector. The private system was called a "supplementary system." During the 1990s, about 24.5 percent of the Brazilian population held private health insurance, while 75.5 percent of Brazilians received care—or could potentially receive it— in the public system.

Under these arrangements, private entities that worked under contract with the government provided some services for the public system, which reimbursed providers for the services provided. For example, private hospitals delivered most inpatient services with public reimbursement; about 80 percent of hospitals that delivered such services to the public system were private facilities. In contrast, public facilities provided about 75 percent of outpatient care.[15] Because the Brazilian constitution treated health care as a constitutional right guaranteed by the federal government for all Brazilians,[16] about 43 percent of the privately insured population also utilized the public system, particularly for more complex and costly diagnostic procedures or treatment.[17] Despite the large proportion of the population that obtained services from the public system, this sector gradually became more fragmented and underfunded.

The Federal Constitution enacted in Brazil during 1988 had sought to implement a Unified Health System (*Sistema Único de Saúde*, SUS). Throughout the country, the Public Health Movement (*Movimento Sanitário*), a large coalition that included professional associations, unions, and community-based organizations, promoted the SUS, partly as a criticism of the prior model that financed the private sector with public resources while undermining the public sector.[18] Under the 1988 constitution, private enterprises could participate in the SUS, but only in a supplementary manner and by means of public contracts and agreements. Such enterprises were to provide services free of charge to the population when the SUS financed the services. Laws enacted to provide regulatory procedures consistent with the constitution prohibited allocation of public funds to aid or to subsidize profit-oriented private institutions.[19]

Officially the SUS's basic principles included universality, equity of care, and integrity of actions, which meant that the public system should provide the same comprehensive services to the entire population without restrictions and according to individual needs. Financing was to come mainly from the social welfare budget of the federal government, states, federal district, and municipalities.[20] Measures to establish the mechanisms of funding allocation and to define the managerial model for the SUS emerged during the 1990s through ministerial regulations such as the Basic Operational Norms (*Normas Operacionais Básicas* [NOB] 91, 93, 96). NOB 96 redefined the roles and responsibilities of the states, federal district, and federal government in the health sector.

Beginning in the mid-1990s, reforms in the SUS implemented the Family Health Program as a mechanism to transfer financial resources from the federal government to municipalities. The Ministry of Health regulated this program, and municipalities gave little input into its implementation. This program proved consistent with the "basic health services packet for the poor," which the World Bank had actively promoted in less developed countries, instead of the comprehensive care mandated by the 1988 Brazilian constitution.[21] NOB 96 also allowed for management of large public hospitals as "social organizations" (*Organizações Sociais*), a model that dissociated public institutions from municipal governments and facilitated implementation of managed care in the public sector.[22]

During the late 1990s, the Brazilian federal government implemented a series of regulatory changes that contradicted principles of the 1988 constitution.[23] By explicitly allowing direct or indirect participation of foreign corporations in health care, these regulatory changes did not adhere to the constitutional principles that prohibited public-sector subsidization of the for-profit private sector. By 1999 Aetna, CIGNA, and other large U.S. insurance companies had made sizable investments in Brazil. Their subsidiaries initiated for-profit managed care operations, in joint ventures with Brazilian firms that circumvented restrictions on the activities of foreign corporations within Brazil.[24]

Penetration by Multinational Corporations

During empire present, policies of international financial institutions therefore fostered "reform" decisions in Mexico and Brazil that supported and expanded the role of multinational corporations based mainly in the United States. In particular, the international financial institutions advocated reforms that privatized public-sector services and opened them to corporate ownership and/or administration. The reforms encouraged a wide range of profit-making activities by managed care organizations, financed by those countries' social security systems.

Undeniably, important problems existed in health care prior to the reforms in both countries. Lack of financial resources affected personnel, maintenance of equipment and facilities, and supply of medications. These problems led to deterioration in working conditions and in delivery of services. A decrease in public-sector resources, however, derived in large part from structural adjustment policies undertaken in the 1980s. These policies caused major reductions in health-care budgets, as well as extensive unemployment and low wages, which further reduced contributions to the social security systems.[25] Corruption and inefficiency, which characterized the health systems of both countries before "reform," did not change substantially under privatization.

The impacts of corporate managed care on health care and public health programs in Mexico and Brazil proved dramatic. These effects included restricted access for vulnerable groups of patients and reduced spending for clinical services as a result of higher spending on administration and return to investors. Because copayments required under managed care plans created barriers to access, they led to increasing use of and strain in public hospitals and clinics.[26]

Effects of Reform in Mexico

In Mexico, the World Bank supported reforms of both the health-care and the pension components of the social security system, with loans of $700 million and $25 million for the former and two loans of $400 million each for the latter.[27] These reforms facilitated the penetration of private capital into the social security system. In health reform, the penetration occurred partly by allowing patients to opt out of coverage by the social security system and into coverage by managed care organizations. The World Bank itself pointed out the reform's potential to weaken the social security system's financial underpinnings due to adverse selection and "cream skimming"—practices that channeled the healthiest clients into the private sector and the sickest patients into the public sector. These practices moved "good risks" from the social security system to managed care organizations, while leaving the social security system with the relatively "bad risks," who contributed less to the system but made more use of it.[28] Despite these concerns, one of the World Bank's conditions for Mexico to access the loans that supported reform was that some managed care organizations would be operating by the year 2000.[29]

The Mexican health reform included a package for the "uninsurable" population in rural or poor urban areas. Proponents portrayed the measure as an "essential health package" that would provide "universal coverage." The package contained selected public health interventions and "cost-efficient" clinical services offered outside hospitals (cost efficiency was estimated in disability-adjusted life years, DALYs; for a critique of the DALYs methodology, see Chapter 7). Components of the package included basic sanitation at the household level; family planning; Pap smear screening for cervical cancer; prenatal, delivery, and postdelivery care; child nutrition and growth surveillance; immunizations; ambulatory care at clinics for people with diarrhea; family antiparasite treatment; ambulatory treatment of acute respiratory disease; prevention and ambulatory care of hypertension and diabetes; accident prevention and first-aid; and community training for self-care.[30] These elements of the package became the basis of national reforms in 2004 under the center-right party (*Partido de Acción Nacional*, PAN), which in 2000 had gained control of the federal government.[31] Despite these covered services, the essential health package excluded treatment for many important conditions, including heart disease, stroke, children's congenital disorders, gastrointestinal diseases other than diarrhea, kidney disease, and cancer. The essential health package closely resembled the basic packages promoted by the World Bank in other less developed countries, reflecting the Bank's fundamental role in designing the Mexican reforms.

Although provided free of charge, the essential package therefore excluded many services that the Ministry of Health traditionally provided to the poor. For example, although the essential package included preventive screening by Pap smears for cervical cancer and ambulatory care for hypertension and diabetes, it did not cover treatment of cervical cancer detected by Pap screening or inpatient treatment for the complications of hypertension and diabetes, such as heart disease, kidney disease, and stroke. Concretely, this gap in coverage meant that all services not included in the package would be charged directly to the patient or would be financed by state governments in Mexico with limited capacity to make independent decisions or to collect taxes. Services not included in the package had to be contracted through public or private insurance; this approach called for major participation by private, for-profit managed care organizations in delivering these services.[32]

Predictably, patients who developed problems requiring services excluded under the essential package either did not receive adequate services or received limited care at public-sector health institutions that experienced cutbacks of funding due to the reform. Prior to the reform, the combination of social security coverage and the services provided by the Ministry of Health remained far from comprehensive for the whole population. Nonetheless, the social security system had offered at least some coverage to all members, while the Ministry of Health had provided a large variety of services for the uninsured population.

Under the reform, although private health insurance plans varied, several key issues emerged, even for those who could afford to buy private policies. Copayments for routine appointments with physicians could reach as high as 65 percent of charges for the appointments. For specialized care, the deductible could amount to about 30 percent of total coverage. Private insurance usually excluded prescriptions for medications. Employers could offer private insurance coverage without premiums paid by employees; therefore, it was promoted as a "free" plan within benefits packages. When an employer provided premiums without employee contributions, the corporation could claim a tax-deductible expense. Although employees were not required to make contributions to premiums, substantial copayments usually proved necessary, and employees could not choose between social security and other types of private insurance. Employees often had to purchase additional coverage, beyond what was offered as a fringe benefit of employment.

Effects of Reform in Brazil

Private companies in Brazil also implemented several classic features of managed care. For instance, they employed mechanisms to restrict utilization, including denial of care, refusal to reimburse physicians for procedures, arbitrary termination of contracts with physicians, and preferred networks of private providers. Private health insurance plans increased, as did the number of patients' complaints due to denials of services.[33] Although the 1998 Health Plans Law (*Lei* 9,656) officially protected consumers from the arbitrary practices of insurance companies, such as fragmentation of plans and unanticipated premium increases, the companies found ways to circumvent the law. Complaints about rising premiums, restrictions on physician visits and hospitalizations, and contracts that did not conform to the legislation continued after the law was enacted. New contracts frequently did not cover the minimum services that the legislation required. At the same time, insurance companies reported high profits.

By late 2000 a special commission appointed by the Brazilian Congress initiated financial investigations concerning these companies' practices.[34] Legislation eventually forced companies to comply with insurance laws and to some extent curtailed "cream-skimming" practices. These actions increased costs for companies, which raised premiums to maintain profits. A decrease in the number of privately insured people from 41 million in 1998 to 35.1 million in 2003 reflected the inability of many clients to afford the higher premiums.[35] These changes also highlighted the public system's financial difficulty in absorbing those who moved from the private to the public system.

Disinvestment in the public sector led to reduced provision of services. A reduction of 2.5 percent of the funds allocated to the public health sector took place in the 1999–2000 budget,[36] and in general the budget did not keep pace with population growth. Paradoxically, specialized and expensive medical procedures still took place largely in the public sector, and those covered by private insurance utilized public facilities when they needed such services.[37] Some professionals argued that to provide health care to private patients without affecting services to SUS patients, public hospitals needed to increase their number of beds. This change occurred initially at the University of Rio de Janeiro's hospital, which expanded with financial support from the National Bank of Economic and Social Development to provide care for privately insured patients.[38] The increasing mix of private-public financing in public hospitals exerted financial pressures that threatened access for patients who depended only on the public sector.

Vicissitudes of Privatization and Corporatization

During empire present, privatization and the opening of public-sector services to corporate participation led to injurious effects throughout the less developed world. As shown by the examples of Mexico and Brazil, international financial institutions and multinational corporations influenced reforms that, though favorable to corporate interests, worsened access to needed services and strained the limited public-sector institutions that remained. Reform decisions continued despite research verifying predictions that the policies would worsen access and health-care outcomes among the most vulnerable populations. Reforms supported by the World Bank and other international financial institutions threatened the countries' social security systems while providing "packages" of basic services that left many needs unmet.

The legitimacy of such policy changes often contributed to the dismantling of the public sector. In Mexico, for example, "a gestation period of almost a decade," during which public institutions were slowly undermined and discredited, was necessary to legitimize the reform.[39] Yet the worsening crisis in the public system, such as medication shortages and deteriorating conditions at public hospitals and clinics, derived from political decisions made by the same actors who became advocates of privatization. These examples showed how governments, in collaboration with international financial institutions and multinational corporations, could create artificial crises and then use them to build their cases for privatization.

*   *   *

Why did people throughout the world consent to privatization schemes and the penetration of corporations into their health systems? New ideological discourses arose during empire present that challenged the role of public-sector services and transformed people's expectations in the face of growing crises. "Experts" in health policy constructed a new common sense, which justified policies that led to a dismantling of public systems and the imposition of privatized systems. How the ideological underpinnings of these policies gained ascendance becomes the next focus in our journey through empire present.

CHAPTER 10

THE "COMMON SENSE" OF HEALTH REFORM

How was health reform constructed ideologically during empire present?[1] During earlier historical periods, discussions of health reform arose periodically. Most of the concepts that received attention later—efficiency, effectiveness, cost-benefit analysis, freedom of choice, decentralization, community participation, etc.—also appeared during the 1950s and 1960s, to motivate transformations in health-care organization.[2]

For instance, two consultation reports on health-care organization in Argentina, presented in 1957 by experts of the Pan American Health Organization, conveyed clear examples of earlier policy positions.[3] These extensive reports recommended that the Argentine government restructure the health system, starting with decentralization of administrative authority. The reports also argued in favor of training health-care personnel to use techniques of cost-benefit analysis and related administrative principles. A central purpose was to achieve more efficient institutions that could maintain an adequate cost-benefit relationship. Health policies were seen partly within an overall economic model of capitalist accumulation. This model was based on full employment, production of goods and services by state enterprises, and a supply of healthy and educated manpower. In this context, the concepts used in proposals for reorganization of health systems included a conception of health as a public good and state responsibility.[4]

Beginning in the mid-1980s, early during empire present, some "experts" in the health-care field recaptured these concepts, which, they argued, could respond to an ongoing crisis of financing health systems. Prior concepts changed, and their new meaning emerged in a different political-economic context. Emerging concepts of reform tried to address a crisis in the model of capitalist accumulation that had occurred since the mid-1970s: intermittent global recession, profound transformations in the forms of production including informatics and robotization, an expanding domain of finance capital in the world economic system, the growing internal and external indebtedness of Third World countries, growth of the fiscal deficit, high inflation, problems in balance of payments, and unemployment.[5]

This situation implied fundamental changes in the role of the state. As part of structural adjustment policies, international financial institutions demanded contraction of public expenditures, control of monetary expansion, and reform of the state structure itself. This vision identified the state as the cause of the crisis, due to its inefficiency in managing productive enterprises (oil, steel, etc.) and services (communications and transportation), as well as its growing social expenses (health, education, and social security). Requirements for state reform included four main elements, which tended to remain hidden or implicit in policy discourse: an increased need for private capital to support areas of production and services that the state previously supported; an increased need to invest large surpluses of liquid capital; a decreased need for labor, which derived partly from a transformation of production due to developments in computer science; and reduced risk for economically dominant countries whose elites wished to invest in less developed countries.[6] New dimensions of ideology provided a justification for reforms that met these requirements.

Ideological Underpinnings of Health Reform

In the previous two chapters, I examine the exportation of managed care from the United States and the role of multinational corporations and international financial institutions in the major health reforms that took place in Mexico and Brazil during empire present. Here, I reexamine these processes to focus on their ideological underpinnings. Such ideologies emerged in official discourses that accepted the inexorability of the proposed reforms as part of a new "common sense" about the position of the state in relation to the economic activities of private corporations.[7]

Administrative and financial reforms involving managed care considered growth of health-care costs to be the main cause of the health sector's crisis. For that reason, the reforms called for an intermediary between providers and users, to separate financial administration from the delivery of services. Proposals for managed care implied the introduction of enterprises (state, private, or mixed) that administered financing under the concept of shared risk (capitated systems). These enterprises contracted with groups of professionals, who provided the state-supported services.[8]

Ideological Assumptions in a Silent Process of Reform

In the construction of public-sector budgets, administrators planned reforms so that they responded to demand rather than supply of services. This approach allowed a reduction of fixed costs and a more efficient management of resources, since excess services were controlled and financing was directed toward providers of presumably higher quality. According to this logic, to obtain financing, providers—including those in the public sector, such as public hospitals and clinics—were forced to lower their costs and to offer services of at least superficially higher quality (attempts to convey quality often involved cosmetic improvements like more frequent painting and purchase of more stylish furnishings). Discourses supporting these policies emphasized the assumption that if purchasers felt in control of their payment for services, they would help to control costs and to improve quality, because purchasers chose providers that offered the best services at the least cost.[9] These discourses also assumed that public-sector services had proven inefficient and unpopular, leading to widespread dissatisfaction among consumers, even though there was little evidence showing more dissatisfaction with public sector as opposed to private-sector services.

Reform proposals, whose frame of reference derived mainly from the United States, produced fundamental changes in clinical practice. These changes involved the subordination of health professionals to an administrative-financial logic. In addition, a drastic reduction of independent professional practice took place, as professionals needed to offer their services to insurance companies or the proprietors of large medical centers.[10]

The political process that accompanied these reforms was usually a silent one, restricted to the executive branch of government. Achieving a silent process of policy making constituted an explicit goal, which emerged from understandings between executive branch officials and administrators of international financial institutions such as the World Bank.[11] This silence generally segmented the policy-making process and therefore reduced political conflict. Reform policies sequentially targeted the public sector, the private sector, or the social security system, but they did not adopt a unified approach to the health system as a whole. In general, policy implementation bypassed discussion in the legislative branch. For this reason, presidential decrees or ministry regulations became the most common ways that the executive branch implemented reform policies.[12]

At each stage, the officials who planned and implemented the reforms involved only those who participated in each subsector (public, private, or medical social security); this approach hindered a societal perspective on reform. Within each subsector, participants tried to accommodate the reform process, without recognizing the impact on other subsectors. For instance, policy changes directed toward the private subsector were not considered within the purview of actors in the public subsector or in the social security subsector. This tendency of segmentation separated the participants in professional associations, professional and nonprofessional unions in the state subsector, unions that administered social security systems, managers in ministries of health, and businesspeople in the private sector.[13] Nevertheless, partly due to the silence of the reform process, the resulting policy changes actually achieved a profound articulation of the three subsectors, not achieved previously in most Latin American countries despite a long expressed need for this articulation. Private interests and especially multinational finance capital, however, controlled the articulation.

A Transformation of Common Sense

Responding to the financial crisis of the 1990s, most Latin American governments accepted the ideological positions of international financial institutions: the World Bank, the Inter-American Development Bank, and the International Monetary Fund. Favored policies implied increased indebtedness, the opening of national economies to multinational finance capital and production, and the restructuring of the state via privatizations and decreased expenditures, which affected both industrial production and public expenditures for health and other human services.[14] This orientation, usually involving ideological assumptions that supported the role of the private sector over that of the public sector, gave impetus to structural adjustment plans, whose execution depended on access to additional international financial resources.[15] In health reform, structural adjustment implied acceptance by Latin American governments of the reform projects initiated by these lending agencies, especially the World Bank. By consenting to the requirements of structural adjustment, governments gained access to loans but also consented to major cutbacks in public services.

In Argentina, for example, at the end of 1991, the reformulation of health projects that received financing from the World Bank began. World Bank loans previously targeted four spheres of activity: hospital decentralization, development of human resources, implementation of health information systems, and health promotion and disease prevention. Under the World Bank's changed policies, the loans required that new projects center on reform of public medical care institutions (hospital self-management) and the deregulation of social security funds. The purpose of these policies was to reduce state participation in the financing, administration, and delivery of services, and to enhance the role of the private sector.[16]

Gradually, conceptualization of health, illness, and health services transformed into a new "common sense." Health reform projects, carried out with international loans, involved an elaboration of legal norms (laws, ordinances, and ministry reso- lutions) that resonated with the new discourse, linked to the crisis of the welfare state. In official pronouncements, health care no longer remained a universal right for whose fulfillment the state assumed responsibility, but rather became con- verted into a good of the marketplace that individuals could acquire by purchase. With this fundamental change in meaning, health transmogrified from a public good to a private good.[17] This metamorphosis of common sense manifested itself not only in discourses concerning health reform, but also in the population's lived experiences in obtaining services. Ultimately, this transformation extended to many other areas of collective life—including education, transportation, commu- nications, and criminal justice—in addition to health care. Policies governing all these spheres eventually adopted a similar ideological framework.

Ideology and the Reconstruction of Common Sense

Little by little during empire present, populations throughout the world accepted, usually without much criticism or opposition, official discourses that called for policy reforms to address a carefully constructed image of crisis. Such reforms included privatizing public enterprises and services as well as reducing social expenditures. In the firmness of the official discourses, people found a source of hope and reencountered a sense of shared social project. Specifically, the shared social project was that required by structural adjustment: to reduce the role of the public sector and to enhance private, market-oriented processes. In this way, social situations became more comprehensible, and lived experience came to be viewed as inevitable, even though daily life might seem unjust and painful.

A transformed common sense thus became a central component of the social cement that filled the breaches, softened contradictions artificially, and made possible a comfortable coexistence of antagonisms. This transformation of consciousness accomplished a shared subjective experience of social conditions, even when individuals occupied very distinct positions in the social structure. A resulting subjectivity became a socially shared truth, in the acceptance of a common direction for society as a whole.[18]

In health policy, many of those referred to as experts contributed to the con- struction of this new common sense, by sustaining several ideas as fundamentals from which to rethink the system:

- The crisis in health stemmed from financial causes.
- Management introduced a new and indispensable administrative rationality to resolve the crisis.

- It was essential to subordinate clinical decisions to this new rationality if cost reduction was desired.
- Efficiency increased if financing was separated from service delivery, and if competition was generalized among all subsectors (state, social security, and private).
- The market in health was to be developed because it was the best regulator of costs and quality.
- Demand rather than supply was to be subsidized.
- Making labor relationships flexible constituted the best mechanism to achieve efficiency, productivity, and quality.
- Private administration was more efficient and less corrupt than public administration.
- Payments for social security were each worker's property.
- Deregulation of social security allowed the user freedom of choice and an ability to opt for the best administrator of his or her funds.
- The passage of the user/patient/beneficiary to client/consumer ensured that rights were respected.
- Quality was ensured by fostering the client's satisfaction.

These components of ideology, summarized briefly here, shaped people's experiences most keenly in those countries where these processes were introduced most forcefully, such as Argentina and Chile. In other countries, such as Brazil and Ecuador, these ideological processes encountered civil societies more disposed to question such proposals. In many less developed countries, however, varying degrees of transnationalization, privatization, and reorganization under managed care corporations took place. These changes, supported by international financial institutions, achieved justification ideologically through a profound reconstruction of common sense, by which populations' lived experiences were interpreted and understood.

During empire present, the reform of health systems manifested a characteristic logic, promulgated by international financial institutions and multinational corporations. Within this logic appeared the diagnoses of socially constructed problems and crises that required a certain type of reform. The logic applied to those reforms carried out by governments, those carried out by multilateral agencies of credit and cooperation, and those initiated by corporations of national and international finance capital. Reform proposals conveyed diagnoses that contained a certain degree of veracity in their critique of the state and the public sector. For that reason, the common sense conveyed by these proposals gained acceptance at the ideological level, both for the population as a whole and for many workers and intellectuals in the health-care field.

From this perspective, diagnoses that spoke of inefficiency in the management of state institutions and social security, of shortages in resources that limited accessibility, of excessive bureaucratization, of limited capacity to respond to the population's demands, of escalating costs, etc.—all these constructed realities became veracities, increasingly shared by users and health workers as part of their lived experiences. These experiences created a supportive substrate for the acceptance of a discourse that became taken for granted as the basis for reform projects, as the reform proposals integrated such experiences into their own rationalities, revealed as natural and evident. This condition made possible an ideological modification of common sense concerning the processes of health, illness, and services, little by little making appear natural a conception that sought to commercialize all the relationships established in these processes.

Assumptions sustained during many years, especially for public health advocates, that conveyed the idea that health constituted a responsibility of the state and a public good, gave up their place to discourses of economics and policy analysis, which conveyed a construction of complexity. In the latter discourse, people and their problems tended to disappear, and nearly everything became transformed into abstract questions of financial resources and their shortage, or of ineffective administration. From this ideological position, the only important goal became a reorganization of institutions, so that they might act efficiently and maintain an appropriate cost-benefit ratio. The central question became how to manage state institutions and social security funds under private, for-profit auspices.

With certainty about the indispensability of change in the health system, many actors linked to reform accepted the instruments developed by managed care organizations, the private insurance industry, other multinational corporations, and international financial institutions. Such actors elaborated discourses that, while trying to differentiate themselves from the neoliberal project, in many cases remained trapped in that logic. Technical proposals thus were framed in the possibilism characteristic of postmodern thought. This orientation recognized no alternatives to negotiate reality other than those that already had presented themselves.[19] As a result, discourses that in many instances did not commit themselves to the neoliberal project in its whole nevertheless facilitated implementation of reform under corporate leadership.

Against the diagnostic veracities of common sense during empire present, those that offered solutions on behalf of the general population but that actually represented the most concentrated sectors of finance capital, some tried to think and to speak more critically. Such voices argued that the common sense did not constitute truth, but rather the imposition of norms defined largely by financial interests. Critical thought, as analyzed by Benasayag and Charlton in a formulation that became influential especially in Latin America and Europe, involved a reflexive movement of the consciousness regarding commonly enunciated views, the ability to "denounce" these views as they were constructed. Not necessarily oppositional, nor at a level superior to common sense, critical thought from this viewpoint operated in another register that questioned the hegemonic ideologies of the times. While common sense presumably functioned as a sixth sense able to apprehend the order of the external world and to enunciate what was "normal and natural," critical thought turned itself toward commonly enunciated views and problematized that which seemed evident.[20]

Viewed through a critical lens, health reform as sought by official discourses constituted not the only option, nor necessarily the best, to address a population's health. On the contrary, late in empire present, many groups worked on alternative projects. In Latin America, to consider only one region, numerous organizations defended health as a public good. These groups gradually attained more influence, as they questioned the common sense of health reform and proposed alternatives, usually those calling for a strengthened, rather than weakened, public sector that guaranteed access to health care as a fundamental human right. Despite the enormous impact that the new common sense exerted on health reform during empire present, efforts to build alternative projects, carried out in specific spaces (institutional, community, municipal, or state), did not lose sight of the countervailing ideas that eventually would carry the day as empire exhausted itself.

*   *   *

Despite living and working under the ideologies expressed in the common sense of health reform, people confronting the key problems of medicine and public health during empire present constructed their realities in quite different ways. How did the protagonists in government agencies, international financial institutions, international health organizations, and multinational corporations formulate their positions? How did people who rejected the common sense and tried to build alternative projects express their own views? The next chapter tries to answer these questions.

CHAPTER 11

STAKEHOLDERS' CONSTRUCTIONS
OF GLOBAL TRADE, PUBLIC HEALTH,
AND HEALTH SERVICES

During empire present, widely divergent views emerged about the impact of global trade on public health and health services. Interpretations connecting trade and health varied, depending on the institutional interests and ideologies of the protagonists.[1] Visions of favorable or unfavorable effects of trade on health reflected more general assumptions about how market forces affect health and well-being.

This chapter examines the attitudes, decisions, and actions of major groups participating in policy debates about globalization, public health, and health services: government agencies, international financial institutions and trade organizations, international health organizations, multinational corporations, and advocacy groups.[2] The official construction of such organizations' policies, as revealed in formal documents and informal comments during interviews, differed—in some cases quite markedly—from the organizations' actions in the arena of global trade. Instead, these constructions more closely matched the ideological "common sense" of health policy, as revealed in the last chapter.

Government Agencies

The policy orientations of U.S. government agencies during empire present emphasized the importance of public health and health services in fostering U.S. interests worldwide. Rather than viewing health as an end in itself, public statements of such agencies usually promoted health initiatives as a way to advance U.S.

interests. For instance, at one point the official global health website of the U.S. Department of Health and Human Services clarified this emphasis on the role of the country's national interests in promoting health around the world: "The health of Americans is a global concern. The United States must engage health policy globally to protect Americans' health and to protect America's vital interests."[3] This vision corresponded to the U.S. government's long-standing policy orientation regarding globalization, as enunciated by Henry Kissinger, which emphasized the country's dominance among nations: "The basic challenge is that what is called globalization is really another name for the dominant role of the United States."[4] The policy orientations of U.S. government agencies emphasized the importance of public health and health services in fostering U.S. interests worldwide.

Officials in the U.S. government described the importance of balance between trade and health in policy decisions and recognized contradictions that arose in the promotion of trade. From this viewpoint, officials responsible for trade negotiations weighed the advantages for trade against the disadvantages for health. As the director of negotiations for a major international trade agreement under the Office of the U.S. Trade Representative stated in an interview,[5] this task raised challenges:

> There is a sense that health policy is as important as trade policy. There is a balance that exists between them, that includes protecting human health and protecting trade, the rights of investors, intellectual property rights; the goal is to find the balance.

The respondent then described this balance in more detail:

> Without that balance, the system breaks down, you don't get investment if you can't protect it; but if you can't protect the people's health, and activities that protect their health, you don't get their support and then don't get investment in the system.

This construction acknowledged that trade could impact health adversely, and that this problem's adjudication became the responsibility of government officials like himself.

From this viewpoint, global trade generated improved economic conditions, which in turn led to improved health services. Similarly, trade agreements between governments achieved prosperity and enhanced access to care:

> I think that one analysis is that removing barriers to trade and investment helps prosperity and improves living standards of people in the countries involved. In

turn, as the standard of living rises, so do things like the quality of health care available and health policies put in place by governments and demanded by citizens, etc.

To achieve such changes, government-based trade negotiators aimed toward uniform policies among nations. However, policies that favored global trade also could lead to negative consequences if not prevented by trade agreement negotiators:

> If done right, it [globalization] helps the world economy, raises living standards, and removes barriers to development. If done wrong, it can do some pretty serious damage to those elements, and to other things like the environment and public health. If one isn't careful, it can create perverse incentives that in the long run aren't to anyone's benefit. The trick is to balance them out.

In this way, the goals of this government official and others like him, as they negotiated the terms of international trade agreements, emphasized achieving balance in the impacts on trade and health.

In contrast to expression of U.S. policy, both officially through website-based pronouncements and unofficially through interviewers, government representatives in Latin America expressed pessimism about the impact of global trade on public health and health services. This viewpoint emerged regardless of their political affiliation or current position. For instance, when asked for a definition of economic globalization, the director of health services in one of Mexico's largest cities responded: "[Globalization is] the imposition of a new model of global accumulation which privileges the financial sector." From this perspective, the purposes of globalization involved financial goals that had little to do with public health or the fairness of trade. About the possibly beneficial effects of international trade agreements, the same respondent commented: "I do not think [there is any]. The information flow does not change." Regarding detrimental effects, the respondent answered: "Actors in the free trade area have power over policies. The government is desperate to attract investors.... They become private actors in policies ... especially the insurers." This vision of globalization and international trade agreements closely resembled Kissinger's earlier formalization that emphasized the overlap between globalization policies in general and U.S. interests in particular.

Other public health leaders in Latin America expressed similar views. One respondent, who directed a major foundation and served as an adviser to the national Ministry of Health, described adverse effects of global trade on health:

There is a possibility that U.S. or foreign corporations could come and invest. What are the corporations' objectives? Usually they want to increase the production of their capital.... If not guaranteed, you will not see a positive effect for the health system, despite a positive effect for them [the corporations].

Similarly, as a definition of economic globalization, the dean of a large, public-sector health sciences center stated:

[It is] subordination to the policies of the International Monetary Fund, the World Bank, and the transnationals [corporations]. The U.S. gets a cold; we get pneumonia. [It is] subordination to multinational organizations. The concept of the nation disappears under globalization.

Across the spectrum of Latin American respondents, little variation arose in the concern expressed about adverse effects of global trade. Informants consistently responded that Latin American governments historically defined health as a right and health care as a public good. They noted that this orientation changed due to the structural reforms imposed by international financial institutions. Latin American respondents also perceived that, in practice, U.S. health policies placed profit before the needs of the population and that this emphasis entered Latin America with deleterious effects as international trade agreements took effect.

International Financial Institutions

Representatives of international financial institutions emphasized the importance of private market mechanisms to achieve efficient and cost-effective policies. As a World Bank official expressed, the institution's mission was "a world without poverty"; the main obstacle to the institution's mission involved governments that remained uncommitted to reforming their public-sector services by open-ing them up to participation by private corporations. By encouraging economic development and prosperity, in this construction, international trade agreements enhanced health outcomes:

The evidence supports a view that these agreements increase people's real income. It's not a zero sum game. Creating a larger trading area makes everyone better off materially. There is a link between material improvement (people get richer) and health outcomes like infant mortality.

In this scenario, market mechanisms encouraged by trade agreements affected health outcomes through economic development, rather than through specific organizational structures for health services. As opposed to health services, in this vision, public health demanded a strong public sector:

> In helping communities meet objectives, the economic framework holds that public goods can't be provided through markets. Government has to do these things due to externalities.... Traditionally, if you try to address malaria by wiping out some types of mosquitoes, it's hard to imagine that the private market would take care of that. It's hard to sell that activity, as opposed to aspirin, where you can have a market. To eradicate mosquitoes, you must have collective action. You can divide up interventions to determine what is not comprehensively provided by private providers.

The World Bank's emphasis on privatization thus approached a limit, since public health problems required public-sector actions unattractive to private providers and investors.

In a related construction of the World Bank's policies, the Bank encouraged self-determination in policy making at the local level. By this construction, the Bank lacked a specific overall policy toward public health and health services throughout the world. One respondent claimed:

> It's a common misperception that the World Bank has views on things, but there are few areas in which the World Bank has official views. There are not many official views on health policy.... Our role is to help communities implement innovations ... and evaluate them.

Like the World Bank's published documents, this respondent and others expressed an official position that the international financial institutions' economic policies did not infringe on countries' autonomy to make their own policy decisions about public health and health services. The respondent argued that economic analyses worked best in a context of freedom:

> The World Bank is not an ideological institution. We're interested in results.... The model is to help communities identify objectives; if you want to meet objectives by contracting out to private firms, then let's do an analysis of the results.... I believe in freedom. In the end, societies have to develop what they want. Economists help with tradeoffs in their deciding what they want.

From this pragmatic viewpoint, the freedom of the private marketplace led to more cost-effective health services, while the public sector could assist with public health necessities that the private sector could not sell. Whether a country accepted a recommendation tied to a World Bank loan, according to this construction, occurred in a process of local determination and freedom of decision making. To the extent that they followed these principles, international financial institutions presumably did not coerce countries that received loans to follow policies that its staff members recommended. Instead, from this viewpoint, the institutions provided technical support in helping a country to determine its own path.

International Health Organizations

Since international health organizations began to coordinate their activities more explicitly with international financial institutions and trade organizations, these three seemingly disparate types of organizations adopted increasingly similar policies. Respondents in the World Health Organization and the Pan American Health Organization, mirroring the official publications of these organizations, favored collaborations that strengthened private-sector, market-oriented policy reforms. Health officials also supported international trade agreements and the reorganization of health services to enhance trade—as long as they themselves could represent the interest of public health in these processes. As a respondent at the Pan American Health Organization noted:

> PAHO was created to facilitate trade in the region.... Right now we are taking positively that countries are involved and discussing trade agreements. But trade agreements may have positive or negative aspects of health.

In this construction, international health organizations took an active role in trade negotiations, so the new agreements would protect public health.

> For example, five years after MERCOSUR [the Common Market of the South] was created, after public health people weren't interested, they approved more than 200 resolutions with little input from the health sector. Then we decided to change our approach ... participate to expand the health agenda in those agreements, to make sure that health priorities are taken into consideration, to influence agreements to avoid negative implications.

This outlook attributed no inherent conflict between global trade and public health, provided that international health organizations could encourage consideration of health issues during trade negotiations. The same scenario manifested itself in the World Trade Organization's and World Health Organization's commitment to collaborate in issues of trade.[6]

From the perspective of international health organizations, the supranational governance achieved through trade agreements exerted favorable rather than adverse effects on health. According to a respondent at the Pan American Health Organization:

> They [international trade organizations] are telling governments what they should do. Countries are expected to incorporate decisions made at the supranational level into their internal policies.... Most decisions are positive. For instance, they are discussing medicines, cooperation about medicines, use of excess capacity in production of a given service.... They can exchange that capacity at a regional level, ... by the recognition of [professional] diplomas, and [harmonized regulations about] ... the importation and exportation of food.... Under subregional arrangements, I don't see many problems of negative implications.

Trade negotiations among less developed countries, according to the respondent, also provided an opportunity to practice and to refine skills for more challenging negotiations with developed countries and multinational corporations:

> Countries in subregional [trade] organizations get experience, expertise, and negotiating capacity, before they engage in a negotiation, for example, with the United States or Canada.... It's a very inefficient process right now. For example, the case of pharmaceuticals is discussed by MERCOSUR and Andean countries at seven different venues.... MERCOSUR, PAHO, FTAA, WTO, etc.... It's challenging for less developed countries to be effective in so many instances.

By this construction, a pragmatic approach prepared the less developed countries to participate more effectively in trade negotiations and agreements. Subsequently, this participation strengthened countries' capacities to negotiate agreements favorable to their populations' health services and outcomes.

Multinational Corporations

Corporate interests, as shown in Chapter 6, figured in virtually every international trade agreement. Among multinational corporations, pharmaceutical companies played a crucial role in policy decisions linking global trade, public health, and health services. These corporations influenced several trade agreements, especially the Agreement on Trade-Related Aspects of Intellectual Property Rights (TRIPS), which protected patented medications.

Interviews showed the importance of intellectual property protections in the constructions of corporate strategies among pharmaceutical executives. These executives saw patent protections as essential in facilitating voluntary efforts to deal with the health problems of less developed countries. Unexpectedly, they emphasized that such noneconomic goals figured more prominently than anticipated profits in corporate policy decisions. For example, the vice president for international operations at one of the world's largest pharmaceutical companies stated that protection of intellectual property under the TRIPS agreement proved especially important for scientists in less developed countries:

> There are people who can do research, biotechnology, they need legislation to protect their discoveries and innovations. In that context, TRIPS is ... a platform for emerging countries to work as partners in innovation, clinical research, and biotechnology.... People in emerging markets need to receive a just reward for their work—just as we ask here for a just reward for the billions of U.S. dollars that we put at risk each year.

In this construction, intellectual property provisions extended beyond ensuring profitability for the corporation, as they also helped foster the work of investigators in countries where career advancement otherwise would prove difficult.

A related construction expressed a connection between intellectual property protections and corporate responsibility to provide medications for the needy:

> The environment must be characterized by strong intellectual property rights and freedom of pricing.... These characteristics are not antagonistic to social responsibility to those patients out of work, out of health care protection, who can't afford to pay for new drugs. We have our own foundations.... We do a lot of these activities.

In the same interview, the executive provided examples of corporate responsibility facilitated by intellectual property rights:

> We don't operate in isolation but have social responsibility. The best example of a private company working with government is our partnership with South Africa and Sub-Saharan Africa. We bring [patented antifungal medication] free of charge to populations that cannot pay. We also help with infrastructure and education of thousands of people, for example in the International Trachoma Initiative. Today, we provide [patented antibiotics] free of charge to people in Morocco, Mali, and Vietnam, even in locations where we don't have a business at all, or where [business is] unlikely in the future.

Responding to a probe about tax advantages or public relations benefits of such contributions, the respondent emphasized the humanitarian mission. He asserted that considerations of money and public image did not figure prominently in decision making:

> There may be some tax benefits particularly in this country. But I don't think this is an issue. It takes a tremendous decision to fly to South Africa and say to the government: you have a large population dying from fungal infections. We are going to bring our drug, [name of patented antifungal medication], free of charge, [for] people who can't pay 10 dollars or 10 cents.... You won't believe the time and efforts that I and the chairman have spent on this issue ... in the World Economic Forum, the United Nations, advocating for other companies to do the same with the poor African who cannot afford to pay.... We have our core mission ... we want to be seen as the most valued company in the world. We have more assets in emerging markets than any other company.

Such commentary construed a broad range of corporate goals, among which profitability constituted only one. Regarding the need for medications in less developed countries, images of corporate beneficence conveyed a scenario very different from the organizational behavior cited in critiques of patents as a major barrier to access.

Regarding noneconomic motivations, ideas about freedom and social justice served as stronger expressed motivations than concerns about profitability in corporate decision making. For one pharmaceutical executive, such ideas derived in large part from personal experiences of poverty. When asked about resistance to globalization and alternative projects linking global trade and health policies, he stated:

> It's really a shame.... I hear comments that globalization is a cause of poverty in country A or country B. I'm surprised because these countries are where globalization hasn't been. I manage the African countries. I came from a poor family in [a country in northern Africa]. I lost my father at the age of 9; I had to work early to take care of my family. Africa needs democracy. No serious person can incriminate globalization as a source of the ongoing unfortunate economic difficulties in Africa.

This construction emphasized notions of freedom and social justice as motivations in corporate decision making, rather than concerns about profitability. Intellectual property rights then became part of a broader construction of corporate profitability balanced by corporate responsibility.

Advocacy Groups

Spokespersons for advocacy groups emphasized adverse effects of global trade on public health and health services. For instance, one respondent explained that the TRIPS agreement negatively impacted the availability of urgently needed medications, especially for AIDS and other endemic infections in Africa:

> Intellectual property agreements are horrible. But there is so much activism around the world to curtail the TRIPS agreement and then get that codified. Then there would be a way that trade agreements could do some good for public health, for a change. Pharmaceutical companies don't see it that way at all and will fight tooth and nail.

Here, mirroring comments of respondents in several advocacy groups, the corporate motivation for intellectual property protection in medication patents derived from economic interests rather than an effort to foster scientific productivity or humanitarian commitment.

Spokespersons for advocacy groups portrayed a system wrought with contradictions between international trade agreements and free trade as envisioned in economic theory. One respondent argued that trade agreements often restricted free trade:

> Free trade agreements have nothing to do with free trade as defined in the economic literature. They are actually complex, detailed agreements about managed trade: which countries can sell which products and services to whom and when. The global economy is being intricately managed and regulated. The question is: who is doing the managing and in whose interest.

This respondent referred to the history of such contradictions:

> Those who articulate the free trade paradigm have always been disingenuous. Even when British economists like Adam Smith and David Ricardo spewed free trade rhetoric, it was disingenuous, since all countries that successfully had developed industrial capacity had used trade restrictions and state subsidies. This has been a major role of the state in industrialized countries. The rhetoric of free trade principles had little to do with how countries had industrialized.

From this perspective, the notion of freedom conveyed by the term "free trade agreements" contradicted the provisions of these agreements, which substantially constrained the freedom to trade. Instead, these agreements imposed a large set of new regulations and requirements, introducing a strong form of management that dictated the terms under which trading partners could operate.

Another respondent, who directed the global trade division of a major consumer rights organization, agreed with this construction and argued that trade agreements intruded into arenas far removed from trade, while maintaining the symbolism of free trade:

> They're not free trade.... If free trade, [the agreements] would be three pages long, with few restrictions.... Instead, they have more than 900 pages of rules under agreements, and even longer laws.... By using the leading edge of trade, they've introduced many other policies. They use international negotiations as a vehicle to change domestic health, pension, and labor policies. Some are anti-competitive, for example, TRIPS.... We want the World Trade Organization to shrink or to sink ... for example, cut back to proper scope ... but its role should not be subjectively to set policy decisions about how much pesticide residues on vegetables worldwide, or whether a country decides to set up national health program, or whether a country provides medications.

From this perspective, trade rules extended corporate dominance inappropriately into many new arenas, including public health and health services:

> The current economic globalization is simply the imposition worldwide of a comprehensive set of policies, which go beyond economics to include health, human rights, labor, environment, consumer safety.... Decisions are being shifted up and away; for example, decisions affecting a local water system are shifted to the state, then federal level, then WTO [World Trade Organization], where absolutely no accountability or access [exists] for individual citizens of the countries affected. If someone finds that they can't get medicines for granny, it's not likely that she will protest at WTO's headquarters on the shores of Lake Geneva.

Pursuing the theme of protest, this respondent also presented a construction of resistance to globalization, as well as alternative projects. These efforts included struggles to protect access to health services and medications:

> Probably the most powerful fight-backs are the incredible efforts in the global south to reverse health care privatization. Brazil's standing up to the U.S. that we are going to produce and distribute AIDS drugs. The U.S. took Brazil to WTO. Brazil fought back in WTO. They also launched a PR [public relations] campaign across the world—the U.S. wants to kill people in Brazil by depriving drugs. In El Salvador, they reversed the privatization of health care.... They won. What's

happening as policies kill people around the world, when day to day life is not survivable, people become ungovernable.

Because of such resistance, this respondent and several others expressed optimism that organizing efforts could reverse some of the adverse effects of global trade on public health and health services.

Social Constructions of Trade and Health

During empire present, the protagonists who confronted the realities of trade and health on a day-to-day basis revealed diverse constructions of social reality. Although policy changes linking trade and health often occurred silently—with little attention by legislators, the public media, professional associations, or other organizations of civil society—stakeholders representing key organizations manifested intense and divergent viewpoints:

- The constructions of global health policies by U.S. government agencies focused on U.S. national interests. Government officials perceived a balance between trade and health, which they adjudicated through their roles as regulators and negotiators. The U.S. position differed markedly from those of other governments, particularly in Latin America, which instead emphasized the right to health.
- As international financial institutions and trade organizations assumed a growing role in public health and health services, they presented a model that favored privatization of health services, as well as a limited role for public-sector activities focusing mainly on unprofitable but necessary public health functions. Respondents speaking for these organizations acknowledged a "balance" between trade and health and viewed their jobs as essential in regulating this balance. Trade agreements favored by international financial institutions and trade organizations supported the entry of multinational corporations into international health-care markets.
- Executives of multinational corporations aligned their motivations with broad humanitarian service to humanity, rather than financial interests based on profitability. They emphasized the importance of intellectual property rights for fostering scientists' work and careers in less developed countries. In addition, they claimed credit for donating medications in specific low-income countries where they chose to intervene, especially to address endemic infections.

- Representatives of advocacy organizations constructed a reality of unfavorable effects on public health and health services imposed by the policies of trade organizations, international financial institutions, and multinational corporations. They focused criticisms especially on fees that reduced access to services and intellectual property provisions that restricted access to essential medications. "Free" trade agreements, from the advocates' perspective, invoked a restrictive, corporate approach to regulating trade, which extended inappropriately into many new areas of public health and health services.

Social constructions concerning trade and health reflected broad ideologies regarding the impacts of market processes, along the same lines as the "common sense" of health reform discussed in the last chapter. Such constructions manifested features of a creed, especially concerning the role of the market in advancing human purposes and meeting human needs. While emphasizing humanitarian benefits of market processes, these notions also provided a rationale for corporate interests grounded in globalized investment and profit-making opportunities. To a surprising extent, interviewees and official documents of international health organizations like the World Health Organization and Pan American Health Organization also enunciated a faith in market processes and trade agreements to advance the cause of public health.[7]

During interviews and in written presentations of organizational policies, representatives of government agencies, international financial institutions, trade organizations, multinational corporations, and international health organizations shared a wide agreement with the position that trade organizations, trade agreements, and intellectual property would likely improve health conditions worldwide. In this construction, official experts regulated trade to enhance patent guarantees through intellectual property rules and to balance the goals of trade and health. Such experts used their ideas to advance the interests of the particular social groups that they represented or for which they spoke.[8]

Except those from Latin America, respondents not working for advocacy organizations manifested optimism that economic globalization would foster public health and access to health services worldwide.[9] They continued to express an ethical purpose in enabling unfettered market activities en route to human betterment. In this sense, constructions of reality concerning trade and health resembled earlier scenarios that conveyed economic competition as a quasi-religious value— for instance, in the divine "invisible hand" that reconciled in the marketplace the individual interests of buyers and sellers for the overall benefit of society as a whole, and in the "Protestant ethic and the spirit of capitalism" by which entrepreneurs imbued their economic activities with a sense of idealist purpose.[10]

The creed linking trade and health also manifested "economism," a belief system based in "confidence of the markets." With this belief system, as Bourdieu[11] argued, policy makers based decisions on technocratic assumptions that market processes achieved the broadest good across social classes in both economically developed and less developed countries. Imparting such beliefs, experts in multinational corporations, international financial institutions, and international health organizations called upon political leaders to take their advice in policy decisions about public health and health services.

Constructions of advocacy organizations usually highlighted relationships of political and economic power that worsened conditions of work, the environment, nutrition, financial security, and access to services and medications for poor people, minorities, the disabled, the elderly, and other disadvantaged groups. As an alternative vision, respondents speaking for advocacy organizations depicted a struggle serving groups that lacked economic resources and political power. Such respondents manifested this orientation when they referred, for instance, to the adverse effects of trade agreements on the availability of needed medications and on the ability of countries to establish national health programs.

Similar to other social constructions, those concerning trade and health involved political symbolism and political spectacle.[12] Although largely hidden from ordinary citizens and their political representatives, the key organizational stakeholders continued to battle largely behind the scenes about policies concerning trade and health that potentially would impact much of the world's population. With public health systems and health services at stake around the world, the linkages between trade and health began to receive more critical attention. Those concerned with health and security worldwide no longer could not afford to ignore the profound changes generated by global trade. Recognizing and demystifying some constructions of social reality put forward by the key stakeholders in trade and health became one step among many that eventually contributed to the end of empire present.

*   *   *

Throughout the history of empire, economic expansion and domination presupposed military might. As corporations extracted natural resources and entered the marketplaces of less developed countries, they predictably met with resistance from the peoples previously dwelling there, and the ideological constructions that justified empire could exert only limited effects to suppress opposition. Under such conditions, the use of military force took over where ideology was not fully succeeding. The next chapter examines militarism as an underpinning of political and economic policies affecting medicine and public health.

CHAPTER 12

MILITARISM, EMPIRE, AND HEALTH

Empire ultimately depended on the threat or actual exercise of military intervention. Resistance to empire could take many forms. For instance, leaders who opposed the various exploitations of empire won democratic elections and, through this tradition of democratic change, assumed the presidencies of nations. Or, in countries ruled by dictatorships, social revolutions empowered leaders who were less cooperative with the economic and political arrangements of empire. (Chapter 4 analyzes both these forms of resistance by considering the course of empire past in Chile and Cuba.)

Through such processes, involving either nonviolent or violent tactics, new governments implemented agendas less conducive to prior patterns of economic and political domination. To prevent such opposition to empire, and to suppress resistance when it did arise, stood the military forces of those countries that sought to maintain the old order. Moreover, military intervention stimulated the growth of sluggish economies by requiring expanded production of military goods and by creating additional jobs to provide services needed for military operations.

During the waning years of empire present, militarism took a new turn in support of economic goals. As had occurred during empire past, war remained a useful method to protect the extraction of natural resources, especially petroleum. In addition, as markets for products and services became increasingly saturated worldwide, war could open new markets more directly by destroying the infrastructures of invaded countries; the disasters generated by war then required the reconstruction that capitalist enterprises could provide for a price.[1] Although such symbols as terrorism and security usually provided a rationale for the militarism of empire present, such constructions of reality gradually became less compelling when assessed in relation to the costs of war for life and health, in both invaded and invading nations.[2] In this chapter I consider the human experience of militarism, especially in terms of physical and mental health, as empire slowly unraveled.

The Physical and Psychic Impact of War on Military Personnel

In the service of empire, militarism exerted profound effects on the health not only of the peoples in invaded countries but also of those who carried out military policy. For instance, toward the end of empire present, combat operations in Iraq, Afghanistan, and elsewhere took the lives of military personnel and damaged the physical and mental health of many who survived. Despite military officials' publicly stated intention to implement high-quality military health care,[3] reports originating both inside and outside the military called attention to the unmet medical and psychological needs of service personnel.[4] The physical and emotional injuries sustained by U.S. soldiers and their families gradually became a public health epidemic that continued to stress the country's already overextended health and mental health systems.[5]

Several challenges interfered with access to medical and mental health services for active-duty military personnel. During the wars of empire present, GIs[6] experienced a command system and a medical care system where illness and injury could be viewed as obstacles to the military mission, inconveniences to local commands, or malingering.[7] GIs faced deployment to combat zones before full evaluation of physical illnesses. Those with mental health problems such as depression or post-traumatic stress disorder (PTSD) often reentered combat when newly diagnosed and just beginning a trial of medication, usually a tranquilizer, an antidepressant, and/or an antipsychotic drug.

During empire present, the problem of double agency pervaded the provision of health and mental health services in the military. Double agency referred to the dual allegiances of military health and mental health professionals that inevitably arose in their relationships with clients. Despite the requirements of the Hippocratic Oath to consider the client's needs first and foremost,[8] professionals working in the military also were required to serve the needs of the military command. Personnel shortages and pressure to deploy and redeploy troops rapidly to Iraq and Afghanistan placed increasing pressure on military physicians, psychiatrists, and psychologists. As they encountered GIs with health and mental health problems, military professionals by necessity considered the goals of maintaining the numbers and readiness of combat forces.[9] These military goals frequently contradicted the goal of helping the individual patient. The dual role of military professionals raised inherent tensions that reduced the chances that GIs could receive suitable care and increased the likelihood of their seeking services in the civilian sector.

Civilian Services for Military Personnel

Such tensions during the wars of empire present led to the creation of networks involving civilian professionals who sought to meet the medical and mental health needs of GIs, without the burden of double agency. These networks provided services that paralleled those that the military officially offered but failed to deliver effectively. Some experiences of one such organization showed the challenges of addressing the physical and psychological injuries that military personnel sustained in the service of empire.[10]

The Civilian Medical Resources Network worked as a small, national network of professionals established to offer GIs an alternative to the military health and mental health-care system.[11] Including professionals in primary care medicine, psychiatry, psychology, social work, and public health, the network tried to address the needs of active-duty U.S. military personnel when they sought medical and psychological care in the civilian sector. Because other civilian resources at least partly addressed the needs of veterans, the network focused on active-duty GIs who needed medical or psychological help.

Those who created the network had gained experience in similar support activities during the Vietnam War in the late 1960s and early 1970s, as well as during and after the Persian Gulf War in the 1990s. In those conflicts, groups such as the Medical Committee for Human Rights and the Medical Resistance Union organized efforts to provide physical and mental health services for individuals who sought medical exemption from the military draft and for GIs who requested care in the civilian sector. Due to the lack of a compulsory draft, efforts during later years targeted active-duty GIs.

Recruitment of clinicians for the network occurred initially through personal outreach to professional colleagues. In addition, two national organizations, Physicians for Social Responsibility (with a focus on peace) and Physicians for a National Health Program (with a focus on health-care access), announced the program to their members. Ultimately, approximately one hundred professionals participated in the network. Participants included mainly primary care and mental health practitioners, based in all regions of the United States. Professionals received a brief training in the types of support and documentation the GIs required.

Referrals to the network came from the GI Rights Hotline, a national effort maintained by twenty-five religious and peace organizations, as well as the

Military Law Task Force of the National Lawyers Guild. Legal professionals provided advice to the network and assisted clinicians with documentation of GIs' medical and mental health problems as needed to support their requests for discharge or reassignment.[12] At its height, the hotline received approximately three thousand calls per month from active-duty GIs and their families. When a GI or family member called the hotline and described unmet needs for physical or mental health services, a counselor could, at his or her discretion, contact the network, which then set up a referral to one or more participating professionals.

Because GIs generally did not have financial resources or insurance coverage to pay for civilian services, network professionals provided care free or at greatly reduced cost, as volunteers. When possible, GIs visited network professionals in person; if a face-to-face visit proved unfeasible due to geographical distance, network professionals assisted GIs through telephone and e-mail consultations. In addition to communication with GIs based in the United States, professionals conducted assessments and treatment interventions with GIs on the front lines in Afghanistan and Iraq who were decompensating emotionally, with suicidal or sometimes homicidal intentions. (More details follow.) Volunteers coordinated the referral procedures and relationships with the hotline and Military Law Task Force.

The network provided independent evaluation and treatment for both medical and psychological problems. In some cases GIs suffering from acute and life-threatening conditions, typically suicidal or homicidal ideation, were referred to local health or mental health facilities. Network professionals intervened in these situations to ensure adequate physical and/or psychological treatment.

For less acute situations, GIs sought independent assessment of diagnoses made by military medics or physicians, or advice about treatment options and the impact of military service on their illnesses or injuries. Other GIs requested independent evaluations for their own peace of mind, or independent treatment because of concerns about the adequacy of services in military clinics. Actions by civilian professionals helped GIs to gain access to military physicians, particularly specialists. This work also reduced the likelihood that commanding personnel would block or oppose visits to medical personnel during "sick call" at medical units in the field during military operations or at military hospitals.

GIs' Physical and Mental Health Problems

What problems were experienced by those who provided the military support for empire present?[13] In a statistical review of the network's clients, most were men

(91 percent), and women constituted a somewhat smaller proportion of clients (9 percent) than their overall proportion among active-duty military personnel (15 percent). The vast majority of clients reported that they and their families were low-income. About half the clients were Absent Without Leave (AWOL). Typical physical and mental health problems appear in the box below.

Among the GIs who sought civilian-sector services from the network, physical problems constituted about 20 percent of referrals. Certain physical disorders appeared relatively minor, while others proved potentially life-threatening. Minor physical disorders included musculoskeletal symptoms, such as back pain, foot pain, and rashes. Potentially life-threatening problems involved unexplained seizures, numbness following fractured vertebrae, double vision following fracture of an eye socket in a shrapnel injury, and persistent bleeding from an ear after a head injury. Most of the more serious physical problems, which the clients felt

---

Box 12-1 Examples of GIs' Physical and Mental Health Problems

• A GI with two fractured vertebrae experienced severe numbness in his legs. When he wore a flak jacket, he could not move his legs. He previously suffered a fractured eye socket, after which surgeons inserted a metal plate; he still experienced double vision and could not focus. Other problems included rectal bleeding and renal insufficiency. When he contacted the GI Rights Hotline, he was scheduled to be deployed to Iraq in about two weeks. Seeking a medical discharge, he went to sick call. He stated that a medic told him that he was in bad shape but that the army needed him and so would not discharge him. Instead, he was told that he could get physical therapy in Iraq. He had a hard time seeing a doctor because his sergeant kept telling him that he shouldn't go to sick call. The GI requested documentation in connection with his request for discharge and secondarily also sought care for his physical problems.

• During his tour in Iraq, a GI witnessed the violent deaths of several close friends as well as Iraqi civilians. One of his assignments involved removal of blood and body parts from military vehicles. After he returned to the United States, he suffered from depression, PTSD, and generalized anxiety. He entered a psychiatric hospital temporarily after one of four suicide attempts. After he learned that his unit was to be redeployed to Iraq, he went AWOL. When he contacted the GI Rights Hotline, he was living with his wife and infant son in a rural area and was working in odd jobs. He learned that military police and the local sheriff's department were trying to find him. During a phone interview, the GI expressed suicidal ideation, as well as an intent to kill specific officers if he were returned to his original unit.

had received insufficient attention from military physicians, resulted directly from combat or other incidents that caused injuries during military service.

Among the 80 percent of clients with mental health diagnoses, PTSD, anxiety, depression, and substance abuse predominated. Some GIs experienced acute psychiatric emergencies, usually linked to traumatic events. Most GIs with the latter problems feared redeployment to Iraq or Afghanistan. Approximately 20 percent of clients reported suicidal ideation and/or suicide attempts, and 5 percent revealed homicidal ideation, usually directed toward officers who would not acknowledge the seriousness of their psychological symptoms. Adverse childhood experiences such as abuse or neglect, a history of sexual assault, and female gender increased the likelihood of GIs' PTSD and depression.[14]

Several features of clients' distress pertained to families. These problems occurred both while GIs remained in combat zones and after they returned home. The problems involved challenges of caretaking responsibilities for non-military family members, intimate-partner violence, and marital or partnership dissolution.[15]

Themes from Encounters Between Military Personnel and Civilian Clinicians

Several recurrent themes emerged from encounters with military clients who engaged in the service of empire. These themes illustrated the circumstances GIs encountered in the military during empire present and the nuances of the physical and psychological challenges they experienced.

The Economic Draft

First, due to the adverse economic conditions in the United States during empire present, most GIs reported that they had enlisted because of financial challenges or lack of employment opportunities. In addition to experiencing low-income financial conditions, many GIs came from ethnic/racial minority backgrounds or grew up in less developed countries.

Deception

Psychological problems among GIs and reservists included perceived deception in recruiting processes. Most of these clients reported that they had received inaccurate assurances about deployments, combat requirements, salaries and benefits, and support for families. Longer and more frequent tours of duty than promised became a source of major distress. Reservists usually did not expect combat duty.

Ethical Dilemmas and Violence Without Meaning

For these military clients, physical and emotional problems derived in large part from the ethical conflict of witnessing or perpetrating violence without a sense that the violence led to progress in meeting military, political, or social goals. Having not been briefed explicitly about the military's role in supporting empire present, GIs reported that they did not understand the purpose of military involvement in Afghanistan or Iraq. Many of the violent acts perpetrated against civilians, especially children, generated guilt, depression, and PTSD. Such violence frequently involved intentional actions, some ordered by commanders, and some resulting from GIs' suspicions of armed attacks by combatants presenting themselves as civilians.

Barriers to Care

GIs who remained with their units experienced barriers in attempts to contact the hotline and to receive evaluations through the network. These barriers resulted primarily from the geographic isolation of military bases. In addition, scheduling problems due to work demands inhibited appointments with civilian professionals. Those GIs who were AWOL encountered fewer difficulties in travel or scheduling problems; however, they experienced deep fears about capture and return to their units.

Privatization of Services

Many clients contacting the network reported difficulties that they or their families had experienced in obtaining privatized services from managed care organizations contracting with the military. Inconvenience in obtaining services and managed care practitioners' diminishing the importance of clinical problems motivated GIs and their families to seek services from network professionals. (In a moment I return to privatization of military health services as a neoliberal health policy that characterized empire present.)

Torture and Human Rights Abuses

Although most GIs using the network did not engage in torture or other forms of abuse, they expressed awareness of these practices as part of military operations.[16]

In their training, GIs learned that such practices contradicted rules of war, such as the Geneva Convention, as well as specific regulations that governed actions by U.S. military forces. In practice, many GIs also learned that officers tolerated and sometimes encouraged the use of torture and similar abuses. This contradiction created stress, stigma, and shame about unethical actions perpetrated by military colleagues. Professionals working with GIs in the network noted high levels of shame, a situation that inhibited GIs from seeking help.

The Changing Health Effects of Militarism

Even aside from effects on the health of the invaded, the invaders who provided support for the economic and political goals of empire present manifested a changing and increasingly untenable constellation of health and mental health problems. Civilian professionals in the network and in other organizations focusing on GIs' rights documented the unmet needs of active-duty U.S. military personnel as well as contextual problems both creating and sustaining those unmet needs.

These contextual problems spoke to the larger social issues of an all-volunteer military force in an increasingly militarized society. During the Vietnam War, which spanned many years during empire past, a military draft led to the induction of young people from a broad range of social positions. A volunteer army during empire present, however, depended on men and women predominantly from low-income and minority backgrounds. Military and veterans' medical care periodically entered public consciousness during empire present, especially after scandals (as in the case of Walter Reed Army Hospital during 2007) and acute crises (for instance, after the shootings by a stressed military psychiatrist at Fort Hood, Texas, during 2009). However, the predominantly working-class origins of those serving in war, as opposed to the more privileged class position of officials in government and industry who made key decisions about initiating and expanding war, limited the attention that the injuries of war among front-line warriors received from policy makers. For instance, during the wars in Iraq and Afghanistan, only a handful of legislators in the U.S. Congress had children in the military.

Due to a new cluster of ethical conflicts related to changing military operations in the service of empire, mental health problems predominated during this period among those participating or anticipating participation in combat. GIs reported suicidal ideation that went unrecognized or unacknowledged when they sought care in the military system. Military statistics indicated rapid increases in suicides, suicide attempts, and self injuries among active-duty GIs. Toward the end of empire present, between sixteen and twenty U.S. soldiers were killing themselves each month, and the predicted death rate from suicides among GIs became higher than the predicted death rate from combat.[17] In one calendar year, the U.S. Army reported approximately 2,100 suicide attempts and self-injuries, a rate of more than five per day, much increased from prior years; these data did not include events involving marines or other combat forces. The probability of suicide increased with the number of deployments and time spent in Afghanistan or Iraq. Suicides committed outside combat zones remained underreported.

The epidemic of mental health problems in the military coincided with an unprecedented privatization of medical and mental health services for active-duty GIs and their families. Although the military previously offered such services within its own facilities, private corporations later received substantial contracts from the military to provide these services. This policy change reflected the same neoliberal principle that favored privatization of services previously provided by public hospitals and clinics for underserved populations. As a result of privatizing military health and mental health services, the chief executive officer who benefited the most financially from the Iraq War did not head a corporation traditionally considered part of the military-industrial complex, but rather a large managed care organization (Health Net), whose contractor (ValueOptions) provided mental health services for GIs and their families.[18]

For GIs who sought help within the military sector for PTSD, depression, and other mental health problems, military psychologists increasingly diagnosed personality disorder. Since military policy considered personality disorder as a pre-existing condition that antedated military service, GIs who received this diagnosis lost financial and health benefits after discharge, creating major concern for the GIs and their families.[19] This policy applied even though military officials did not diagnose personality disorder during GIs' mental health evaluation when inducted into the armed forces.[20]

During the wars of empire present, military leaders implemented strategies that involved less combat engagement with identified combatants and more violence involving civilians. Reports from GIs, including those using the network, emphasized violence committed against civilian noncombatants.[21] In a context where both torture and systematic human rights abuse occurred, it is not surprising that soldiers suffered from high levels of psychological distress and pathology. Resistance to the war thus became increasingly medicalized. With accumulated injuries—both physical and psychological—GIs turned to professionals in the civilian sector as a route to less dangerous assignments or to discharge.

Efforts to deal with the physical and mental health damage caused by war during empire present rarely addressed the linkages among empire, militarism, and health. As recurrent financial crises devastated less developed countries and eventually began to plague the dominant nations as well, war increasingly became one of the few remaining methods to stimulate a failing global economy. The physical and emotional suffering of soldiers, who over time occupied an ever more marginalized position in the dominant societies, apparently seemed an acceptable price for economically driven war. For those who might otherwise have called a halt to militarism without a clear narrative to justify it, the symbolism of terrorism and security provided a justification.

*   *   *

Early in the twenty-first century, the paths of neoliberalism and militarism became overgrown with the brambles of ill health, unnecessarily early death, emotional distress, and environmental consequences of economic progress that were making the world itself unlivable. Equating economic progress with the financial well-being of a tiny segment of humanity became discredited, along with the assumption that the wealth of the few eventually would lead to more favorable conditions for the many. The possibility of expanding or even maintaining empire itself became less tenable.

In short, empire as historically organized was ending, and a new vision for medicine and public health in a post-empire world was emerging. These changes were occurring gradually, almost imperceptibly at times. But by the second decade of the twenty-first century, the transformations became undeniable.

Turning now to the final part of the book, I examine in the next chapter a vision of a world beyond empire that grew influential initially in Latin America and later worldwide. Then I offer an account of the social movements that were creating a new order, where empire no longer would threaten the physical and mental health of the world's peoples.

PART THREE

EMPIRE FUTURE

CHAPTER 13

HEALTH AND PRAXIS

SOCIAL MEDICINE IN LATIN AMERICA

Social medicine in Latin America addresses the links among empire, public health, and health services, as well as strategies to move toward a healthier future, post-empire. Already widely respected in Latin America, this field encompasses research, teaching, clinical practice, and activism toward change. Partly through its emphasis on praxis—the creative uniting of theory and practice—social medicine provides a model of intellectual and practical work, offering a helpful vision for the transition to a more health-supportive world as empire declines.

The accomplishments of this field remain little known outside Latin America, as major publications remain untranslated from Spanish and Portuguese. A lack of attention also reflects an erroneous assumption that the intellectual and scientific productivity of the less developed world manifests a less relevant and rigorous approach to the important questions of our age. After describing the history of the field and depicting the challenges of leadership and sometimes dangerous work conditions that practitioners have faced, I analyze the major themes and debates. Prior and more recent work in the field points to the new links between health and praxis that the future will require.[1]

Productivity and Danger

Many who have worked in Latin American social medicine have experienced dramatic personal histories. Three such histories show how the very nature of their work—to the extent that it reveals the origins of health problems in the structure of society—can become seen as dangerous to sectors of the society that control wealth and wield power.[2]

The public health expert is about to receive torture by electric shock applied to his testicles. His crimes have been to teach medical and other health science students in a model community clinic, one of the major teaching sites for the University of Chile. A graduate of the Harvard School of Public Health, he also is accused of conducting research on the relationships between poverty and health outcomes in local communities. He knows that several of his colleagues already have been killed for similar crimes. In his interrogation he has been asked to provide information about many friends and colleagues, but so far has refused.

The torturer, a clean-cut and matter-of-fact person whose military affiliation isn't quite clear, orders the public health expert to pull down his pants. He complies, looking at the electrodes in the torturer's right hand. Just then, the torturer glances at the watch on his right wrist.

"Okay," the torturer says, "it's five o'clock—time to go home," and leaves the room. The public health expert pulls his pants back up and waits for a guard to take him back to his cell.

Recalling this experience in an interview, he mentions Max Weber's work on the sociology of bureaucracy[3]—"bureaucratized torture," he calls it.

* * *

The chief of surgery at a public hospital in a working-class neighborhood of Santiago, Chile, sits in his dimly lit office, his tall frame bent over a notebook computer. He had trained on the surgical services at Massachusetts General Hospital. Salvador Allende chose him as minister of health for the *Unidad Popular* (Popular Unity) government. Known as an outstanding surgeon and medical educator, he convened a "council of elders" from the University of Chile's School of Public Health to advise the Ministry of Health.

On September 11, 1973, he was the last person in the line of government officials who walked down the stairs to the first floor of *La Moneda*, the presidential palace, which was on fire after the air force's precision bombing, to surrender to the military victors of the coup d'état. As the last person to see Allende alive, he notes simply that Allende was not killed but instead committed suicide, in the tradition of José Manuel Balmaceda, the reformist president of Chile who killed himself in 1891 rather than surrender to a military coup.

After his own arrest, the surgeon and former minister of health was tortured and sent to prison for a year on frigid Dawson Island near Antarctica. Later he worked in exile for fourteen years as a professor of surgery in Caracas, Venezuela. Following the Chilean plebiscite in 1988 that led to an elected government, he returned as chief of surgery to the same public university hospital where he worked before the coup.

He writes mainly for the clinical journal that health professionals and workers at his hospital have produced intermittently since 1953. Currently he is working on a series of articles that he has introduced with a quote from *Alice in Wonderland:* "Could you tell me please what road I should take?" These articles describe the deterioration of Chile's public health system under both the dictatorship and the country's subsequent civilian regime, whose policies call for further privatization of public industries, housing, education, and health programs.

* * *

The former dean of the medical school of the University of Buenos Aires explains why, at age seventy-three, he lives hand to mouth on small teaching and consulting fees and royalties, without a pension or other regular income. Before the dictatorship took control in Argentina during 1976, he had enjoyed a prominent career, applying the social sciences to medicine and public health administration. His articles and books in health planning had achieved international recognition. He frequently was asked to consult with the World Health Organization and the Pan American Health Organization, and to give presentations at universities and professional organizations throughout the Americas.

When the military took control, he and his family happened to be outside Argentina. He was not to return for more than ten years. His neighbors told him that they watched helplessly as soldiers knocked down the doors of his home and proceeded to ransack and burn his library. The burning of books and journals in this case and many others (sometimes voluntarily by the owners of the publications for fear that the military would find them and use them as evidence of subversion justifying imprisonment, torture, and death) makes the Argentine intellectual productivity of the 1960s through the 1980s difficult to locate except in rare books collections. The former dean points proudly to the bookshelf that contains his own publications, many of which were given to him as gifts after his return to his homeland, by friends who had hidden them for many years.

During various periods in the history of Latin American social medicine, the work of its leaders has proven threatening to those who governed their societies. The risks of working in this field have reflected a critique of the existing social order, a focus on the health problems of oppressed peoples, and a vision of a healthier and more just future. After depicting social medicine's history, I analyze its more recent productivity, its sources of danger, and its pertinence to medicine and public health during empire future.

History of Latin American Social Medicine

To understand Latin American social medicine, as well as its importance for the present and future, one can step back in time to examine its origins during empire past, its flowering during empire present, and its growing influence as empire draws to a close. Most Latin American accounts of social medicine's history refer to its origins in Europe, frequently citing the work of Rudolf Virchow in Germany.[4] Through his political activism in the reform movements that culminated in the revolutions of 1848, as Chapter 2 describes, Virchow initiated a series of pathbreaking investigations concerning the effects of social conditions on illness and mortality. Presenting pathologic observations and statistical data, he argued that the solution of these problems required fundamental social change, rather than specific medical interventions. Virchow defined the new field of social medicine as a "social science" that focused on illness-generating social conditions.[5]

Adherents of Virchow's vision immigrated to Latin America near the turn of the twentieth century. Virchow's followers helped establish departments of pathology in medical schools and initiated courses in social medicine. Max Westenhofer, a prominent German pathologist, directed the department of pathology at the medical school of the University of Chile for many years and influenced a generation of students, including Salvador Allende, a medical student activist and future president of Chile.[6]

The "Golden Age" of Social Medicine in Chile and the Role of Salvador Allende

While the roots of Chilean social medicine date back to the mid-nineteenth century, the most sustained activities began after the nationwide strikes of 1918 that focused in the mining industry. Luis Emilio Recabarren, a charismatic leader among the saltpeter workers, emphasized malnutrition, infectious diseases, and premature mortality as themes to address in organizing. During the next three decades, Recabarren and his political allies agitated for economic reforms as the only viable route to improvements in patterns of illness and mortality that affected the poor. During the 1920s and 1930s, social medicine flourished in Chile, partly as a response to demands of the labor movement.

Allende's experiences as a physician and pathologist shaped much of his later career in politics. Acknowledging debts to Virchow and others who studied the social roots of illness in Europe, Allende set forth an explanatory model of medical problems in the context of underdevelopment. Although parallel developments in social medicine were occurring during the same period in North

America and Europe,[7] Allende's writings did not indicate a direct influence of this latter work.

As noted in Chapter 2, Allende presented his analysis of the relationships among social structure, disease, and suffering in his classic book, *La Realidad Médico-Social Chilena* (The Chilean Medico-Social Reality).[8] *La Realidad* conceptualized illness as a disturbance of the individual fostered by deprived social conditions. Breaking new ground in Latin America at the time, Allende described the "living conditions of the working classes" that generated illness. He emphasized conditions of underdevelopment, international dependency, and the effects of foreign debt and the work process. In *La Realidad*, Allende focused on several specific health problems, including maternal and infant mortality, tuberculosis, sexually transmitted and other communicable diseases, emotional disturbances, and occupational illnesses. Describing issues that had not been studied previously, he analyzed illegal abortion, the responsiveness of tuberculosis to economic advances rather than treatment innovations, housing density in the causation of infectious diseases, and differences between generic and brand-name pricing in the pharmaceutical industry.

The Ministry of Health's proposals that concluded *La Realidad* took a unique direction by advocating social rather than medical solutions to health problems. Allende proposed income redistribution, state regulation of food and clothing supplies, a national housing program, and industrial reforms to address occupational health problems. Rather than seeing improved health services as a means toward a more productive labor force, Allende valued the health of the population as an end in itself and advocated social changes that exceeded the scope of the medical realm.

Allende's analytic position in social medicine influenced much of his political work until his death in 1973 during the military coup d'état. As an elected senator in the early 1950s, Allende introduced the legislation that created the Chilean national health service, the first national program in the Americas that guaranteed universal access to services. He linked this reform to other efforts that aimed to achieve more equitable income distribution, job security, improved housing and nutrition, and a less dominant role for multinational corporations within Chile. Similarly, as a senator during the 1960s and elected president between 1970 and 1973, Allende sought reforms in the national health service and other institutions that, if not cut short by the coup d'état, would have achieved structural changes throughout the society. Due to his advocacy of a unified health service in the public sector, the Chilean national medical association (*Colegio Médico*) feared the effects of Allende's policies on private practice and therefore frequently opposed him.

Social Medicine Versus Public Health Elsewhere in Latin America

Other Latin American countries did not advance as far in adopting the perspectives and activism that characterized Chile during the 1930s. Public health efforts throughout Latin America provided a background to which contemporary practitioners of social medicine responded.[9] For instance, leaders of social medicine in many Latin American countries reacted critically to the Rockefeller Foundation's public health initiatives, which (as discussed in Chapter 1) emphasized the productivity of labor in enhancing the ventures of U.S.-based multinational corporations.[10]

Both historically and more recently, leaders in Latin America have distinguished social medicine from traditional public health. In this perspective, public health has tended to define a population as a sum of individuals. By contrast, much work in social medicine envisions populations, as well as social institutions, as totalities whose characteristics transcend those of individuals.[11] Social medicine therefore analyzes problems and seeks solutions with social rather than individual units of analysis. Applying this broader focus, the population can be analyzed through such categories as social class, economic production, reproduction, and culture, as opposed to simply measuring and summing up the characteristics of individuals.[12]

Another distinction between social medicine and traditional public health concerns the static versus dynamic nature of health versus illness, as well as the effect of social context. Social medicine conceptualizes "health-illness" as a dialectic process, rather than a dichotomous category that views disease as either present or absent. As in Engels's earlier and Levins and Lewontin's more recent interpretations of dialectic processes in biology,[13] critical epidemiologists have studied disease processes in a contextualized model, considering the changing effects of social conditions over time. The epidemiological profile of a society or group within a society requires a multilevel analysis of how social conditions such as economic production, reproduction, culture, marginalization, and political participation affect the dynamic process of health-illness. In this theoretical vision, models in public health that analyze disease as a dichotomous variable, either present or absent, obscure health-illness as a dialectic process.[14]

In Argentina during the 1920s, a group led by Juan B. Justo challenged the public health initiatives of the time, known as "hygienic" interventions (*higienismo*), which emphasized infection control, improved sanitation, nutrition, and similar efforts to improve population health.[15] *Higienismo* aimed to improve labor force productivity, in the interest of national development and international investment. Justo, a surgeon, became a founding leader of the Socialist Party and provided an early Spanish translation of Marx's *Capital*. Resembling Allende's stance, Justo called attention to the pervasive effects of social class on health services and outcomes.[16] This work led to regional and national organizing efforts that sought broad social change primarily as the basis of improved health, as opposed to enhanced economic productivity. Justo's efforts remained in a minority position, however, as *higienismo* gained dominance.

Another line of work in social medicine that grew from Argentine roots was that of Ernesto "Che" Guevara. Guevara's childhood asthma, as well as role models in his family, led him to enter medical school and eventually to specialize in allergic diseases. After medical school, he toured South America by motorcycle. Through experiences of poverty and suffering during this trip, he developed his views about the need for revolution as a prerequisite for improving health conditions.[17]

In his speeches and writings on "revolutionary medicine," Guevara called for a corps of physicians and other health workers who understood the social origins of illness and the need for social change to improve health conditions.[18] Guevara's work profoundly influenced Latin American social medicine. Predictably, Guevara's views might have developed partly from knowledge about Allende, Justo, and others who preceded him, but apparently this was not the case. Sources close to Guevara, including an uncle who served as a role model in medicine, claimed that throughout his medical training and career, Guevara remained unexposed to earlier works in Latin American social medicine and that he developed his analysis connecting health outcomes with social conditions largely through experiences during his motorcycle trip.[19]

In Ecuador, leaders in social medicine traced their local roots back more than 200 years. During the early eighteenth century, the physician Eugenio Espejo linked his work as a physician to the revolutionary struggles against Spain.[20] In efforts to control epidemics, similar to Virchow's later work in Germany, Espejo became convinced that poverty, inadequate housing and sanitation, and insufficient nutrition fostered such outbreaks. Later, in the early twentieth-century movement toward social security, Pablo Arturo Suárez's book on the working class and peasantry provided epidemiological data on adverse health outcomes.[21] During the 1930s, the physician Ricardo Paredes found extensive occupational lung diseases and accidents among Ecuadorian miners working at a U.S.-owned mining company.[22] In addition to legislation that improved working conditions, Paredes's efforts led to a broad consciousness in Ecuador about the adverse effects on health of multinational corporations' operations during empire past.

The 1960s and Later

Among the changes that occurred worldwide during the 1960s, the Cuban Revolution of 1959 emerged as one of the most important for social medicine. Cuba's improved public health system flowered as part of a social revolution, where accomplishments in health occurred as an integral part of broad structural changes in the society as a whole.[23] The social transformations underlying Cuba's achievements in primary care, public health, medical education, planning and administration, and epidemiological surveillance, as described in Chapter 3, inspired activists and scholars in other countries.

If Cuba provided a positive model for Latin American social medicine, Chile's policies created ambivalence. Social medicine groups took keen interest when Allende and the *Unidad Popular* government achieved victory during 1970, and many people in social medicine came to Chile to work with the new government. Allende had proposed a peaceful transition to socialism through electoral rather than military means—the first such transition in history. The government moved toward a "unified" national health program, in which the contradictions of coexisting private and public sectors would be reduced. Allende's plan for socialized medicine crumbled after the violent coup d'état of 1973, when repression of the population and especially of health workers reached unprecedented levels of violence.[24] The failure of the peaceful road to socialism served as a reminder of danger throughout Latin America for those who pursued social medicine.

Nicaragua's 1979 revolution also inspired social medicine activists, although many worried about the Sandinista government's social policies linked to health. Leaders of social medicine from several countries contributed to the new Nicaraguan government's health reforms, including extensive programs that dealt with infectious diseases and maternal and child health.[25] These leaders' concerns focused on contradictions of the Nicaraguan revolution that, for instance, permitted a continuing major role for private practice, even involving health professionals who worked full time for the national health service. Government representatives argued that such policies enhancing the private sector of the economy would prevent a similar exodus of health professionals as had occurred in Cuba. Due to such contradictions, some social medicine leaders eventually reduced their support activities, especially after the Sandinistas' electoral losses.

Liberation theology became a source of inspiration for many social medicine activists. Priests such as Frei Betto in Brazil advocated participation in "base communities" that fused religious piety with struggles for social justice.[26] These struggles included efforts to improve health and public health services. Certain leaders of liberation theology grew skeptical about nonviolent processes in base communities. Influenced by Camilo Torres, a priest who joined the revolutionary movement in Colombia, some social medicine activists entered armed struggle in several countries and later returned to practicing social medicine.[27]

Another important influence on social medicine stemmed from the educational innovations of Paulo Freire and coworkers in Brazil. Through adult literacy campaigns, Freire encouraged people in poor communities to approach education as a process of empowerment. In the efforts that led to his classic book, *Pedagogy of the Oppressed*,[28] Freire fostered the organization of small educational "circles," where local residents could link their studies to solving concrete problems in their communities. Activists later began to extend this approach to public health education and organizing to improve health services.[29] Freire himself became more interested in applying empowerment strategies to health.[30] While Freire's orientation also has affected public health in the United States,[31] the impact proved far greater in Latin American social medicine.

During the 1970s, a leader emerged who profoundly affected the course of social medicine, from a base in Washington, D.C. Trained as a physician in Argentina and as a sociologist in Chile, Juan César García served as research coordinator within the Pan American Health Organization (PAHO) from 1966 until his death in 1984. García himself produced seminal works on medical education, the social sciences in medicine, social class determinants of health outcomes, and the ideological bases of discrimination against Latinos.[32] Although his Marxist social philosophy manifested itself in several works published under his own name while he was working for PAHO, he also published more explicitly political articles under pseudonyms.[33]

García affected social medicine through financial and socioemotional support that he provided through PAHO. With his colleague at PAHO, María Isabel Rodríguez, who was living in exile after serving as dean of the school of medicine at the University of El Salvador, García orchestrated grants, contracts, and fellowships that proved critical for social medicine groups throughout Latin America. PAHO funding helped established the first influential training program in social medicine at the Autonomous Metropolitan University, Xochimilco, in Mexico City, which attracted students from throughout Latin America. Subsequently, social medicine leaders consistently referred to García's initiative and tenacity, despite opposition that he received within PAHO.

Political Repression and Work Challenges

Many leaders of social medicine in Latin America have suffered political repression, including torture, imprisonment in concentration camps, exile, exclusion from government jobs, loss of economic security and work stability, reduced professional prestige, and restriction from political activity. A focus on the social origins of illness and early death tends to challenge patterns of economic and political power. As a result, participation in social medicine has led to suffering and even death for some of its most talented and productive adherents.

The work process in social medicine varies widely, depending on political and economic conditions. After the dictatorships in Argentina and Chile, people in social medicine have faced great difficulties during attempts to reintegrate themselves into universities or medical schools. Most have held multiple jobs, usually in clinical or administrative work, and pursue social medicine as largely unpaid activities.

In countries without dictatorships, or where dictatorships proved somewhat less brutal (such as Brazil), fewer people needed to emigrate and more remained at work in universities or teaching hospitals. Due to the tradition of violence in Colombia, however, prominent leaders of social medicine (including the dean and several faculty members at the national school of public health) have perished or entered exile, despite the presence of elected governments. In other countries, such as Mexico, Ecuador, and Cuba, participants in social medicine have maintained relatively stable academic positions. Recently, the most favorable institutional conditions for social medicine exist in Mexico, Ecuador, Brazil, Venezuela, and Cuba. Although conditions in Argentina, Chile, and Colombia have remained more adverse, participants in social medicine in those countries also struggle to achieve high levels of productivity.

Theory, Method, and Debate

Latin American social medicine emphasizes theory.[34] Practitioners of social medicine have argued that a lack of explicitly stated theory in North American and European medicine and public health does not signify an absence of theory. Instead, an atheoretical or antitheoretical stance means that the underlying theory remains implicit, subtly supporting the status quo and the ideological positions of dominant groups in society. Through this prism, Latin American critics have interpreted the tendency to focus on biological rather than social components of such problems as cancer, hypertension, and occupational illnesses. The biological focus, from this perspective, reduces the unit of analysis to the individual and thus obscures social causes amenable to societal-level interventions.[35]

Referring to the linkage between theory and practice, practitioners of social medicine frequently use the term "praxis," as developed in Italy by Gramsci.[36] Latin American leaders have emphasized that theory both informs and takes inspiration from efforts toward social transformation. Research and teaching activities often take place in collaboration with labor unions, women's groups, coalitions of indigenous peoples, and community organizations.[37]

Social medicine has focused on social class, as defined by the relations of economic production. As in Marxist theory, practitioners of social medicine have argued that the most important characteristic of social class involves ownership of the means of economic production and control over the productive process. From this perspective, the exploitation of labor remains an inherent condition of economic production, especially in less developed countries.[38] As a result, Latin American social medicine has maintained a vision of social class rooted in economic production, rather than in such demographic characteristics as income, education, and occupational prestige. This theoretical position concerning economic production has led to research questions that focus on the labor process itself in both industrial and agricultural settings. The social medicine groups in Mexico, Chile, Ecuador, and Brazil have initiated studies of such key issues as work hierarchies, the production process in factories, and the impact of work conditions on health and mental health outcomes.

A second focus for social medicine involves the reproduction of economic production. This focus questions how the capitalist system can reproduce inherently exploitative relations of production across generations. Among the supporting institutions that accomplish this reproduction, the family figures most prominently, particularly through the patterning of gender roles. On the issue of gender roles and family relationships, Latin American social medicine examines the exploitation of workers linked to the exploitation of women. From this perspective, economic production requires the reproduction of the labor force, mainly through the activities of women within families.[39] In contemporary societies, women often bear the "triple burden" of wage labor, housework, and child-rearing. For this reason, social medicine groups in several countries have collaborated in research that focuses on female workers and the effects of their roles in economic production and reproduction.[40]

Ideology constitutes a third theoretical focus in Latin American social medicine.[41] Some theorists have adopted Althusser's perspective in arguing that ideology represents individuals' imagined relationship to the material conditions of their existence.[42] A "hegemonic" ideology tends to justify the interests of the class that dominates a society during a specific historical period. Demystification of this dominant ideology then becomes a task for theoretical and political work.[43] The social medicine groups in Latin America have accepted this task of demystification as a priority. During earlier years, the work of demystification focused on "developmentalist" policies, fostered by North American and European governments.[44] More recently, demystification efforts have emphasized the health policies of the World Bank and other international financial institutions. Critical studies have clarified the increasing indebtedness, privatization, and cutbacks in public services that these institutions have fostered, based on macroeconomic, market-oriented principles.[45]

The theory of health-illness as a dialectic process has generated criticisms of traditional approaches to causal inference in medicine and public health.[46] At a basic level, social medicine practitioners have criticized monocausal explanations of disease. From a similar perspective as Virchow's, simplistic explanations that a specific agent causes a particular disease do not adequately consider the social conditions that increase the likelihood of that disease. However, even multi-causal models, including those that consider interactions among agent, host, and environment, still define disease in a relatively static fashion. As noted already, critiques from the standpoint of social medicine have argued that by dichotomizing the presence or absence of a disease, traditional multicausal models do not adequately consider the dynamic linkages by which social conditions affect the dialectic process of health-illness. These analyses have suggested an approach to causality where social and historical conditions receive more explicit emphasis.

Anticipating later methodological trends in the United States and Europe, leaders in Latin American social medicine have used a multimethod and multi-level approach that triangulates complementary methods at both individual and societal levels of analysis.[47] Even in early research, Mexican and Ecuadorian researchers combined quantitative, multivariate analyses with qualitative, in-depth interviews that they often conducted in group situations ("collective interviews"). For instance, such work clarified environmental and occupational health problems by applying a variety of methods, including in-depth interviews in communities and workplaces.[48] Recent approaches to multilevel research have included quantitative techniques, such as structural equation modeling, combined with qualitative techniques, such as focus groups and computerized content analysis. These investigations have advanced policy changes in such realms as infant mortality in low-income communities and in reducing the risk of illness from pesticides in companies that produce flowers for export.[49]

Emerging Themes

Social Policies, Empire, and Health

Social medicine groups throughout Latin America have emphasized the effects on health of international policies under empire. Historically this work has analyzed the extraction of raw materials and the exploitation of inexpensive labor during empire past. More recently, social medicine groups have focused on international macroeconomic policies during empire present, as well as the political power of multinational corporations and international financial institutions. The burden of foreign debt in less developed countries has emerged as a grave concern. Public-sector cutbacks, privatization of public services, and the opening of markets in health care to multinational corporations have received critical attention by social medicine groups in several countries. As one example, an assessment of managed care as a privatization initiative by multinational corporations and international financial institutions has emphasized the detrimental effects on access to services as the public-sector "safety net" deteriorates and has demystified claims that market-oriented practices improve conditions for the poor.[50]

Social medicine links policy research with organizing efforts aiming to achieve progressive change in political systems. These actions aim to expand public debate and to redirect reform initiatives toward meeting the needs of vulnerable populations. Social medicine groups have collaborated with the opposition Party of the Democratic Revolution and the Zapatista Army of National Liberation in Mexico, the coalition of indigenous and labor organizations in Ecuador, the Workers' Party in Brazil, the Central Organization of Argentine Trade Unions, and elected governments in Venezuela, Ecuador, and Bolivia that have implemented the perspectives of social medicine in their national health policies. Applying theory, methods, and findings from social medicine, these efforts have contributed to broader social changes linked to fundamental modifications of public health practices and health services.

Social and Cultural Determinants of Health and Illness

Several groups have pioneered research on social and cultural determinants of health outcomes.[51] Researchers in Ecuador have focused on urban ecology, economic changes stemming from petroleum production, the relationships between gender and the work process, and the impact of pesticides in explaining local morbidity and mortality patterns.[52] The Ecuadorian group has pioneered the use of quantitative techniques to conduct multilevel research on social determinants, using data at the individual, social, and cultural units of analysis.[53] Brazilian researchers have also used multilevel and multimethod approaches—including anthropological methods in epidemiology—to clarify mechanisms at the community, family, and biological levels that mediate the impact of social inequalities.[54]

Relations Among Work, Reproduction, the Environment, and Health

This focus emerged from a theoretical emphasis on economic production and reproduction, as well as a recognition that such problems represent some of the chief threats to health in less developed countries. Mexican researchers have worked with industrial unions and local communities to clarify health and mental health problems that derive from the work process and environment. As noted already, the investigators have pioneered in this research such methods as the collective interview.[55] The Ecuadorian group has emphasized the differing health outcomes that women experience in industrial and agricultural work environments.[56] In Chile, the social medicine group has carried out research that links gender, work, and environmental conditions.[57] Microlevel research on the work process in Brazilian health institutions has informed the policy efforts of the national Workers' Party.[58]

Violence, Trauma, and Health

Partly reflecting the violent conditions that practitioners of social medicine themselves have confronted, research and political action to address violence and trauma have received priority in several countries. In Colombia, the social tradition of violence—previously linked to poverty and cycles of rebellion but more recently reflecting narcotics traffic and paramilitary operations—has generated research on the effects of violence on health outcomes.[59] Chilean investigators have studied families whose members experienced torture, exile, or death during the dictatorship.[60] Influenced by psychological studies of violence in El Salvador by Ignacio Martín-Baró, a U.S.-trained psychologist who himself was assassinated by paramilitary forces, researchers in Argentina have analyzed the extensive psychosocial problems among survivors of the more than thirty thousand individuals who "disappeared" during the Argentine dictatorship.[61]

The Future of Social Medicine

While social medicine groups have achieved varying influence on medical practice, public health programs, and medical education in their respective countries, they have pioneered a praxis that offers a standard for the future. For the most part, their work has not attained publication in English and remains little known outside Latin America. Wider knowledge of this work would prove helpful, not least because of the courage of the individuals and groups that have continued their efforts under dangerous working conditions.

Practitioners of Latin American social medicine have utilized theories and methods that distinguish their efforts from those of traditional public health. In particular, a focus on the social and historical contexts of health problems, an emphasis on economic production and social causation, and the linkage of research and education to political practice have provided innovative approaches to some of the most important problems of our age. Despite the challenges of struggling against the stream of the dominant paradigms, the themes and findings of Latin American social medicine have much to offer as medicine and public health throughout the world enter a period of profound transformation.

*   *   *

The praxis of Latin American social medicine provides a guide for an alternative future, as empire draws to a close. A series of popular struggles oriented to social medicine show the contours of social reconstruction that increasingly will occur worldwide. As the exploitations of empire present end, along with ideas that have justified these exploitations, a new vision of medicine and public health is emerging. The last chapter examines the enactment of this vision, as we leave the world of empire and enter a new one.

CHAPTER 14

RESISTANCE AND BUILDING
AN ALTERNATIVE FUTURE

With Rebeca Jasso-Aguilar[1]

Conditions during the twenty-first century have changed to such an extent that a vision of a world without empire has become part of an imaginable future. Throughout the world, diverse struggles against neoliberalism and privatization illustrate the challenges of popular mobilization. In addition to these struggles *against*, groups in several countries have moved to create alternative models of public health and health services. Because empire, at least as we have known it, has ended, these efforts—especially in Latin America—have moved beyond the historical patterns fostered by capitalism and empire.

The paragraphs that follow consider a series of popular struggles in which we have been involved during the past decade as researchers and activists. These struggles include resistance against the privatization of health services in El Salvador and against the privatization of water supplies in Bolivia, as well as efforts to expand public-sector health services in Mexico and Venezuela. We also describe recent struggles in the centers of empire, especially the United States, that focus on the creation or preservation of national health programs that do not involve reliance on the private marketplace and that do not commodify health services. Such scenarios convey a picture very different from that of the historical relation between empire and health—a picture that shows a diminishing tolerance among the world's peoples for the public health policies of empire and a growing demand for public health systems grounded in solidarity rather than profitability.

The Struggle Against Privatization of Health Services in El Salvador

One of the first outbreaks of sustained resistance to imperial policies in public health and medicine took place during the late 1990s in El Salvador. This struggle focused on privatization policies initiated by the World Bank, in collaboration with a right-wing political party that ruled El Salvador at that time. Efforts to resist privatization of health services and the public health system in El Salvador emerged as a model for analogous social movements elsewhere in Latin America. The example of El Salvador also illustrated similar processes that were to occur in many other countries throughout the world during the early twenty-first century, as imperial policies met with sustained resistance.[2]

In 1998–1999 the health-care sector in El Salvador fell into political turmoil, when conflict broke over various issues. First, unionized workers from the Salvadoran Institute of Social Security (*Instituto Salvadoreño del Seguro Social*, ISSS) mobilized for a salary increase in 1998, when an agreement was reached but not honored by ISSS authorities. Second, an unfavorable revision of the collective bargaining contract in 1999 further strained the relationship between workers and the ISSS administration. And third, in 1999 the administration began to contract private entities to deliver services to the ISSS hospitals, the first signs of privatization within the ISSS. In line with this possibility, two major public hospitals under renovation remained closed for several months, waiting to have their services contracted out to private entities instead of being returned to the ISSS.[3]

Such actions constituted part of a strategy, favored by the World Bank, to privatize public hospitals and clinics. Simultaneously the government had tried to gather public sympathy for the privatization of health care while avoiding the term "privatization," on the basis of alleged corruption and inefficiency in the ISSS. Several conditions, however, called into question the credibility of such allegations. For instance, those directly responsible for the functioning of the ISSS, such as hospital directors and ISSS officials, for the previous thirteen years had been appointed by the party in power (the Republican Nationalist Alliance, *Alianza Republicana Nacionalista*, ARENA). Many ARENA politicians who supported the privatization effort held a financial stake in it. In addition, the health budget remained underspent, creating an artificial shortage of medications and delays in services, elements that proponents of privatization used to build the case for "modernization" and "democratization" of the health-care system.[4]

These issues led to partial and temporary strikes in San Salvador. Workers mobilized on the streets where specific public hospitals were located. In November 1999 unionized workers belonging to the Union of Workers of the Salvadoran Institute of Social Security (*Sindicato de Trabajadores del ISSS*, STISSS) began a national strike—an indefinite, escalating strike. In December 1999, negotiations between the ISSS administrative authorities and STISSS workers collapsed. This collapse combined with a growing concern among doctors with the issue of privatization, providing the ground for an alliance between the STISSS workers and the doctors of the recently created Medical Union of Workers of the Salvadoran Institute of Social Security (*Sindicato Médico de Trabajadores del ISSS*, SIMETRISSS). The medical profession, with little or no history of unionization, therefore began to join the national strike. An alliance of STISSS and SIMETRISSS produced a document labeled "Historical Agreement for the Betterment of the National Health System" (*"Acuerdo Histórico por el Mejoramiento del Sistema Nacional de Salud"*). This document contained a key demand for ending privatization in the national health system: "No to the Privatization of the National Health System" (*"No a la Privatización del Sistema Nacional de Salud"*).[5]

A government commitment not to privatize health services ended the conflict temporarily in March 2000. But instead of honoring the commitment, the Ministry of Health and ISSS authorities continued to contract out hospital services to private entities, leading to an ongoing conflict that lasted until 2003.[6] For about three years beginning in late 1999, the workers from the STISSS and the doctors from SIMETRISSS organized strikes and rallies that gradually drew the support of many other groups. Strikes varied in length, and participants had to walk a fine line to avoid alienating the population at large. During strikes, doctors tended to acutely ill patients on the sidewalks, a strategy to gain the support of the general population as much as a humanitarian action. Another strategic action involved "handing the hospitals to the administrators" and walking out, a symbolic gesture to demonstrate that the hospitals could not run without doctors. The government responded with repression, using tear gas, rubber bullets, and high-pressure water against strikers; doctors were fired and replaced with new personnel.[7]

This solidarity and organization resulted, during November 2002, in congressional approval of Decree 1024 (Decree of State Guarantee of Public Health and Social Security, *Decreto de Garantía Estatal de la Salud Pública y la Seguridad Social*). President Francisco Flores threatened to veto the decree, but legislative pressure in Congress and pressures from civil society through street demonstrations forced him to comply with it. Besides guaranteeing that health care would remain public, the decree effectively voided any health care–related contract that the government had signed with the private sector since the conflict began.[8]

This victory proved short-lived because the party in power, ARENA, formed an alliance that produced enough votes during December 2002 to repeal Decree 1024. The conflict continued for months with several more marches and demonstrations taking place in San Salvador. These were massive rallies where demonstrators dressed in white as a symbol of peace and as a sign of solidarity with doctors and nurses wearing white uniforms. The demonstrations drew from 25,000 to 200,000 participants—in a city of about 800,000 people. Many doctors sold their homes, cars, and home appliances to obtain the financial means for continuing the struggle.[9]

The nine-month-old strike ended with a decision by the World Bank to reverse a privatization clause in a loan earmarked for modernizing the public health system. On June 13, 2003, union leaders and government representatives reached an agreement to halt the privatization of the public health system. All the members of the STISSS and SIMETRISSS were reinstated under previous conditions of salaries and seniority. The agreement also called for the establishment of a commission to follow up on health-care system reforms. The commission included medical professionals, government officials, and representatives of unions and civil society.[10] Efforts to maintain and to expand public-sector health care have continued, especially after the 2009 election of left-oriented Mauricio Funes as president.

Resistance to Privatization of Water in Bolivia

Toward the end of empire present, availability of clean water supplies emerged as a fundamental goal of public health throughout the world. On the one hand, contaminated water supplies generated epidemics of infectious and environmental diseases, which philanthropic foundations and international health organizations targeted in public health campaigns—especially (as discussed in Chapter 1) when such epidemics threatened corporate financial ventures. On the other hand, the world's declining supplies of freshwater emerged as a new frontier for corporate profit, as major corporations whose intent was to sell water as a private commodity sought to privatize public water sources.[11] In this context, the long-term resistance against privatization of water in Bolivia shows how a previously marginalized population can organize to win a struggle against powerful corporate forces that seek to commodify a critical public health resource.

Climate and environmental conditions made the province of Cochabamba, Bolivia, a prime agricultural area, yet historically the region experienced serious problems with its water supply. For decades, agricultural workers (called irrigators, or *regantes*) managed dwindling water resources through irrigation practices rooted in cultural traditions known as "uses and customs" (*usos y costumbres*). However, accelerated urbanization increased the demand for drinking water and water for domestic uses, aggravating an already serious problem of insufficient supply. Newer policies depleted underground water resources and favored urban development at the expense of the rural population, pitting the two groups against each other.[12]

In 1999 the World Bank promoted privatization of the public water utility, based on a rationale of eliminating public subsidies, securing capital for water development, and attracting skilled management—elements viewed as crucial to solve Cochabamba's water shortage problem. During the same year, new legislation on water, *Ley* 2029, allowed a private corporation, *Aguas del Tunari*, to lease Cochabamba's public water and sewer company, the Municipal Service of Potable Water and Sewerage (*Servicio Municipal de Agua Potable y Alcantarillado*, SEMAPA). The contract awarded a private corporation monopoly control over water services in the area for forty years.[13] By the end of 1999, only a few weeks after the contract was signed, water bills increased by an average of 200 percent, an action known as the "rate hike" (*tarifazo*).

A "war of water" (*guerra del agua*) ensued. Community-based groups initiated roadblocks and mobilized support in towns and villages throughout the province. The federation of irrigator organizations in Cochabamba (*Federación Departamental Cochabambina de Organizaciones Regantes*, FEDECOR) had organized roadblocks to reject *Ley* 2029 as early as October 1999, fearing that it represented a threat to their water supply and their traditional irrigation practices. But the *tarifazo* mostly affected the urban population of Cochabamba, and outraged citizens began to mobilize.[14]

A Coalition for the Defense of Water and Life emerged in November 1999 to coordinate mobilizations and protests around the water issue. This coalition included farmers, factory workers, professional people, neighborhood associations, teachers, retirees, the unemployed, and university students. Aided by local professional groups, the coalition uncovered information about the corporation intending to control water supplies, as well as the terms of the contract and other dealings with the government. For instance, the coalition learned that *Aguas del Tunari* did not hold the necessary capital to invest in infrastructure required to alleviate the water shortage in Cochabamba. Instead, the corporation constituted a "ghost consortium" of enterprises grouped together in an improvised manner. Eventually the coalition also discovered that *Aguas del Tunari* was a subsidiary of Bechtel, a large U.S.-based corporation, and that well-known Bolivian politicians maintained economic interests in this consortium. The water contract sought to secure the participation of this private, multinational corporation by providing preferential treatment in every aspect of the project. Basing the project's viability on the increase in water rates, the contract essentially guaranteed profitability regardless of management performance and quality of services.[15]

Outraged at the water rate increases and the newly discovered information about the corporation, the coalition initiated strikes and roadblocks. In January 2000 such actions paralyzed the city of Cochabamba. Citizens refused to pay their water bills and staged symbolic acts where they publicly burned their receipts. When the government refused to consider the coalition's demands, the coalition engaged in the "peaceful takeover of Cochabamba" (*toma pacífica de Cochabamba*), when tens of thousands of citizens marched from different points of the city to converge at the main plaza and to hold an open town meeting (*cabildo*). The government responded to this event with police and military actions lasting two days. In the repression's aftermath, citizens' outrage grew. Additional people, previously not active in the movement, began to participate in the mobilizations.[16]

In March 2000 the coalition called for a cancellation of the contract altogether and organized a popular referendum, where responses showed that citizens overwhelmingly rejected the contract and the water rate hikes. The referendum also showed that citizens were aware that *Ley* 2029 contained elements opening the door to privatization, which the government previously had denied. Local media praised the referendum as an advance in the exercise of democracy. On the other hand, the government trivialized the event, calling the results illegal and refusing to negotiate with the coalition.

Faced with this lack of response, the coalition heightened the confrontation, again calling not only for the contract's cancellation but also for the immediate modification of *Ley* 2029. By April 2000, Cochabamba's economic activity essentially came to a halt. Citizens barricaded every street in their neighborhoods. Thousands of people occupied the main plaza to hold daily *cabildos*, while the government declared that "there was nothing to negotiate" and "the situation in the country is completely normal."[17] When the government offered to negotiate, police arrested the coalition's negotiators and violently dispersed a popular gathering at the city's central plaza. Coalition members and much of the general public perceived this act as government trickery and galvanized themselves further; "almost no citizen in Cochabamba was indifferent to the mobilizations."[18] Citizens increased the blockades, and about seventy thousand people occupied the plaza. As repression by the government intensified, citizens opened their doors to offer the protesters food, water, and shelter.

Under the equivalent of martial law, the government took further actions to repress the uprising over water. An official curfew went into effect. The government initiated a disinformation campaign—one instance was the announcement that drug traffickers were financing the struggle against the privatization of water. Angered by these accusations, people intensified the mobilizations and blockades, not even allowing bicycles to circulate. Despite intense repression, protesters continued to occupy the streets and the central plaza, often clashing with police. Eventually an unarmed seventeen-year-old youth died from gunfire; television footage caught the shooting, perpetrated by an army captain dressed in civilian clothing. The youth's funeral drew tens of thousands of angry protesters.

On the afternoon of the funeral, *Aguas del Tunari* announced that it was rescinding the contract and leaving Cochabamba.[19] SEMAPA remained a public company, and several policy changes occurred as a result of the preceding struggle. The composition of the new board of directors reflected less government control and more community participation: three members now came from the population at large through elections, the mayor's office appointed two members, the city's professional schools elected one member, and the water workers' union designated one member. Underlying these changes was a goal of creating a "Public Institution of Basic Services," a new public entity without profit motive or interference from political parties, but with broad social participation in management. Elected community representatives became accountable to social organizations and the population at large. Comanagement of the company in turn strengthened social organizations such as water committees and local community organizations. By 2005, SEMAPA expanded drinking water and sewer services to a wider geographical area.

The struggle to defeat privatization and to strengthen public water supplies between 2000 and 2005 constituted the first in a wave of mobilizations and uprisings that "broke the hegemonic trajectory of neoliberalism" in Bolivia.[20] To the extent that community participation in the management of SEMAPA realized its goals, the defeat of prior neoliberal policies became more consolidated and visible. In addition, the water war contributed substantially to the election in December 2005 and reelection in December 2009 of Evo Morales, Bolivia's first indigenous president.

Social Medicine's Coming to Power in Mexico City

Bold new health policies, linked to the election of a progressive government in the Federal District of Mexico City, illustrate what an alternative vision of the possible can accomplish under conditions of broad sociopolitical change. In the election of 2000, the left-oriented Party of the Democratic Revolution gained control of the government in the Federal District of Mexico City, which comprises the equivalent of a state, while the conservative Party of National Action won the presidential election. Thus, political life in Mexico during the first decade of the twenty-first century saw the strengthening of two distinct political and economic projects: an anti-neoliberal position in Mexico City, represented by Andrés Manuel López Obrador (known popularly as "AMLO"), and a neoliberal one at the federal level, embodied by President Vicente Fox. The two projects led to very different results.

As governor, AMLO initiated wide-ranging reforms of health and human services. To the post of secretary of health he appointed Cristina Laurell, a widely respected leader of Latin American social medicine.[21] Laurell and colleagues began a series of ambitious health programs, modeled according to social medicine principles. They first focused on senior citizens and the uninsured population, with a goal of guaranteeing the constitutional right to health protection.

The fourth article of the Political Constitution of Mexico granted this right, and later federal health legislation granted universal coverage and free care through public institutions.[22] However, because these documents did not clarify what entity had the obligation to provide health services, this right in practice often came to be seen as merely "good intentions." On the other hand, an assumption underlying these documents was that public institutions should provide health protection. This assumption provided a legal justification to make the state—presumably the guardian of public interest—the provider of this right.[23] The Mexico City Government (MCG) made use of this legal justification to design and to implement health and human services policies that targeted vulnerable groups, thus making "the right to health protection a reality."[24] Broad goals that guided the MCG's approach to health policy were:

> To democratize health care, reducing inequality in disease and death and removing economic, social, and cultural obstacles to access; to strengthen public institutions as the only socially just and economically sustainable option granting equal and universal access to health protection; to attain universal coverage; to broaden services for the uninsured population; to achieve equality in access to existing services; and to create solidarity through fiscal funding and the distribution of the costs of disease among the sick and the healthy.[25]

Health policies of the MCG derived from a concept of social rights. Leaders of the MCG saw the creation of social rights—those that the state is required to guarantee—as one of the Mexican Revolution's most important gains.[26]

Two major programs initiated by the MCG aimed to improve public health and medical services. First, the Program of Food Support and Free Drugs for Senior Citizens created a social institution that granted all seniors a new social right. This program started in February 2001 and by October 2002 had become virtually universal, covering 98 percent of Mexico City residents age seventy years or older. Citizens received a monthly stipend for the cost of food for one person (the equivalent of U.S. $70) and free health care at the city government's health facilities.[27]

A second initiative, the Program of Free Health Care and Drugs, focused on uninsured Mexico City residents. By December 2002, about 350,000 of the 875,000 eligible families had enrolled. Later, by the end of 2005, 854,000 family units had registered in the program, which effectively amounted to universal coverage of the target population. The program provided all personal and public health services; MCG health facilities offered primary and hospital care for individuals and families.[28]

Financing these programs proved possible due to the MCG's commitment to curb administrative waste and corruption. An austerity program beginning in 2000 implemented a 15 percent pay cut for top government officials and eliminated superfluous expenses. AMLO explained these changes under the widely quoted slogan "We can pay for these services because the government isn't robbing you anymore." The austerity measures yielded savings of U.S. $200 million in 2001 and $300 million in 2002. Simultaneously, the government undertook crackdowns against tax evasion and financial corruption. These savings allowed the government to increase the health budget by 67 percent, meaning that 12.5 percent of the Mexico City budget went for public health and health services.[29]

Such community-oriented initiatives achieved wide admiration and contributed to the party's electoral successes. While in 2000 the Party of the Democratic Revolution's victory in Mexico City had been tight, by April 2003 the approval rate for AMLO reached an unprecedented 80–85 percent. The party swept the 2003 midterm election and took control of the Mexico City legislature.

After AMLO narrowly lost the national presidential election during 2006—an election that generated wide dispute and that showed extensive evidence of fraud—the "Legitimate Government of Mexico" took office. In this parallel, unofficial government, AMLO served as president, and Laurell became minister of health. The parallel government kept the social medicine vision alive as a viable policy alternative. According to Laurell, the Legitimate Government of Mexico "is not a shadow government understood as a reaction to official actions of the other government.... [It is] much more proactive, [with the capacity] to elaborate and discuss original proposals using as a starting point another idea of what we want our nation to be."[30]

On the other hand, the Popular Insurance (*Seguro Popular*), the federal health coverage program proposed and partly implemented by Vicente Fox's administration between 2003 and 2006, comprised a service package with limited coverage, cost-sharing by families, and gradual enrollment of the uninsured population. Limited coverage disrupted the provision of comprehensive care. Cost-sharing amounted to 6 percent of family income, a financial burden for poor families. Services not included had to be purchased through private insurance.[31] The latter signaled a further push toward the privatization of health care, which was in line with Fox's neoliberal agenda and the earlier health reforms in Mexico promoted by the World Bank (as discussed in Chapter 9).

The different ways in which Fox and AMLO treated policies regarding public health and health services illustrated two discrepant visions of development. In 2006 the Mexican presidential election became so contested because it served as a kind of referendum on these projects with the potential to create very different countries. As Laurell notes:

> In 2006 what was at play was not just the election of a candidate, the future of the country was at stake.... We lost the opportunity to rebuild our country and to make it less unequal, of building a nation for everyone, in which social rights are guaranteed and built, that is what we lost with this electoral fraud.... What we are trying to do with the Legitimate Government and with the mobilization of citizens is to keep the hope alive.[32]

Mexico City's example of enhanced public-sector services and the Legitimate Government's enduring program for change convey a vision of an alternative future that will continue to inspire, within Mexico and elsewhere, during the post-empire era.

Other Examples of a New Vision: Venezuela, Uruguay, and Brazil

Although we have focused attention on El Salvador, Bolivia, and Mexico City, the emergence of alternative visions and policies that do not accept the historical assumptions of empire and neoliberalism has occurred worldwide. Among many examples, events in Venezuela, Uruguay, and Brazil provide a multifaceted picture of new approaches to public health and medicine. The cumulative experience of such efforts during the early twenty-first century convey an overall impression that the historical linkages among empire, medicine, and public health have dissolved and that this emerging trajectory will prove difficult to reverse.

Under the presidency of Hugo Chávez, Venezuela enacted path-breaking innovations based on social medicine principles. Influenced partly by social medicine leaders such as María Urbaneja, Francisco Armada, and Oscar Feo (the first two serving as national ministers of health), the country embarked on a far-reaching series of organizational changes.[33] Although Chávez and his government advocated accessible, public-sector health services as part of its program after winning the national election in 1999, key barriers stood in the way of achieving that vision. First, the Ministry of Health in the Chávez government continued to operate in a top-down, bureaucratic manner that impeded outreach to underserved urban and rural communities. Second, the Venezuelan medical profession opposed proposals to expand public-sector services.

In the impasse, the Libertador municipality within the boundaries of Caracas initiated a grassroots effort to improve services for the poor. The municipality issued a call for physicians to live and work in the community. When only a small number of Venezuelan doctors responded, the municipality's mayor, Freddy Bernal, approached the Cuban embassy. Within several months a contingent of Cuban doctors arrived.

This approach spread throughout Venezuela. The name of the initiative, *Misión Barrio Adentro* ("mission of the barrio within") referred to the grassroots, bottom-up emergence of a parallel public-sector health system. Low-income communities throughout the country organized to provide their own health services, with the assistance of more than twenty thousand primary care physicians from Cuba. Communities constructed their own health facilities and designed services that addressed the perceived needs of specific neighborhoods. These changes occurred with some support but for the most part independently from the national Ministry of Health. *Misión Barrio Adentro* later attracted attention as a model for change in many other Latin American countries, particular in Bolivia under the presidency of Evo Morales.

After the 2004 election of Tabaré Vázquez, an oncologist, Uruguay also initiated dramatic reforms influenced by Latin American social medicine. In particular, a decentralization of health institutions, guided by extensive neighborhood participation, integrated health services with local governments at the municipal level. These changes occurred with the leadership of Miguel Fernández, a social medicine scholar and teacher who served as subsecretary in the Ministry of Health. During the Vázquez presidency, public-sector services received prioritization, and the neoliberal model fell into decline as, for instance, Uruguay refused to participate in a new free-trade agreement initiated by the United States. In November 2009 Uruguayan voters elected José Mujica, a former guerrilla leader, as Vázquez's successor. Mujica promised to maintain Vázquez's economic policy orientation and vowed to strengthen even further Uruguay's public-sector health services.

"Collective health," the term that characterized social medicine in Brazil, profoundly affected health policies under the government of Luiz Inácio Lula da Silva, a former trade unionist elected in 2002 and again in 2006 to two successive terms as president. Leaders of collective health participated as activists within the Workers' Party and contributed to many of Lula's electoral and substantive accomplishments. Several leaders of collective health served as influential officials in the national Ministry of Health. In municipalities, collective health activists worked in such efforts as community-determined budgets to address local needs. Due to anticipated adverse effects on health and health services, some collective health leaders opposed Lula's policies that favored the interests of international financial capital, including the renewal of agreements with the International Monetary Fund. On the other hand, Lula received wide praise for his support of policies to strengthen public-sector services and for his willingness to oppose U.S. policies in such venues as the World Trade Organization. With the election of Dilma Rousseff, Lula's chosen successor within the Workers' Party, as Brazil's first woman president in October 2010, a further strengthening of public-sector services at the national and municipal levels likely will continue.

Struggles for National Health Programs in the Heart of Empire

Since at least the 1920s, in the midst of empire past, people in the United States have organized in support of a national health program that would provide universal access to comprehensive medical services. In Europe, these struggles began even earlier. For instance, in 1883, Germany became the first country in the world to establish a national health program, as part of Otto von Bismarck's social legislation that largely aimed to prevent a more wide-reaching social revolution. Although many initiatives have tried to privatize the European national health programs in part or in whole, as noted in Chapter 8, these efforts have achieved little lasting success.[34]

In the United States, the latest of many attempts to achieve a national health program involved President Barack Obama's efforts, which resulted during March 2010 in the passage of the highly contested Patient Protection and Affordable Care Act. Earlier in his career, Obama had supported a single-payer, public-sector program of universal health care. However, in his 2008 presidential campaign, he received approximately three times more contributions from the private for-profit insurance industry than did his Republican Party opponent, John McCain. Unsurprisingly, the Patient Protection and Affordable Care Act called for the preservation and strengthening of the private insurance industry through vastly increased public payments to the industry for the care of uninsured and underinsured people.[35]

Despite the complexity of the Patient Protection and Affordable Care Act, its basic components resembled those of many health reform proposals favored by international financial institutions and multinational insurance corporations throughout the world during empire present. As I discuss in Part 2, such proposals aimed to enhance access by corporations to public-sector health and social security trust funds. An ideology favoring for-profit corporations in the marketplace justified these reforms through unproven claims about the efficiency of the private sector and about enhanced quality of care under principles of competition and business management. Such reforms usually have dealt with health care as a commodity to be bought and sold in a competitive marketplace, rather than as a fundamental human right to be guaranteed by government according to the principle of social solidarity.

The contrast between a single-payer approach and the Patient Protection and Affordable Care Act resembles the contrast between public-sector versus market-based reform proposals that occurred worldwide during empire present. As noted, political and economic elites supported market-based reform as a route to enhance investment opportunities and profitability for multinational corporations selling private health insurance, medications, and equipment. As advocated by the leadership of those corporations and international financial institutions such as the World Bank, these market-based proposals sought to use public-sector funds, usually in the target countries' social security systems, to subsidize private-sector corporate expansion.

Like many national health programs around the world, a single-payer program in the United States basically would extend Medicare to the entire population. Although Medicare has not been without problems, people over sixty-five years of age have widely supported the system and have expressed satisfaction with it. Under Medicare, the government occupies a very small role. The government collects payments from workers, employers, and Medicare recipients and then distributes funds to health-care providers for the services that Medicare patients receive. Because it is such a simple system, the administrative costs under Medicare average between 3 percent and 5 percent, according to most studies. This small percentage means that the vast majority of Medicare expenditures pay for clinical services as opposed to administrative expenses.

On the other hand, private insurance generally shows administrative expenses between 20 percent and 30 percent,[36] and there is little evidence that administrative waste will decrease substantially under the Patient Protection and Affordable Care Act. This much larger percentage means that about one-quarter of every dollar spent on health care goes to administrative costs. Many of these expenditures pay for activities such as billing, denial of claims, supervision of copayments and deductibles, scrutiny of preexisting conditions that disqualify people from care (the Patient Protection and Affordable Care Act would prohibit such practices based on preexisting conditions, but the prohibition would be phased in over a period of years), and exorbitant salaries for executives (in some cases totaling between $10 million and $20 million per year).

A single-payer national health program would achieve universal access to care by drastically reducing administrative waste.[37] All people would receive the care that they need without copayments, deductibles, or other expenses at the point of service. Under a single-payer system, the average family and the average business would spend the same or less than they previously spent on medical expenses. Despite lack of support by the Obama administration and many congressional representatives, national polls consistently have shown that a majority or plurality (depending on the poll) of people in the United States have favored the single-payer approach.[38]

The Obama administration's proposal, as well as the highly modified Patient Protection and Affordable Care Act (which eventually passed Congress by a narrow majority as part of the budget reconciliation process rather than as stand-alone legislation), involved a "mixed" approach to linking the public and private sectors. In the mixed model, private health insurance corporations receive public-sector funds, deriving mostly from tax revenues. These funds subsidize private insurance, which insurance corporations continue to administer. Although the Obama administration also proposed a "public option," to be operated by the federal government, Obama eventually dropped the public option, largely due to opposition from the private insurance industry and from the industry's supporters in Congress.[39]

As a result of this process, the overall national health program, as enacted in the Patient Protection and Affordable Care Act, retained the previous private insurance industry as the main administrative entity and therefore projected a much higher level of administrative costs than a single-payer approach. Because the mixed approach would not significantly reduce administrative waste, the anticipated costs of the proposal predictably would become prohibitive, despite assurances to the contrary. Concern about these high costs became a key focus of debate in Congress and throughout the United States. Moreover, even in the best-case scenario, the Patient Protection and Affordable Care Act would leave nearly one-half of the previously uninsured population, about 23 million people, still uninsured.[40]

Obama and his core staff members consistently argued that it was important to preserve the for-profit private insurance industry, with even more tax subsidies for the industry. The Patient Protection and Affordable Care Act essentially would compel families and individuals to buy insurance from the private industry, with the poor assisted through a means-testing approach requiring huge administrative costs. In prior state-level programs that involved a mixed private and public approach, these programs failed to achieve universal coverage and generated crippling cost overruns (for instance, in Massachusetts, frequently cited as a model for the Obama proposal).[41]

Other countries that have implemented mixed private-public systems have encountered challenges. Although some European systems have received critical attention,[42] several middle-income countries in Latin America also have tried to implement mixed systems. As discussed in Part 2, these initiatives resulted largely due to the requirements of international financial institutions like the World Bank and International Monetary Fund, which demanded a reduction of public-sector services and an expansion of private-sector services as a requirement of new or renegotiated loans.[43]

In these countries, neither the conversion of public-sector to private-sector insurance, nor the expansion of private insurance through enhanced public financing and participation by corporate entrepreneurs, succeeded in ensuring access to needed health services. Expansion of private insurance often generated additional copayments. Privatization of social security and other public-sector trust funds for health services generally favored private corporations by providing publicly subsidized insurance and by increasing the capital these corporations held. In addition, privatization led to higher administrative costs.

The impact of mixed private-public systems varied across countries. For Argentina, these policies led to increasing economic crisis and major cutbacks of services, especially for older and disabled people. In Chile, where privatization occurred largely during the military dictatorship, private managed care organizations (subsidized by public tax funds) prospered as they covered relatively healthy groups in the population, while a constricted public sector continued to provide services to the uninsured. Mexico faced pressures from the World Bank to privatize its social security system, including public-sector health services; as avenues opened to the participation of private corporations, public-sector institutions encountered budget reductions that led to eroded services.

If we are serious about working to improve the devastating problems of access to services in the United States and other countries, we need to move beyond conventional wisdom about the positive impact of market-based policies like mixed private-public systems. Strategies that channel public funds into private insurance corporations have failed to achieve the goal of universal access. Unfortunately, such policies may even further worsen the conditions faced by vulnerable groups. Based on empirical realities, our work must find ways to enhance the delivery of public-sector services, rather than continuing to implement the mostly failed policies of privatization. In the United States, the center of empire present, these failed policies will continue to exhaust the already fragile national economy, while leaving a large part of the population with inadequate access to services.

Because the Patient Protection and Affordable Care Act very likely will fail to achieve its purposes of universal access and cost control, especially after the increased opposition generated in the mid-term elections of November 2010, organizing to achieve a public-sector national health program based on single-payer principles will continue.[44] As the United States remains the only economically advanced country without a viable national program that ensures access to needed care, the single-payer approach will come to be seen as the only way to avoid the failures that have plagued the country for so many years. In the long run, we might take hope from Winston Churchill's much-quoted observation, "The United States invariably does the right thing, after having exhausted every other alternative."[45]

The End of Empire?

At the end of the twentieth century, trade agreements were strengthening the political and economic positions of the United States and other dominant nations in North America and Europe, but the twenty-first century has seen a rapid deterioration of this mechanism of empire building and maintenance. As only one key example, collective actions led to the failure of attempts to pass the Free Trade Area of the Americas, an agreement that would have converted the Western Hemisphere into a single free-trade zone, along the lines of the North American Free Trade Agreement. With rare exceptions like the Dominican Republic–Central American Free Trade Agreement, similar actions have forced the U.S. government to implement bilateral free-trade agreements sporadically with single countries, instead of reaching regional agreements that could achieve compliance to imperial principles by a wider spectrum of countries.

The collapse of the World Trade Organization's round of negotiations in 2008 implied the probable end of U.S. and Western European hegemony in trade agreements. This collapse resulted from resistance, partly to agricultural tariffs, by an emerging coalition: the Common Market of the South (MERCOSUR in Latin America, led by Brazil and also involving Argentina, Paraguay, Uruguay, and Venezuela as full members), China, and India. This transition will continue to change profoundly the prior adverse effects of trade agreements on public health and health services.

Alternative trade agreements not involving the United States or Western European countries have emerged.[46] The first such agreement in Latin America was the MERCOSUR. Another increasingly influential agreement is the Bolivarian Alliance for the Peoples of Our America (*Alianza Bolivariana para los Pueblos de Nuestra América*, or ALBA). Initiated by Venezuela, ALBA includes Cuba, Bolivia, Nicaragua, Ecuador, Dominica, Saint Vincent and the Grenadines, and Antigua and Barbuda. These alternative trade agreements create collaborative trade activities that minimize the dominant and often exploitative efforts previously exerted by the United States and other countries of the North. Several of the agreements involve cooperation in public health and medical care, such as Cuba's sending physicians to work in Venezuela and Bolivia, in exchange for oil and natural gas.

Considering only Latin America, progressive governments have come to power as a result of electoral victories in Venezuela, Ecuador, Bolivia, Chile, Argentina, Uruguay, Brazil, Nicaragua, Honduras, Paraguay, and El Salvador.[47] These governments generally have rejected the historical principles and relationships associated with empire. Several of the countries (particularly Venezuela and Bolivia) have explicitly adopted visions of a peaceful, electoral transition to socialism—a transition that imperial powers previously would not have tolerated, as in the case of Chile during the early 1970s (discussed in Chapter 4). Empire's deterioration has carried with it a reduced capacity to destroy democratically elected governments that do not defer to imperial expectations. One key policy that typically characterizes such new governments involves a reversal of neoliberal requirements for the reduction of public sector-health services and, instead, a strengthening of those services.

The weakness of capitalist empire in response to these changes became clearer after 2008, with a near collapse of the international capitalist banking system, the socialization through increased government ownership of banks and other large private enterprises like the auto industry, and the overextension and ineffectuality of military operations. So far the expansion of government ownership in the capitalist economy has continued to benefit mainly the rich. But the debility revealed by actions to socialize increasing parts of the capitalist economy became inescapably clear to any who cared to look closely. Likewise, the prospect of endless war, usually perpetrated in the name of antiterrorism, uncovered the underlying desperation of "disaster capitalism."[48] This stage of capitalism maintains itself largely by creating disasters through war so that corporate actors can open new markets and opportunities for investment by strengthening "security" and reconstructing war-torn societies.

Such changes hearken back to prediction of the ever-controversial V. I. Lenin, whose stature as an analyst of capitalism's vulnerability during the era of empire has grown (despite his failure to predict correctly the future of socialism in Europe); more recent analysts such as Immanuel Wallerstein, Chalmers Johnson, and Johan Galtung have reached similar conclusions.[49] Lenin analyzed several tendencies in "late" capitalism that linked the deterioration of empire to a breakdown of the banking system and the emergence of perpetual war that ultimately would weaken the capitalist powers. For instance, he noted the increasing concentration of banking during the late phases of empire, as the fundamental activities of the capitalist economy switch to the expansion of finance capital (more recently termed the "financialization" of economic activities)[50] and away from production of useful goods and services. War figures as a fundamental component of the incessant search of financial capital for new sources of profitability:

> The question is: what means other than war could there be under capitalism to overcome the disparity between the development of productive forces and the accumulation of capital on the one side, and the division of colonies and spheres of influence for finance capital on the other?

And ultimately the late stage of empire implies decay and transformation:

> Monopolies, oligarchy, the striving for domination and not for freedom, the exploitation of an increasing number of small or weak nations by a handful of the richest or most powerful nations—all these have given birth to those distinctive characteristics of imperialism which compel us to define it as parasitic or decaying capitalism.... From all that has been said in this book on the economic essence of imperialism, it follows that we must define it as capitalism in transition, or, more precisely, as moribund capitalism.

These visions of the "moribund" tendencies in capitalist empire emerged more than eight decades before they would play themselves out with much greater clarity during the early twenty-first century. Furious opposition will continue to flow from the centers of finance and power, while the dark flower of empire gradually wilts.

Sociomedical Activism in the Post-Empire Era

The struggles considered here confirm certain core principles of public health: the right to health care, access to clean water and other components of a safe environment, and the reduction of illness-generating conditions such as inequality and related social determinants of ill health and early death. Affordable access to health care and clean water supplies provided by the state, for instance, has become the focus of activism throughout the world. Such struggles reaffirm the principle of the right to organize at the grass roots and to have communities' voices heard and counted in policy decisions. Fostering a sense of dignity, activism that seeks alternatives to neoliberalism and privatization encourages participation by diverse populations, an emphasis on solidarity, and a rejection of traditional political forms. Reinforcing this view, Pierre Bourdieu places such new social movements at the heart of the struggle against neoliberalism, as the state and civil society transform.[51]

As William Robinson argues, such popular struggles and organized resistance respond to the exploitative practices of global capitalism and empire but also move beyond those practices. He situates these struggles within the context of the transnational state, noting that "the challenge is how to reconstruct the social power of the popular classes worldwide in an era in which such power is not mediated and organized through the nation state."[52] From this perspective, mobilization by civil society opens counter-hegemonic spaces, in which the given wisdoms that foster empire become demystified and unacceptable.

The challenge is to develop strategies for activism that can extend these counter-hegemonic spaces to broader social change. A goal of the social movements that we have described is not simply to win but also to encourage public debate and to raise the level of political consciousness. This new consciousness rejects the inevitability of empire and also fosters a vision of medicine and public health constructed around principles of justice rather than commodification and profitability. As the era of empire passes, no other path will fulfill our most fundamental aspirations for healing.

NOTES

Preface

1. Howard Waitzkin and Hilary Modell, "Medicine, Socialism, and Totalitarianism: Lessons from Chile," *New England Journal of Medicine* 291 (1974): 171–177.

2. Salvador Allende, *La Realidad Médico-Social Chilena* (Santiago, Chile: Ministerio de Salubridad, 1939).

Chapter 1

1. Among the extensive works on the social history of empire past, Wallerstein's masterful account of how the modern world system emerged from the 1500s onward remains especially helpful: Immanuel Wallerstein, *The Modern World-System, vol. I: Capitalist Agriculture and the Origins of the European World-Economy in the Sixteenth Century* (New York/London: Academic Press, 1974); *The Capitalist World-Economy* (Cambridge: Cambridge University Press, 1979); *The Modern World-System, vol. II: Mercantilism and the Consolidation of the European World-Economy, 1600–1750* (New York: Academic Press, 1980); *The Modern World-System, vol. III: The Second Great Expansion of the Capitalist World-Economy, 1730–1840's* (New York: Academic Press, 1989).

2. Andrew Carnegie, *The Gospel of Wealth & Other Timely Essays* (New York: Century Company, 1901).

3. Carnegie, *The Gospel of Wealth*, p. 176.

4. E. Richard Brown, *Rockefeller Medicine Men: Medicine and Capitalism in the Progressive Era* (Berkeley: University of California Press, 1979); Anne-Emanuelle Birn, *Marriage of Convenience: Rockefeller International Health and Revolutionary Mexico* (Rochester, NY: Rochester University Press, 2006); Anne-Emanuelle Birn, Yogan Pillay, and Timothy H. Holtz, eds., *Textbook of International Health: Global Health in a Dynamic World* (New York: Oxford University Press, 2009), chapter 2; Marcus Cueto, ed., *Missionaries of Science: The Rockefeller Foundation and Latin America* (Bloomington: Indiana University Press, 1994).

5. Howard Waitzkin, "Report of the World Health Organization's Commission on Macroeconomics and Health—A Summary and Critique," *Lancet* 361 (2003): 523–526; Anne-Emanuelle Birn, "Gates's Grandest Challenge: Transcending Technology as Public Health Ideology," *Lancet* 366 (2005): 514–519.

6. Ellen R. Shaffer, Howard Waitzkin, Rebeca Jasso-Aguilar, and Joseph Brenner, "Global Trade and Public Health," *American Journal of Public Health* 95 (2005): 23–34.

7. James D. Wolfensohn (President, World Bank), Address to the World Parks Congress,

Durban, South Africa, September 8, 2003, http://web.worldbank.org/WBSITE/EXTERNAL/
NEWS/0,,contentMDK:20127038~menuPK:34472~pagePK:34370~piPK:34424~theSitePK:
4607,00.html, accessed June 18, 2010.

8. Shaffer et al., "Global Trade and Public Health."

9. Ilona Kickbusch, "The Development of International Health Policies—Accountability Intact?" *Social Science & Medicine* 51 (2000): 979–989; Shaffer et al., "Global Trade and Public Health."

10. Shaffer et al., 2005; Howard Waitzkin, Rebeca Jasso-Aguilar, Angela Landwehr, and Carolyn Mountain, "Global Trade, Public Health, and Health Services: Stakeholders' Constructions of the Key Issues," *Social Science & Medicine* 61 (2005): 893–906.

11. Marcos Cueto, *The Value of Health: A History of the Pan American Health Organization* (Rochester, NY: Rochester University Press, 2007), chapter 1.

12. Ibid., chapter 2.

13. Ibid., chapter 5; Elizabeth Fee and Theodore M. Brown, "100 Years of the Pan American Health Organization," *American Journal of Public Health* 92 (2002):12–13.

14. Andy Haines, Richard Horton, and Zulfiqar Bhutta, "Primary Health Care Comes of Age. Looking Forward to the 30th Anniversary of Alma-Ata: Call for Papers," *Lancet* 370 (2007): 911–913; World Health Organization, "Declaration of Alma-Ata: International Conference on Primary Health Care," Alma-Ata, USSR, September 6–12, 1978, www.who.int/hpr/NPH/docs/declaration_almaata.pdf, accessed June 18, 2010; Marcos Cueto, "The Origins of Primary Health Care and Selective Primary Health Care," *American Journal of Public Health* 94 (2004): 1884–1893.

Chapter 2

1. Early works that considered the social origins of illness, but with a different analytic perspective, include: George Rosen, "What Is Social Medicine?" *Bulletin of the History of Medicine* 21 (1947): 674–733; George Rosen, *A History of Public Health* (New York: MD Publications, 1958), especially pp. 192–293; René Sand, *The Advance to Social Medicine* (London: Staples Press, 1952), especially pp. 295–343, 507–589; Henry E. Sigerist, *Civilization and Disease* (Ithaca, NY: Cornell University Press, 1944), pp. 6–64. For more extensive discussion of this history, see Howard Waitzkin, *At the Front Lines of Medicine: How the Health Care System Alienates Doctors and Mistreats Patients ... And What We Can Do About It* (Lanham, MD: Rowman & Littlefield, 2001), pp. 41–75.

2. Due to the varying usages of the term *political economy,* a brief definition may prove helpful. In this chapter, political economy refers to the political conditions under which economic production is organized. This definition follows the usage of the term in Marxian and neo-Marxian studies, as well as their prior antecedents in the works of Adam Smith and David Ricardo. In this sense, *political economic systems* refer to the different political frameworks for organizing economic production, such as capitalism and socialism. From this viewpoint, class structure, particularly the distinction between those who do own or control the means of production (capitalists) and those who do not (workers), composes a key focus of political economy.

3. Friedrich Engels, *The Condition of the Working Class in England in 1844* (1845; Moscow: Progress Publishers, 1973).

4. For a sympathetic critique, see Steven Marcus, *Engels, Manchester, and the Working Class* (New York: Vintage, 1974).

5. Engels, *Condition*, p. 135.

6. Ibid., pp. 141–142.

7. Ibid., pp. 142–143.

8. Ibid., pp. 190–193.
9. Ibid., p. 200.
10. Ibid., pp. 279–284.
11. Erwin H. Ackerknecht, *Rudolf Virchow: Doctor, Statesman, Anthropologist* (Madison: University of Wisconsin Press, 1953), p. 52.
12. Rudolf Virchow, *Disease, Life, and Man,* trans. L. J. Rather (Stanford, CA: Stanford University Press, 1958), pp. 27–29. Unless otherwise noted, I have prepared the translations from German and Spanish.
13. Virchow, *Gesammelte Abhandlungen,* vol. 1, pp. 121–122; Ackerknecht, *Rudolf Virchow,* pp. 125–129.
14. Rudolf Virchow, *Werk und Wirkung* (Berlin: Rütten & Loenig, 1957), p. 110.
15. Ibid., p. 55; Ackerknecht, *Rudolf Virchow,* pp. 131–138.
16. Virchow, *Werk und Wirkung,* pp. 127, 108.
17. Ibid., p. 106.
18. Ibid., p. 117; Virchow, *Disease, Life, and Man,* p. 106.
19. Salvador Allende, *La Realidad Medico-Social Chilena* (Santiago, Chile: Ministerio de Salubridad, Prevision y Asistencia Social, 1939).
20. Ibid., pp. 6, 8.
21. Ibid., p. 86.
22. Ibid., p. 105.
23. Ibid., p. 119.
24. Ibid., pp. 189–190.
25. Ibid., p. 191.
26. Ibid., p. 198.

Chapter 3

1. Adam Smith, *An Inquiry into the Nature and Causes of the Wealth of Nations* (1776; London: Methuen, 1904), chapter 9; David Ricardo, *On the Principles of Political Economy and Taxation* (1817; Harmondsworth, UK: Penguin, 1971), chapter 6; Karl Marx, *Capital: A Critique of Political Economy* (1894; London: Electric Book Company, 1998), vol. 3, pp. 279–306 ("The Law of the Tendency of the Rate of Profit to Fall"); Fred Moseley, *The Falling Rate of Profit in the Post-War United States Economy* (New York: St. Martin's Press, 1991).
2. United States Department of Health, Education, and Welfare, Heart Disease and Stroke Control Program, *Guidelines for Coronary Care Units.* DHEW Publication No.1824 (Washington, DC: Government Printing Office, 1968).
3. Metropolitan Life Insurance Company, "Geographical Distribution of Coronary Care Units in the United States," *Statistical Bulletin* 58 (July–August, 1977): 7–9.
4. Osler L. Peterson, "Myocardial Infarction: Unit Care or Home Care?" *Annals of Internal Medicine* 88 (1978): 259–261; Editorial, "Antidysrhythmic Treatment in Acute Myocardial Infarction," *Lancet* 1 (1979): 193–194; Editorial, "Coronary-Care Units—Where Now?" *Lancet* 1 (1979): 649–650; Howard Waitzkin, "How Capitalism Cares for Our Coronaries: A Preliminary Exercise in Political Economy," in *The Doctor-Patient Relationship in the Changing Health Scene,* ed. Eugene B. Gallagher (Washington, DC: Government Printing Office, DHEW Publication No. [NIH] 78-183, 1978); Samuel P. Martin, et al., "Inputs into Coronary Care During 30 Years: A Cost Effectiveness Study," *Annals of Internal Medicine* 81 (1974): 289–293.
5. Stefan Hofvendahl, "Influence of Treatment in a CCU on Prognosis in Acute Myocardial Infarction," *Acta Medica Scandinavica* (Suppl.) 519 (1971): 1–78; Ingelise Christiansen, Kasper Iversen, and Arne P. Skouby, "Benefits Obtained by the Introduction of a Coronary-Care Unit:

A Comparative Study," *Acta Medica Scandinavica* 189 (1971): 285–291; J. Donald Hill, Greg Holdstock, and John R. Hampton, "Comparison of Mortality of Patients with Heart Attacks Admitted to a Coronary Care Unit and an Ordinary Medical Ward," *British Medical Journal* 2 (1977): 81–83; Karen Astvad, et al., "Mortality from Acute Myocardial Infarction Before and After Establishment of a Coronary Care Unit," *British Medical Journal* 1 (1974): 567–569.

6. H. Gordon Mather, Denise C. Morgan, Neil G. Pearson, et al., "Myocardial Infarction: A Comparison Between Home and Hospital Care for Patients," *British Medical Journal* 1 (1976): 925–929; H. Gordon Mather, Neil. G. Pearson, K. L. Q. Read, et al., "Acute Myocardial Infarction: Home and Hospital Treatment," *British Medical Journal* 3 (1971): 334–338; J. Donald Hill, John R. Hampton, and John R. A. Mitchell, "A Randomised Trial of Home-versus-Hospital Management for Patients with Suspected Myocardial Infarction," *Lancet* 1 (1978): 837–841; Aubrey Colling, Alex W. Dellipiani, Ralph J. Donaldson, "Teesside Coronary Survey: An Epidemiological Study of Acute Attacks of Myocardial Infarction," *British Medical Journal* 2 (1976): 1169–1172; Alex W. Dellipiani, Aubrey Coiling, and Ralph J. Donaldson, et al., "Teesside Coronary Survey—Fatality and Comparative Severity of Patients Treated at Home, in the Hospital Ward, and in the Coronary Care Unit After Myocardial Infarction," *British Heart Journal* 39 (1977): 1172–1178.

7. Ernest Mandel, *An Introduction to Marxist Economic Thought* (New York: Pathfinder, 1970), p. 52.

8. Warner-Lambert, *Annual Report* (1967), p. 7.

9. Ibid. (1968), p. 25.

10. Ibid. (1969), pp. 18–19.

11. Ibid. (1970), p. 19.

12. Ibid. (1975), p. 5.

13. Ibid. (1970), p. 16.

14. *People* & *Taxes*, November 1978, p. 4.

15. Hewlett-Packard Company, *Annual Report* (Palo Alto, CA, 1966), p. 11.

16. Ibid. (1969), p. 11.

17. Ibid. (1966), p. 4.

18. Ibid. (1969), p. 15.

19. Ibid. (1974), p. 2.

20. Ibid. (1971), p. 5.

21. Bernard Lown, et al., "The Coronary Care Unit: New Perspectives and Directions," *JAMA* 199 (1967): 188–198.

22. Anne A. Scitovsky and Nelda McCall, *Changes in the Costs of Treatment of Selected Illnesses, 1951–1964–1971* (Washington, DC: Government Printing Office, DHEW Publication No. [HRA] 77-3161, 1977).

23. American Heart Association, *Annual Report* (New York, 1967), p. 11.

24. Ibid. (1968), pp. 2, 13–14.

25. John A. Hartford Foundation, *Annual Report* (New York, 1963), p. 58.

26. W. R. Hewlett Foundation, *Annual Report to the Internal Revenue Service* (Palo Alto, CA, 1967, 1971).

27. Hughes W. Day, "An Intensive Coronary Care Area," *Diseases of the Chest* 44 (1963): 423–427.

28. Bernard S. Bloom and Osler Peterson, "End Results, Cost, and Productivity of Coronary-Care Units," *New England Journal of Medicine* 288 (1973): 72–78.

29. James O'Connor, *The Fiscal Crisis of the State* (New York: St. Martin's Press, 1973), pp. 64–72, 92–174.

30. United States Department of Commerce, Domestic and International Business Administration, *Global Market Survey: Biomedical Equipment* (Washington, DC: Government Printing Office, 1973).

31. Harry Braverman, *Labor and Monopoly Capital* (New York: Monthly Review Press, 1974), especially pp. 85–152.

32. Edwin F. Rosinski, "Impact of Technology and Evolving Health Care Systems on the Training of Allied Health Personnel," *Military Medicine* 134 (1969): 390–393.

33. Francis J. Moore, "Information Technologies and Health Care: The Need for New Technologies to Offset the Shortage of Physicians," *Archives of Internal Medicine* 125 (1970): 351–355.

34. Glen L. Foster, Gus G. Casten, and T. Joseph Reeves, "Nonmedical Personnel and Continuous ECG Monitoring," *Archives of Internal Medicine* 124 (1969): 110–112; Paul J. Sanazaro, "Physician Support Personnel in the 1970s," *JAMA* 214 (1970): 98–100; G. Otto Barnett and Anthony Robbins, "Information Technology and Manpower Productivity," *JAMA* 209 (1969): 546–548.

35. A later random controlled trial of an "intermediate" CCU, involving less intensive monitoring and treatment than a standard CCU, found no advantage of the intermediate approach but did not reevaluate the standard CCU approach itself: P. C. Reynell, "Intermediate Coronary Care: A Controlled Trial," *British Heart Journal* 37 (1975): i66–i68. For further perspectives on evaluating such studies: Andrew D. Oxman, Mary Ann Thomson, David A. Davis, and R. Brian Haynes, "No Magic Bullets: A Systematic Review of 102 Trials of Interventions to Improve Professional Practice," *Canadian Medical Association Journal* 153 (1995), 1423–1431; Kjell Benson and Artur J. Hartz, "A Comparison of Observational Studies and Randomized Controlled Trials," *New England Journal of Medicine* 342 (2000): 1878–1886.

36. William S. Harris, Manohar Gowda, Jerry W. Kolb, et al., "A Randomized, Controlled Trial of the Effects of Remote, Intercessory Prayer on Outcomes in Patients Admitted to the Coronary Care Unit," *Archives of Internal Medicine* 159 (1999): 2273–2278; Randolf C. Byrd, "Positive Therapeutic Effects of Intercessory Prayer in a Coronary Care Unit Population," *Southern Medical Journal* 81 (1988): 826–829. For contradictory findings: Jennifer M. Aviles, Ellen Whelan, Debra A. Hernke, et al., "Intercessory Prayer and Cardiovascular Disease Progression in a Coronary Care Unit Population: A Randomized Controlled Trial," *Mayo Clinic Proceedings* 76 (2001): 1192–1198.

37. Eugene D. Robin, "Death by Pulmonary Artery Flow–Directed Catheter: Time for a Moratorium?" *Chest* 92 (1987): 727–731; James A. Dalen and Roger C. Bone, "Is It Time to Pull the Pulmonary Artery Catheter?" *JAMA* 276 (1996): 916–918; Monica R. Shah, Vic Hasselblad, Lynne W. Stevenson, et al., "Impact of the Pulmonary Artery Catheter in Critically Ill Patients: Meta-Analysis of Randomized Clinical Trials," *JAMA* 294 (2005): 1664–1670.

38. Valentin Fuster, "Myocardial Infarction and Coronary Care Units," *Journal of the American College of Cardiology* 34 (1999): 1851–1853; Thomas Killip and John T. Kimball, "Treatment of Myocardial Infarction in a Coronary Care Unit: A Two-Year Experience with 250 Patients," *American Journal of Cardiology* 20 (1967): 457–464.

Chapter 4

1. Vicente Navarro, *An Analysis of Cost Expenditures in Latin America for the Period 1965–1970* (Baltimore: Johns Hopkins University, School of Hygiene and Public Health, unpublished manuscript, 1974).

2. Salvador Allende, *English and Spanish Texts of His Political Platform, the Program of the Popular Front, and His Biography* (Washington, DC: Editorial Ardilla, n.d.), pp. 2–6, 39.

3. Fidel Castro, "On Chilean Fascism and Revolution," in *The Chilean Road to Socialism,* ed. Dale L. Johnson (Garden City, NY: Anchor, 1973), pp. 337–359; Dale L. Johnson, ed., *The Chilean Road to Socialism* (Garden City, NY: Anchor, 1973), pp. 35, 47–51, 120, 125–129; North

American Congress on Latin America, "Secret Memos from ITT" (released by Jack Anderson), *NACLA Latin America and Empire Report,* April 1972; International Telephone and Telegraph, "Memorandum," dated September 17, 1970, cited in *New York Times,* March 24, 1972.

4. International Telephone and Telegraph, "Memorandum."

5. Richard M. Nixon, "Policy Statement: Economic Assistance and Investment Security in Developing Nations," press release, January 19, 1972; Frank Bonilla and Robert Girling, eds., *Structures of Dependency* (Stanford, CA: Stanford University Press, 1973).

6. J. Valenzuela Feijoo, "Apostoles y Mercaderes de la Salud," *Punto Final* (Santiago), June 19, 1973, pp. 2–11.

7. North American Congress on Latin America, *New Chile* (Berkeley, CA: Waller Press, 1972), pp. 81–117, 150–167.

8. Oscar Ozlak and Dante Caputo, "The Migration of Medical Personnel from Latin America to the United States: Toward an Alternative Interpretation," presented at the Pan American Conference on Health Manpower Planning, Ottawa, Canada, September 10–14, 1973; Rosemary Stevens and Joan Vermuelen, *Foreign Trained Physicians and American Medicine,* DHEW Publication No. [NIH] 73-325 (Washington, DC: Government Printing Office, 1973); Vicente Navarro, "The Underdevelopment of Health or the Health of Underdevelopment: An Analysis of the Distribution of Health Resources in Latin America," *Politics and Society* 4 (1974): 267–293.

9. Regis Debray, *The Chilean Revolution—Conversations with Allende* (New York: Vintage, 1971), pp. 63–66, 84; North American Congress on Latin America, *New Chile,* pp. 16, 17, 21, 23, 52–58; Richard E. Feinberg, *The Triumph of Allende: Chile's Legal Revolution* (New York: Mentor, 1972), pp. 81, 187, 240; Paul B. Comely, Roberto Belmar, Leslie A. Falk, et al. "Report of the APHA Task Force of Chile," *American Journal of Public Health* 67 (1977): 31–36, 71–73.

10. Eduardo Santa Cruz, "Ejemplo de Lucha poe el Derecho a la Salud," *Punto Final* (Santiago), June 19, 1973, pp. 14–16; Andrew Zimbalist and Barbara Stallings, "Showdown in Chile," *Monthly Review* 25 (October 1973): 1–24; Kyle Steenland, "Two Years of 'Popular Unity' in Chile: A Balance Sheet," *New Left Review* 78 (March–April 1973): 1–25; Paul M. Sweezy, "Chile: The Question of Power," *Monthly Review* 25 (December 1973): 1–11; anonymous contributors, "Worker Control: (1) Its Structure Under Allende; (2) At the Side of the Workers," *Science for the People* 5 (November 1973): 25–32.

11. John Barnes, "Slaughterhouse in Santiago," *Newsweek,* October 8, 1973; Lawrence R. Birns, ed., *The End of Chilean Democracy* (New York: Seabury, 1974), pp. 29–74; R. Rojas Sanford, *The Murder of Allende* (New York: Harper & Row, 1976), pp. 190–220; International Commission of Jurists, Preliminary Report of the ICJ Mission to Chile (Geneva, 1974).

12. Chicago Commission of Inquiry into the Status of Human Rights in Chile, "Terror in Chile. I. The Chicago Commission Report," *New York Review of Books,* May 20, 1974, pp. 38–41; Rose Styron, "Terror in Chile. II. The Amnesty Report," *New York Review of Books,* May 30, 1974, pp. 42–44; A. Argus, "Medicine and Politics in Chile," *World Medicine,* April 10, 1974, pp. 15–24; Chilean Medical Doctors in Exile, "An Appeal," Lima, Peru, March 8, 1974; A. Schester Cortes (military physician), "Policy to Be Followed with Members of the Popular Unity (UP)," Santiago, October 11, 1973. Regarding long-term social and economic impacts of the Chilean dictatorship, see Howard Waitzkin, "Next in Line for NAFTA?: Images from Chile," *Monthly Review* 46 (March 1995): 17–27.

13. Margaret Gilpin and Helen Rodriguez-Trias, "Looking at Health in a Healthy Way," *Cuba Review* 8 (March 1978): 3–15. For detailed accounts of prerevolutionary medicine, see Ross Danielson, *Cuban Medicine* (New Brunswick, NJ: Transaction Books, 1979), pp. 21–125; Vicente Navarro, "Health Services in Cuba," *New England Journal of Medicine* 287 (1972): 954–959; Vicente Navarro, "Health, Health Services, and Health Planning in Cuba," *International Journal of Health Services* 2 (1972): 397–432.

14. Regarding the Cuban mass organizations, see Richard R. Fagen, *The Transformation of*

Political Culture in Cuba (Stanford, CA: Stanford University Press, 1969), especially pp. 69–103; "New Forms of Democracy," *Cuba Review* 6 (September 1976): 1–36; Linda Fuller, *Work and Democracy in Socialist Cuba* (Philadelphia: Temple University Press, 1992); Peter Roman, *People's Power: Cuba's Experience with Representative Government,* 2nd ed. (Lanham, MD: Rowman & Littlefield, 2003).

15. For example, see Pan American Health Organization, *Health in the Americas,* vol. 2 (Washington, DC: The Organization, 2007), http://new.paho.org/hq/index.php?option=com_content&task=view&id=44&Itemid=191&limit=1&limitstart=3, accessed November 12, 2010; Pol de Vos, "'No One Left Abandoned': Cuba's National Health System Since the 1959 Revolution," *International Journal of Health Services* 35 (2005): 189–207; Paul K. Drain and Michele Barry, "Fifty Years of U.S. Embargo: Cuba's Health Outcomes and Lessons," *Science* 328 (2010): 572–573. For ongoing information about the Cuban health system and its outcomes, see: *MEDICC Review: International Journal of Cuban Health and Medicine,* www.medicc.org/mediccreview, accessed November 12, 2010.

16. For discussions of professional dominance in Cuba, see Sarah Conover, Sandy Donovan, and Ezra Susser, "Reflections on Health Care," *Cubatimes* 1 (Winter 1981): 20–25; Julie M. Feinsilver, *Healing the Masses: Cuban Health Politics at Home and Abroad* (Berkeley: University of California Press, 1993); Christina Pérez, *Caring for Them from Birth to Death: The Practice of Community-Based Cuban Medicine* (Lanham, MD: Lexington, 2008).

17. Further details about this orientation toward medicalization of social problems in Cuba appears in Howard Waitzkin, *The Politics of Medical Encounters: How Patients and Doctors Deal with Social Problems* (New Haven, CT: Yale University Press, 1991), chapter 11.

18. Zimbalist and Stallings, "Showdown in Chile"; Sweezy, "Question of Power."

Chapter 5

1. In this chapter, Rebeca Jasso-Aguilar participates as a co-author. The chapter reflects our long-term collaboration in several of the efforts presented in this book.

2. David Harvey, *A Brief History of Neoliberalism* (Oxford: Oxford University Press, 2005).

3. For further perspectives on the impact of neoliberalism in medicine and public health, see: Jim Y. Kim, et al., *Dying for Growth: Global Inequality and the Health of the Poor* (Monroe, ME: Common Courage Press, 2000); Meredith Fort, Mary Anne Mercer, and Oscar Gish, eds., *In Sickness and Wealth: The Corporate Assault on Global Health* (Boston: South End Press, 2004); Vicente Navarro, ed., *Neoliberalism, Globalization, and Inequalities: Consequences for Health and Quality of Life* (Amityville, NY: Baywood, 2007); and Leo Panitch and Colin Leys, eds., *Morbid Symptoms: Health Under Capitalism* (New York: Monthly Review Press [*Socialist Register*], 2009).

4. Hector Guillen Romo, *La Contrarrevolución Neoliberal en México* (Mexico City: Ediciones Era, 1997).

5. Pertinent sources include: Alfred Marshall, *The Principles of Economics* (1920; Amherst, NY: Prometheus Books, 1997); William Stanley Jevons, *The Theory of Political Economy* (1911; Harmondsworth, UK: Penguin, 1970); Léon Walras, *Elements of Pure Economics, or the Theory of Social Wealth* (1899; Philadelphia, PA: Orion Editions, 1984); Adam Smith, *An Inquiry into the Nature and Causes of the Wealth of Nations* (1776; London: Methuen, 1904); David Ricardo, *On the Principles of Political Economy and Taxation* (1817; Harmondsworth, UK: Penguin, 1971).

6. Harvey, *A Brief History.*

7. David C. Korten, *When Corporations Rule the World,* 2nd ed. (San Francisco: Berrett-Koehler, 2001).

8. Ibid.; Kim, et al., *Dying for Growth*; William Robinson, *A Theory of Global Capitalism:*

Production, ·Class, and State in a Transnational World (Baltimore: Johns Hopkins University Press, 2004).

9. Harvey, *A Brief History.*

10. John Maynard Keynes, *The General Theory of Employment, Interest, and Money* (1936; San Diego, CA: Harcourt, Brace, Jovanovich, 1991).

11. Guillen Romo, *La Contrarrevolucion Neoliberal*; Harvey, *A Brief History*; Duncan Green, *Silent Revolution: The Rise and Crisis of Market Economics in Latin America,* 2nd ed. (New York: Monthly Review Press, 2010).

12. Sources include: Friedrich von Hayek, *Economic Freedom* (Oxford, UK: B. Blackwell, 1991), and Milton Friedman, *Capitalism and Freedom* (1962; Chicago: University of Chicago Press, 2002).

13. Harvey, *A Brief History*; Sabina Alkire and Angus Ritchie, "Winning Ideas: Lessons from Free-Market Economics," Oxford Poverty and Human Initiative Working Paper Series, Working Paper No. 6, http://www.ophi.org.uk/working-paper-number-06/, accessed November 12, 2010.

14. Francis Fukuyama, *State-Building: Governance and World Order in the 21st Century* (Ithaca, NY: Cornell University Press, 2004).

15. Leslie Schuld, "El Salvador: Anti-Privatization Victory," *NACLA Report on the Americas* 37, no. 1 (2003): 1; Asa Cristina Laurell, "Health Reform in Mexico: The Promotion of Inequalities," *International Journal of Health Services* 31 (2001): 291–321; Asa Cristina Laurell, *Mexicanos en Defensa de la Salud y la Seguridad Social: Como Garantizar y Ampliar tus Conquistas Históricas* (Mexico City: Editorial Planeta Mexicana, 2001); Celia Iriart, Emerson Merhy, and Howard Waitzkin, "Managed Care in Latin America: The New Common Sense in Health Policy Reform," *Social Science and Medicine* 52 (2001): 1243–1253.

16. The new "common sense" in health policy reform receives attention in Chapter 10.

17. Robinson, *A Theory of Global Capitalism.*

18. Harvey, *A Brief History.*

19. Korten, *When Corporations Rule the World,* p. 87.

20. Public Citizen, "The Medicare Drug War," www.citizen.org/documents/MedicareDrugWarReportREVISED72104.pdf, accessed November 12, 2010.

21. Richard J. Barnet and Ronald E. Mueller, *Global Reach: The Power of the Multinational Corporations* (New York: Simon & Schuster, 1974).

22. Walden Bello, *Dilemmas of Domination: The Unmaking of the American Empire* (New York: Metropolitan, 2005).

23. Barnet and Mueller, *Global Reach.*

24. Green, *Silent Revolution.*

25. Robinson, *A Theory of Global Capitalism.*

26. Ibid. Immanuel Wallerstein developed the theory of hegemonic economic and political power in "Three Hegemonies," in P. Karl O'Brien and Armand Clesse, eds., *Two Hegemonies: Britain 1846–1914 and the United States 1941–2001* (Aldershot, UK: Ashgate, 2002); *World-Systems Analysis: An Introduction* (Durham: Duke University Press, 2004); and *Alternatives: The U.S. Confronts the World* (Boulder, CO: Paradigm, 2004). For related analyses, see Jonathan Friedman and Christopher Chase-Dunn, eds., *Hegemonic Decline: Present and Past* (Boulder, CO: Paradigm, 2005).

27. Robinson, *A Theory of Global Capitalism,* pp. 101–103.

28. We use the term "civil society" in the following sense:

> Civil society refers to the arena of uncoerced collective action around shared interests, purposes and values. In theory, its institutional forms are distinct from those of the state, family and market, though in practice, the boundaries between state, civil society, family and market are often complex, blurred and negotiated. Civil society commonly embraces

a diversity of spaces, actors and institutional forms, varying in their degree of formality, autonomy and power. Civil societies are often populated by organisations such as registered charities, development non-governmental organisations, community groups, women's organisations, faith-based organisations, professional associations, trades unions, self-help groups, social movements, business associations, coalitions and advocacy group[s].
—London School of Economics, "What Is Civil Society?"
www.lse.ac.uk/collections/CCS/what_is_civil_society.htm, accessed June 26, 2010.

29. Michael Hardt and Antonio Negri, *Empire* (Cambridge, MA: Harvard University Press, 2000). Global circuits referred to the spatial routes that were traveled in this era of empire present: commercial/trade/corporative routes (Davos, Geneva, New York, London, Dubai, that is, the places where the International Monetary Fund, World Bank, World Trade Organization, etc., held their large meetings and summits), production and commercialization routes (these were somewhat different for different products, depending on whether they were agricultural, manufactured, etc.), and fashion routes (Paris, Milan, London, New York, etc.). See also Saskia Sassen, "Locating Cities on Global Circuits," *Environment and Urbanization* 14, no. 1 (2002): 13–30.

30. In the following paragraphs, we use the capitalized "Empire" when referring to Hardt and Negri's conceptualization.

31. Hardt and Negri, *Empire*, p. xxii.

32. Ibid., p. 15.

33. Ibid., pp. 24–27.

34. Ibid., p. 31.

35. Ibid., pp. 16–17, 34. Noam Chomsky has criticized such ideological justifications for war under empire present, for instance, in *Imperial Ambitions: Conversations on the Post-9/11 World* (New York: Metropolitan, 2005); *What We Say Goes: Conversations on U.S. Power in a Changing World* (New York: Metropolitan, 2005); and *Making the Future: The Unipolar Imperial Moment* (San Francisco: City Light Books, 2010).

36. Hardt and Negri, *Empire*, pp. 35–36.

37. Ibid., pp. 42–63.

Chapter 6

1. In this and later chapters, I use the past tense to refer to events and trends that arose during what I have called "empire present," lasting from about 1980 to 2010. For an overview of the issues analyzed in this chapter, see Ellen R. Shaffer, Howard Waitzkin, Rebeca Jasso-Aguilar, and Joseph Brenner, "Global Trade and Public Health," *American Journal of Public Health* 95 (2005): 23–34; and Howard Waitzkin, "Global Trade and Public Health [letter]," *American Journal of Public Health* 95 (2005): 192–193. Several other articles offer pertinent perspectives on these themes: Ted Schrecker, Ronald Labonte, and Roberto De Vogli, "Globalisation and Health: The Need for a Global Vision," *Lancet* 372 (2008): 1670–1676; David P. Fidler, Nick Drager, and Kelley Lee, "Managing the Pursuit of Health and Wealth: The Key Challenges," *Lancet* 373 (2009): 325–331; Kelley Lee, Devi Sridhar, and Mayur Patel, "Bridging the Divide: Global Governance of Trade and Health," *Lancet* 373 (2009): 416–422; Chantal Blouin, Mickey Chopra, and Rolph van der Hoeven, "Trade and Social Determinants of Health," *Lancet* 373 (2009): 502–507.

2. Ilona Kickbusch, "The Development of International Health Policies—Accountability Intact?" *Social Science & Medicine* 51 (2000): 979–989.

3. Lori Wallach and Patrick Woodall, *Whose Trade Organization?: A Comprehensive Guide to the WTO* (New York: New Press, 2004).

4. Nick Drager and Carlos Vieira, *Trade in Health Services: Global, Regional, and Country Perspectives* (Washington, DC: Pan American Health Organization, 2002).

5. Lori Wallach, "Accountable Governance in the Era of Globalization: The WTO, NAFTA, and International Harmonization of Standards," *University of Kansas Law Review* 50 (2002): 823–865.

6. Walden Bello, "Reforming the WTO Is the Wrong Agenda," in Kevin Danaher and Roger Burbach, eds. *Globalize This! The Battle Against the World Trade Organization and Corporate Rule* (Monroe, ME: Common Courage Press, 2000).

7. Wallach and Woodall, *Whose Trade Organization?*

8. Sarah Anderson, *Seven Years Under NAFTA* (Washington, DC: Institute for Policy Studies, 2003).

9. Carnegie Endowment for International Peace, *NAFTA's Promises and Realities: Lessons from Mexico for the Hemisphere* (Washington, DC: The Endowment, 2004).

10. Alejandro Nadal, Francisco Aguayo, and Marcos Chávez, "Los Siete Mitos del TLC: Lecciones para América Latina," *La Jornada* (Mexico City), http://colombia.indymedia.org/news/2003/11/7907.php, accessed November 12, 2010.

11. Núria Homedes and Antonio Ugalde, "Globalization and Health at the United States–Mexico Border," *American Journal of Public Health* 93 (2003): 2016–2022.

12. Those who initiated this provision justified it by citing a precedent in the realm of eminent domain, where governments compensated individuals and companies if property was seized to build public works like highways: Richard Epstein, *Takings: Private Property and the Power of Eminent Domain* (Cambridge, MA: Harvard University Press, 1985).

13. U.S. Department of State, "*Metalclad Corporation v. United Mexican States,*" www.state.gov/s/l/c3752.htm, accessed November 12, 2010; Michelle Sforza, "MAI and the Metalclad case," www.greenleft.org.au/1998/331/20498, accessed November 12, 2010.

14. William Greider, "The Right and U.S. Trade Law: Invalidating the 20th Century," *The Nation* 273 (2001): 21–29.

15. Coalition of Service Industries, "Response to Federal Register Notice of March 28, 2000: Solicitation of Public Comment for Mandated Multilateral Trade Negotiations on Agriculture and Services in the World Trade Organization and Priorities for Future Market Access Negotiations on Non-Agricultural Goods," www.uscsi.org/publications/papers/CSIFedReg2000.pdf, accessed November 12, 2010.

16. Karen Stocker, Howard Waitzkin, and Celia Iriart, "The Exportation of Managed Care to Latin America," *New England Journal of Medicine* 340 (1999): 1131–1136; Celia Iriart, Emerson Elias Merhy, and Howard Waitzkin, "Managed Care in Latin America: The New Common Sense in Health Policy Reform," *Social Sciences Medicine* 52 (2001): 1243–1253; Howard Waitzkin and Celia Iriart, "How the United States Exports Managed Care to Third World Countries," *Monthly Review* 52 (2000): 21–35.

17. Meredeth Turshen, *Privatizing Health Services in Africa* (New Brunswick, NJ: Rutgers University Press, 1999); Mohan Rao, ed., *Disinvesting in Health: The World Bank's Prescriptions for Health* (New Delhi: Sage, 1999).

18. World Trade Organization, "General Agreement on Trade in Services," www.wto.org/english/docs_e/legal_e/26-gats.doc, accessed November 12, 2010.

19. John Hilary, *The Wrong Model: GATS, Trade Liberalization and Children's Right to Health* (London, UK: Save the Children, 2001).

20. U.S. International Trade Commission, "U.S. Schedule of Commitments Under the General Agreement on Trade in Services," 1998, http://catalogue.nla.gov.au/Record/3825052, accessed November 12, 2010.

21. Rudolf Adlung and Antonia Carzaniga, "Health Services Under the General Agreement on Trade in Services," *Bulletin of the World Health Organization* 79 (2001): 352–364.

22. Trade Observatory, Institute for Agriculture and Trade Policy, "GATS Requests by State," www.citizen.org/documents/leaked_WTO_Service_requests.pdf, accessed November 12, 2010.

23. Office of the United States Trade Representative, "Trade Facts: Free Trade in Services," www.ustr.gov/sectors/services/2003–03–31-services-tradefacts.pdf, accessed April 8, 2010.

24. Trade Observatory, "GATS Requests by State."

25. Allyson M. Pollock and Dominique Price, "Rewriting the Regulations: How the World Trade Organisation Could Accelerate Privatisation in Health Care Systems," *Lancet* 356 (2000): 1995–2000; Allyson Pollock and Dominique Price, "The Public Health Implication of World Trade Negotiations on the General Agreement on Trade in Services and Public Services," *Lancet* 362 (2003): 1072–1075; Richard D Smith, Rupa Chanda, and Viroj Tangcharoensathien, "Trade in Health-Related Services," *Lancet* 373 (2009): 593–601; Nicholas Skala, "The Potential Impact of the World Trade Organization's General Agreement on Trade in Services on Health System Reform and Regulation in the United States," *International Journal of Health Services* 39 (2009): 363–387.

26. Richard D Smith, Carlos Correa, and Cecilia Oh, "Trade, TRIPS, and Pharmaceuticals," *Lancet* 373 (2009): 684–691.

27. Wallach and Woodall, *Whose Trade Organization?*; Stephen W. Schondelmeyer, *Economic Impact of GATT Patent Extension on Currently Marketed Drugs* (Minneapolis: PRIME Institute, College of Pharmacy, University of Minnesota, 1995).

28. George J. Annas, "The Right to Health and the Nevirapine Case in South Africa," *New England Journal of Medicine* 348 (2003): 750–754; David Barnard, "In the High Court of South Africa, Case No. 4138/98: The Global Politics of Access to Low-Cost AIDS Drugs in Poor Countries," *Kennedy Institute of Ethics Journal* 12 (2002): 159–174; Siripen Supakankunti, et al., "Impact of the World Trade Organization TRIPS Agreement on the Pharmaceutical Industry in Thailand," *Bulletin of the World Health Organization* 79 (2001): 461–470.

29. Editors, "Brazil Fights for Affordable Drugs Against HIV/AIDS," *Pan American Journal of Public Health* 9 (2001): 331–337.

30. World Trade Organization, General Council, "Implementation of Paragraph 6 of the Doha Declaration on the TRIPS Agreement and Public Health," www.wto.org/english/tratop_e/trips_e/implem_para6_e.htm, accessed November 12, 2010.

31. Doctors Without Borders, "Doha Derailed: A Progress Report on TRIPS and Access to Medicines," Cancún, Mexico, 2003, www.doctorswithoutborders.org/publications/reports/2003/cancun_report.pdf, accessed November 12, 2010; John H. Barton, "TRIPS and the Global Pharmaceutical Market," *Health Affairs* 23 (2004): 146–154; Amir Attaran, "How Do Patents and Economic Policies Affect Access to Essential Medicines in Developing Countries?" *Health Affairs* 23 (2004): 155–166; Smith, Correa, and Oh, "Trade, TRIPS, and Pharmaceuticals."

32. Ronald Labonte, "From the Global Market to the Global Village: 'Free' Trade, Health and the World Trade Organization," *Promotion et Education* 10, no. 1 (2003): 23–25, 33–39, 46; Nicolas Checa, John Maguire, and Jonathan Barney, "The New World Disorder," *Harvard Business Review* 81, no. 8 (2003): 70–79, 140; Richard D. Smith, Kelley Lee, and Nick Drager, "Trade and Health: An Agenda for Action," *Lancet* 373 (2009): 768–773.

33. Editors, "Brazil Fights for Affordable Drugs Against HIV/AIDS," *Pan American Journal of Public Health* 9 (2001): 331–337.

Chapter 7

1. World Bank, *World Development Report 1993: Investing in Health* (Washington, DC: World Bank, 1993).

2. Asa Cristina Laurell and Oliva López Arellano, "Market Commodities and Poor Relief: The World Bank Proposal for Health," *International Journal of Health Services* 26 (1996): 1–18;

Mohan Rao, ed., *Disinvesting in Health: The World Bank's Prescriptions for Health* (New Delhi: Sage, 1999); Meredeth Turshen, *Privatizing Health Services in Africa* (New Brunswick, NJ: Rutgers University Press, 1999).

3. Commission on Macroeconomics and Health. *Macroeconomics and Health: Investing in Health for Economic Development* (Geneva: World Health Organization, 2001).

4. Ibid., p. 1.

5. World Bank. *World Development Report 1993.*

6. Jeffrey Sachs, "The Report of the Commission on Macroeconomics and Health," presented at the annual meeting of the American Public Health Association, Atlanta, Georgia, 2001.

7. Commission, *Macroeconomics and Health,* p. 4.

8. Ibid., p. 57.

9. Ibid., p. 101.

10. Ibid., pp. 30–40.

11. Ibid., pp. 57–60.

12. Allyson M. Pollock and David Price, "Rewriting the Regulations: How the World Trade Organisation Could Accelerate Privatisation in Health-Care Systems," *Lancet* 356 (2000): 1995–2000; David Price, Allyson M. Pollock, and Jean Shaoul, "How the World Trade Organisation Is Shaping Domestic Policies in Health Care," *Lancet* 354 (1999): 1889–1892; Ellen R. Shaffer, Howard Waitzkin, Rebeca Jasso-Aguilar, and Joseph Brenner, "Global Trade and Public Health," *American Journal of Public Health* 95 (2005): 23–34.

13. Commission, *Macroeconomics and Health,* p. 7.

14. World Bank, *World Development Report 1993.*

15. World Health Organization, *World Health Report 2000* (Geneva: World Health Organization, 2000).

16. Commission, *Macroeconomics and Health,* p. 60.

17. Ibid., pp. 64–73.

18. Ibid., p. 6.

19. World Health Organization. *World Health Report 2000*; Julio Frenk and Felicia Knaul, "Health and the Economy: Empowerment through Evidence" (editorial on the *Report of the Commission on Macroeconomics and Health*), *Bulletin of the World Health Organization* 80 (2002): 88.

20. Thomas S. Bodenheimer and Kevin Grumbach, *Understanding Health Policy* (Stamford, CT: Appleton & Lange, 2009).

21. Karen Stocker, Howard Waitzkin, and Celia Iriart, "The Exportation of Managed Care to Latin America," *New England Journal of Medicine* 340 (1999): 131–136; Celia Iriart, Emerson Merhy, and Howard Waitzkin, "Managed Care in Latin America: The New Common Sense in Health Policy Reform," *Social Science & Medicine* 52 (2001): 1243–1253.

22. Stocker, Waitzkin, and Iriart, "The Exportation of Managed Care to Latin America."

23. Commission, *Macroeconomics and Health,* pp. 7, 12–13, 109.

24. James Tobin, *The New Economics, One Decade Older* (Eliot Janeway Lectures on Historical Economics in Honor of Joseph Schumpeter) (Princeton, NJ: Princeton University Press, 1974); Kavaljit Singh, *Taming Global Financial Flows: A Citizen's Guide* (New York: Zed Books, 2000).

25. Arguments for a Tobin tax to prevent market volatility include: Lawrence H. Summers and V. P. Summers, "When Financial Markets Work Too Well: A Cautious Case for a Securities Transactions Tax," *Journal of Financial Services Research* 3 (1989): 163–188; Paul Krugman, "Taxing the Speculators," *New York Times,* November 26, 2009, www.nytimes.com/2009/11/27/opinion/27krugman.html, accessed July 3, 2010. Perspectives on a Tobin tax as a method of global poverty reduction include: Duncan Green, "Tobin Tax Update: How Momentum Is Building for a Financial Transactions Tax," www.oxfamblogs.org/fp2p/?p=1589, accessed July 3, 2010; Robert

Lee, "Global Economists Call For Tobin Tax," www.tax-news.com/news/Global_Economists_Call_For_Tobin_Tax_41720.html, accessed July 3, 2010.

26. Commission, *Macroeconomics and Health*, p. 20.

27. Ibid., pp. 12–13, 103–108.

28. Vicente Navarro, "Assessment of the World Health Report 2000," *Lancet* 356 (2000): 1598–1601; Celia Almeida, et al., "Methodological Concerns and Recommendations on Policy Consequences of the *World Health Report 2000*," *Lancet* 357 (2001): 1692–1697.

29. Commission, *Macroeconomics and Health*, p. 21.

30. Ibid., p. 14.

31. Ibid., pp. 14–15.

32. Ibid., pp. 86–91.

33. Amir Attaran and Lee Gillespie-White, "Do Patents for Antiretroviral Drugs Constrain Access to AIDS Treatment in Africa?" *JAMA* 286 (2001): 1886–1892.

34. Richard Horton, "WHO: The Casualties and Compromises of Renewal," *Lancet* 359 (2002): 1605–1611; Editors, "Patently Robbing the Poor to Serve the Rich," *Lancet* 360 (2002): 885; David Wilson, Paul Cawthorne, Nathan Ford, and Saree Aongsonwang, "Global Trade and Access to Medicines: AIDS Treatments in Thailand," *Lancet* 354 (1999): 1893–1895.

35. Anne-Emanuelle Birn, "Gates's Grandest Challenge: Transcending Technology as Public Health Ideology," *Lancet* 366 (2005): 514–519; Anne-Emanuelle Birn, Yogan Pillay, Timothy H. Holtz, eds., *Textbook of International Health: Global Health in a Dynamic World* (New York: Oxford University Press, 2009), chapter 2.

Chapter 8

1. Eli Ginzberg and Miriam Ostow, "Managed Care—A Look Back and A Look Ahead," *New England Journal of Medicine* 336 (1997): 1018–1020.

2. John C. Lewis, "Latin American Managed Care Partnering Opportunities," presented to the Eighth Congress of the Association of Latin American Pre-Paid Health Plans (ALAMI), São Paulo, Brazil, November 8, 1996.

3. George Anders and Ron Winslow, "Turn for the Worse: HMOs' Woes Reflect Conflicting Demands of American Public," *Wall Street Journal*, December 22, 1997, p. A1.

4. Ibid.

5. Ibid.

6. Mary Jane Fisher, "Managed Care Plans Exit Medicare," *National Underwriter*, July 10, 2000, pp. 1–2; Laura McGinley and Ron Winslow, "Major HMOs to Quit Medicare Markets," *Wall Street Journal*, June 30, 2000, p. A2.

7. Rhonda L. Rundle, "Health Care Firms to Cut Medicare, Affecting More Than 500,000 Seniors," *Wall Street Journal*, September 24, 2001, p. B4.

8. Vicky Lankarge, "Medicare HMO Withdrawals in 2001: A State-by-State List of Pullouts," www.insure.com/articles/healthinsurance/medicare-drops-seniors.html, accessed November 12, 2010; see also: Haiden A. Huskamp, Deborah W. Garnick, Kristina W. Hanson, and Constance Horgan, "The Impact of Withdrawals by Medicaid Managed Care Plans on Behavioral Health Services," *Psychiatric Services* 52 (2001): 600–602.

9. Johanna Bennett and Laurie McGinley, "CIGNA Medicare-HMO Retreat May Signal Trend," *Wall Street Journal*, June 5, 2000, p. B2.

10. David Price, Allyson Pollock, and Jean Shaoul, "How the World Trade Organization Is Shaping Domestic Policies in Healthcare," *Lancet* 354 (1999): 1889–1892.

11. David Swafford, "A Healthy Trend," *Latin Finance*, December 1996; Roberto Cisneros, "International Benefits and Risk Management: Managed Care Makes Inroads in Latin America,"

Business Insurance, October 6, 1997; Editors, "Healthcare Dream for Insurers: Will Social Security Changes Lead to Major Surgery on the Medical System?" *Financial Times,* October 23, 1997.

12. Milt Freudenheim and Clifford Krauss, "Dancing to a New Healthcare Beat; Latin America Becomes Ripe for US Companies' Picking," *New York Times,* June 16, 1999.

13. Robert Kuttner, "Must Good HMOs Go Bad?" *New England Journal of Medicine* 338 (1998): 1558–1563, 1635–1639; William A. Glaser, "The Competition Vogue and Its Outcomes," *Lancet* 341 (1993): 805–812; Alan Jacobs, "Seeing the Difference: Market Health Reform in Europe," *Journal of Health Politics, Policy and Law* 23 (1998): 1–33.

14. Alain Enthoven, *Theory and Practice of Managed Competition in Health Care Finance* (Amsterdam: North Holland/Elsevier, 1988).

15. Howard Waitzkin, "The Strange Career of Managed Competition: Military Failure to Medical Success?" *American Journal of Public Health* 84 (1994): 482–489; Donald W. Light, "Lessons for the United States: Britain's Experience with Managed Competition," in John D. Wilkerson, Kelly J. Devers, and Ruth S. Given, eds., *Competitive Managed Care: The Emerging Health Care System* (San Francisco: Jossey-Bass, 1997).

16. Christoph Hermann, "The Marketization of Health Care in Europe," in Leo Panitch and Colin Leys, eds., *Morbid Symptoms: Health Under Capitalism* (New York: Monthly Review Press (*Socialist Register*), 2009). See also Maureen Mackintosh and Meri Koivusalo, eds., *Commercialization of Health Care: Global and Local Dynamics and Policy Responses* (New York: Palgrave Macmillan and United Nations Research Institute for Social Development, 2005).

17. The institutions and investigators participating in the World Health Organization–sponsored study of managed care in Latin America were the University of Buenos Aires, Argentina (Celia Iriart, Silvia Faraone, Marcela Quiroga, and Francisco Leone); the University of Campinas, Brazil (Emerson Elias Merhy and Florianita Coelho Braga Campos); the Group for Research and Teaching in Social Medicine (*Grupo de Investigación y Capacitación en Medicina Social*), Santiago, Chile (Alfredo Estrada, Enrique Barilari, Silvia Riquelme, Jaime Sepúlveda, Marilú Soto, and Carlos Montoya); the Center for Research and Consultation in Health (*Centro de Estudios y Asesoría en Salud*), Quito, Ecuador (Arturo Campaña, Jaime Breilh, Marcos Maldonado, and Francisco Hidalgo); and the University of New Mexico (Howard Waitzkin and Karen Stocker). The study's overall coordinators were Celia Iriart and Howard Waitzkin. An initial report on this work appeared in Karen Stocker, Howard Waitzkin, and Celia Iriart, "The Exportation of Managed Care to Latin America," *New England Journal of Medicine* 340 (1999): 1131–1136.

18. Louise Kertesz, "The New World of Managed Care," *Modern Healthcare* (November 1997): 114–120.

19. Swafford, "A Healthy Trend."

20. Kertesz, "The New World of Managed Care."

21. Celia Iriart, Francisco Leone, and Mario Testa, "Las Políticas de Salud en el Marco del Ajuste," *Cuadernos Médico Sociales* (Argentina) 70 (1995): 5–21.

22. Asociación Gremial de ISAPREs de Chile, *Las ISAPREs: Hacia la Modernidad en Salud* (Santiago, Chile: CIEDESS, 1996).

23. Michael Tangeman, "The Mañana Pension Bonanza," *Institutional Investor* 31, no. 2 (1997): 69–72.

24. Kertesz, "The New World of Managed Care"; J. Welsh, "Here's a Bunch of Doctors Willing to Make House Calls," *World Trade* 8, no. 11 (1995): 24–26.

25. Economic Commission for Latin America and the Caribbean, *Latin America and the Caribbean: Total Gross Domestic Product* (Santiago, Chile: CEPAL, 1997); Frederick Schmitt, "Aetna Stake Gives It Entree into Brazil's Life Insurance Market," *National Underwriter* 101, no. 7 (1997): 57.

26. Inter-American Development Bank, *Latin America After a Decade of Reforms: Economic and Social Progress, 1997 Report* (Washington, DC: Johns Hopkins University Press, 1997).

27. World Bank, *World Development Report 1993, Investing in Health* (Washington, DC: World Bank, 1993).

28. Asa Cristina Laurell and Oliva López, "Market Commodities and Poor Relief: The World Bank's Proposal for Health," *International Journal of Health Services* 26 (1996):1–18.

29. Celia Iriart, "La Reforma del Sector Salud en Argentina," in *Reforma en Salud: Lo Privado o lo Solidario* (Quito, Ecuador: Centro de Estudios y Asesoría en Salud, 1997).

30. Asociación Colombiana de la Salud, "Performance Evaluation of Public Hospitals Under a New Entrepreneurial Form," *Informing & Reforming, Newsletter of the International Clearinghouse of Health System Reform Initiatives* (Mexico City: ICHSRI, 1997), no. 4.

31. Manuel Guitián, *The Unique Nature of the Responsibilities of the IMF*, Pamphlet Series (Washington, DC: International Monetary Fund, 1992).

32. Kertesz, "The New World of Managed Care."

33. Ibid.

34. Stocker, Waitzkin, and Iriart, "The Exportation of Managed Care to Latin America."

35. Ibid.; Anthony J. McMichael and Robert Beaglehole, "The Changing Global Context of Public Health," *Lancet* 356 (2000): 495–499; Kasturi Sen and Meri Koivusalo, "Healthcare Reforms and Developing Countries—A Critical Overview," *International Journal of Health Planning and Management* 13 (1998): 199–215; Celia Iriart, Emerson E. Merhy, and Howard Waitzkin, "La Atención Gerenciada en América Latina: Transnacionalización de Sector Salud en un Contexto de la Reforma," *Cadernos Saúde Pública* (Brazil) 16 (2000): 95–105.

36. Francisco Armada, Carles Muntaner, and Vicente Navarro, "Health and Social Security Reforms in Latin America: The Convergence of the World Health Organization, the World Bank, and Transnational Corporations," *International Journal of Health Services* 31 (2001): 729–768.

37. Debra J. Lipson, "The World Trade Organization's Trade Agenda," *British Medical Journal* 323 (2001): 1139–1140; Simonetta Zarrilli, "Identifying a Trade-Negotiating Agenda," in *Trade in Health Services: Global, Regional, and Country Perspectives,* ed. Nick Drager and Carlos Vieira (Washington, DC: Pan American Health Organization, 2002).

38. Roberto Ceniceros, "Managed Care Makes Inroads in Latin America," *Business Insurance* October 6,1997, pp. 3–4, 6.

39. "Aetna International Sells Canadian Operations to Maritime Life," www.aetna.com/news/1999/pr_19990419b.htm, accessed July 3, 2010.

40. Catherine Smith, "Aetna Announces Letter of Intent to Form Joint Venture in Brazil with Sul America Seguros," www.thefreelibrary.com/Aetna+announces+letter+of+intent+to+form+joint+venture+in+Brazil+with ... -a019085449, accessed November 12, 2010.

41. Ceniceros, "Managed Care Makes Inroads in Latin America."

42. Swafford, "A Healthy Trend."

43. Kertesz, "The New World of Managed Care."

44. Swafford, "A Healthy Trend."

45. Ceniceros, "Managed Care Makes Inroads in Latin America."

46. Kertesz, "The New World of Managed Care."

47. "Fuente de las Empresas del Exxel Group," *Revista Noticias Editorial Perfíl* (Buenos Aires), December 8, 1997.

48. Hugo E. Arce, *Tendencias, Escenarios y Fenómenos Emergentes en la Configuración del Sector Salud en la Argentina* (Santiago, Chile: United Nations, Proyecto CEPAL/GTZ, 1997).

49. "Aetna Completes Sale of Financial Services and International Businesses to ING and Spinoff of Health Business to Its Shareholders," www.aetna.com/news/2000/pr_20001213b.htm, accessed July 3, 2010; "Aetna Announces Actions to Improve Profitability and Competitiveness," www.aetna.com/news/2000/pr_20001218.htm, accessed November 12, 2010.

50. CIGNA Corporation, "Form 10-K Submitted to the U.S. Securities and Exchange Commission for Fiscal Years 1998 and 1999," Lexis-Nexis Academic Universe: Business, accessed

December 15, 2002, www.panoramabrasil.com.br/por/noticia_completa.asp?p=conteudo/
txt/2002/02/08/20276478.htm&.2002, www.panoramabrasil.com.br/por/noticia_completa
.asp?p=conteudo/txt/2003/01/17/20644479.htm&.2003, accessed July 20, 2004.

51. Wharton School, "The Changing Face of Strategic Alliances in Latin America," www62
.homepage.villanova.edu/jonathan.doh/LA.alliances.pdf, accessed November 12, 2010.

52. Mark Sherman, "Medicare: In Shift, HMOs Plan to Cut Premiums, Enhance Benefits,"
Associated Press, February 1, 2004, http://news.google.com/newspapers?nid=1908&dat=
20040201&id=JQYxAAAAIBAJ&sjid=PuAFAAAAIBAJ&pg=5358,102782, accessed November
12, 2010.

53. Alfredo Estrada, Enrique Barilari, Jaime Sepúlveda, and Marisol Soto, *Atención Gerenciada en Chile: Informe Final* (Santiago, Chile: Centro de Investigación y Capacitación en Salud,
1998).

54. Celia Iriart, Francisco Leone, and Mario Testa, *Evaluación de los Hospitales Estatales de la
Provincia de Tierra del Fuego. Ushuaia* (Buenos Aires: Instituto de Servicios Sociales, 1995).

55. Celia Iriart, Silvia Faraone, and Francisco Leone, *Atención Gerenciada en Argentina:
Informe Final* (Buenos Aires: Universidad de Buenos Aires, 1998).

56. Ibid.

57. Estrada, Barilari, Sepúlveda, and Soto, *Atención Gerenciada en Chile.*

58. Ibid.

59. Francisco Hidalgo, "Reforma del Estado y Sociedad Civil en el Marco de Propuestas Alternativas," in *Reforma en Salud: lo Privado o lo Solidario* (Quito, Ecuador: Centro de Estudios y
Asesoría en Salud, 1997).

60. Emerson E. Merhy, *Atencão Gerenciada em Brasil: Relatório Final* (Campinas, Brazil:
Universidade Federal de Campinas, 1998).

Chapter 9

1. I am grateful to Rebeca Jasso-Aguilar and Angela Landwehr for their field observations
and interviews, in Mexico and Brazil, respectively, that contributed to this chapter.

2. Karen Stocker, Howard Waitzkin, and Celia Iriart, "The Exportation of Managed Care
to Latin America," *New England Journal of Medicine* 340 (1999): 1131–1136; Mohan Rao, ed.,
Disinvesting in Health: The World Bank's Prescriptions for Health (Newbury Park, CA: Sage, 1999);
World Health Organization, *World Health Report 2000* (Geneva, Switzerland: World Health Organization, 2000).

3. Jim Y. Kim et al., eds, *Dying for Growth: Global Inequality and the Health of the Poor*
(Monroe, ME: Common Courage Press, 2000).

4. Stocker, Waitzkin, and Iriart, "The Exportation of Managed Care to Latin America"; Celia
Iriart, Emerson E. Merhy, and Howard Waitzkin, "Managed Care in Latin America: The New
Common Sense in Health Policy," *Social Science and Medicine* 52 (2001): 1243–1253.

5. Allyson Pollock and David Price, "Rewriting the Regulations: How the World Trade Organization Could Accelerate Privatisation in Health Care Systems," *Lancet* 356 (2000): 1995–2000.

6. Asa Cristina Laurell, "Health Reform in Mexico: The Promotion of Inequality," *International Journal of Health Services* 31 (2001): 291–321.

7. Ibid.

8. World Bank, "Mexico: Country Strategy and Implementation Review Meetings (CISR)"
(summary minutes, manuscript) (Washington, DC: World Bank, 1995), cited in Asa Cristina
Laurell, "La Reforma del Estado y la Política Social en México," *Nueva Sociedad* 164 (December
1999): 146–158.

9. Asa Cristina Laurell, *Mexicanos en Defensa de la Salud y la Seguridad Social: Como*

Garantizar y Ampliar Tus Conquistas Históricas (Mexico City, Mexico: Editorial Planeta Mexicana, 2001).

10. World Bank, "Mexico: Country Strategy and Implementation Review Meetings (CISR)," p. 6.

11. Ibid., p. 7.

12. Laurell, "Health Reform in Mexico."

13. Scott Hensley, "Brazilian Healthcare at a Crossroads: Private Sector Flourishes as the Government Program Buckles Under Heavy Demand, Lack of Funding," *Modern Healthcare* (May 17, 1999): 34.

14. International Monetary Fund, "Brazil—Letter of Intent," Brazil Memorandum of Economic Policies, 1999, www.imf.org/external/np/loi/1999/070299.htm, accessed November 13, 2010.

15. Pan American Health Organization, "Brazilian General Situation and Trends: Country Health Profile," www.paho.org/English/SHA/prflBRA.htm, accessed November 13, 2010.

16. Brazil, *Lei 9,656/1998*, Senado Federal. Subsecretaria de Informações. Legislação, Lei dos Planos de Saúde, Regulamentação dos Planos Privados de Assistência à Saúde, 1998, www6.senado .gov.br/pesquisa/preparaPesquisaBasica.action?argumento=Lei+9%2C656%2F1998&executa=s, accessed November 13, 2010.

17. Hensley, "Brazilian Healthcare at a Crossroads," p. 34.

18. Gastão Wagner de Sousa Campos, *Reforma da Reforma: Repensando a Saúde,* 2nd ed. (São Paulo, Brazil: HUCITEC, 1997).

19. Brazil, *Lei 9,656/1998.*

20. André Cezar Médici, "A Dinâmica do Setor Saúde no Brasil. Transformações e Tendências nas Décadas de 80 e 90," *Cuadernos de la CEPAL* (Santiago, Chile: Naciones Unidas, 1997).

21. World Bank, *Investing in Health: World Development Report 1993* (Oxford: Oxford University Press, 1993); Emerson E. Merhy and Wanderly S. Bueno, "Organizações Sociais: Autonomia de Quem e para Que?" Faculdade de Ciências Médicas da Universidade de Campinas (UNICAMP), Campinas, Brazil, 1998, www.datasus.gov.br/cns/temas/OSreflex2.htm, accessed November 13, 2010.

22. Brazil, *Norma Operacional Básica do SUS—96* (Basic Operational Norm—96), Ministério da Saúde, Legislação, 1996, http://saude.teresina.pi.gov.br/legislacao/NOBSUS96.htm, accessed November 13, 2010.

23. Merhy and Bueno, "Organizações Sociais."

24. Further details about managed care organizations' penetration of the Brazilian market appear in Chapter 8.

25. Laurell, "Health Reform in Mexico."

26. Iriart, Merhy, and Waitzkin, "Managed Care in Latin America"; Stocker, Waitzkin, and Iriart, "The Exportation of Managed Care to Latin America"; Howard Waitzkin and Celia Iriart, "How the United States Exports Managed Care to Third World Countries," *Monthly Review* 52, no. 1 (2000): 21–35.

27. Francisco Armada, Carles Muntaner, and Vicente Navarro, "Health and Social Security Reforms in Latin America: The Convergence of the World Health Organization, the World Bank, and Transnational Corporations," *International Journal of Health Services* 31 (2001): 729–768.

28. World Bank, *Mexico Health System Reform* (Washington, DC: World Bank, 1998).

29. Laurell, "Health Reform in Mexico."

30. Ibid.

31. Ibid. For an account by the designers of the Mexican reform, see Julio Frenk, et al., "Comprehensive Reform to Improve Health System Performance in Mexico," *Lancet* 368 (2006): 1524–1534.

32. Laurell, "Health Reform in Mexico"; Laurell, *Mexicanos en Defensa de la Salud y la Seguridad Social.*

33. Eduardo da Silva Vas, "Implantação do Managed Care no Brasil," *Jornal da Associação Médica Brasileira* 42 (2001): 11, www.amb.org.br/teste/imprensa/jamb/jamb_2001_mai_jun.pdf, accessed November 13, 2010.

34. Caio Prates, "Planos de Saúde Podem Ter CPI," *O Estado de Sao Paulo,* http://economia.estadao.com.br/busca/Planos%20de%20Sa%C3%BAde%20podem%20ter%20CPI, accessed November 13, 2010.

35. Instituto Brasileiro de Geografia e Estatística, "Pesquisa Nacional por Amostra de Domicílios," 2002, www.ibge.gov.br/home/, accessed November 13, 2010.

36. CNS, Conselho Nacional de Saúde, Ministério da Saúde, "Relatório da Reunião da Comissão do CNS de Acompanhamento do Processo Orçamentário," http://conselho.saude.gov.br, accessed July 3, 2004.

37. Celia Almeida, Claudia Travassos, Silvia Porto, and Maria Eliana Labra, "Health Sector Reform in Brazil: A Case Study of Inequality," *International Journal of Health Services* 30 (2000): 129–162.

38. Estadão, "Retrocesso na Área de Saúde Suplementar," *O Estado de São Paulo,* August 15, 2001, http://www.irb-brasilre.com.br/cgi/clipping/internet/noticiasListar.cfm?dataBase=20010815, accessed November 13, 2010.

39. Laurell, "Health Reform in Mexico."

Chapter 10

1. By "ideology," I refer to the distinct ideas and ideals that characterize a specific social group and that become the basis of key political and economic policies. The theories of ideology that influenced the conceptualization of "common sense" in this chapter include: Karl Marx and Friedrich Engels, *The German Ideology* (1844–1845; Amherst, NY: Prometheus Books, 1998); Louis Althusser, "Ideology and Ideological State Apparatuses," in *Lenin and Philosophy and Other Essays* (New York: Monthly Review Press, 1971); and Slovoj Žižek, *The Sublime Object of Ideology* (London: Verso, 1989). This formulation also resembles Gramsci's exposition of "hegemony," referring to the dominant ideas during a specific historical period (Antonio Gramsci, *The Prison Notebooks* [1929–1935; New York: Columbia University Press, 2007]), as well as Bourdieu's theory of "doxa," referring to ideas about social reality that are taken for granted in any particular society (Pierre Bourdieu, *Outline of a Theory of Practice* [Cambridge: Cambridge University Press, 1977]).

I acknowledge the key roles that my colleagues, Celia Iriart and Emerson Elías Merhy, played in developing the notion of "common sense" in health policy. An earlier version of these themes appeared in Celia Iriart, Emerson Merhy, and Howard Waitzkin, "Managed Care in Latin America: The New Common Sense in Health Policy Reform," *Social Science & Medicine* 52 (2001): 1243–1253.

2. Emerson E. Merhy, *A Saúde Pública como Política* (São Paulo, Brazil: Editora Hucitec, 1992); Celia Iriart, Laura Nervi, Beatriz Olivier, and Mario Testa, *Tecnoburocracia Sanitaria: Ciencia, Ideología y Profesionalización* (Buenos Aires: Lugar Editorial, 1994).

3. O. P. Pedroso, "Informe del Consultor en Administración Hospitalaria," Buenos Aires, Organización Panamericana de la Salud, 1957; Comisión de Consultores, "Estudio de los Servicios de Salud Pública de la República Argentina," Buenos Aires, Organización Panamericana de la Salud, 1957.

4. Mario Testa, *Saber en Salud. La Construcción del Conocimiento* (Buenos Aires: Lugar Editorial, 1997).

5. Benjamin Coriat, *El Taller y el Robot: Ensayos sobre el Fordismo y la Producción en Masa en la Era de la Electrónica* (Mexico City: Siglo XXI Editores, 1992); Roberto Feletti and Claudio Lozano, *Reestructuración Capitalista y Endeudamiento Externo Latinoamericano* (Buenos Aires: Editora Instituto de Estudios sobre Estado y Participación IDEP/CTA, 1997).

6. Feletti and Lozano, *Reestructuración Capitalista y Endeudamiento Externo Latinoamericano*.

7. In this new context, we initiated a comparative investigation of health reforms, carried out by teams in Argentina, Brazil, Chile, Ecuador, and the United States. For information about the participating investigators and institutions, see Chapter 8, note 17.

8. Organización Panamericana de la Salud, *Nuevas Modalidades de Organización de los Sistemas y Servicios de Salud en el Contexto de la Reforma Sectorial: La Atención Gerenciada* (Washington, DC: OPS [HSP/SILOS-40], 1996); Emerson E. Merhy, Celia Iriart, and Howard Waitzkin, "Atenção Gerenciada: Da Micro-Decisão Corporativa à Micro-Decisão Administrativa, um Caminho Igualmente Privatizante?" in *Managed Care: Alternativas de Gestão em Saúde* (São Paulo: Editora PROAHSA/Editora Fundação Getulio Vargas, 1998), pp. 85–115; Rebeca Jasso-Aguilar, Howard Waitzkin, and Angela Landwehr, "Healthcare and Multinational Corporations in the United States and Latin America," *Harvard Health Policy Review* 9 (2008):158–172; Rebeca Jasso-Aguilar and Howard Waitzkin, "El Estado, las Multinacionales y la Medicina Contemporánea," *Palimpsestus* (Bogotá, Colombia, special issue on Ethics, Capitalism and Health), 2009.

9. L. C. Bresser Pereira, "Reforma Administrativa do Sistema de Saúde: Criação das Organizaçoes Sociais," Coloquio Técnico Previo a la XXV Reunión del Consejo Directivo del CLAD, Buenos Aires, 1995; Ministerio de Salud y Acción Social (Argentina), *Hospital Público de Autogestión* (Buenos Aires: Editora MSAS, 1997).

10. Howard Waitzkin, "El Dilema de la Salud en Estados Unidos: Un Programa Nacional de Salud o Libre Mercado," *Salud y Cambio* (Chile) 5, no. 15 (1994): 24–38; Howard Waitzkin and Jennifer Fishman, "Inside the System: The Patient-Physician Relationship in the Era of Managed Care," in *Competitive Managed Care: The Emerging Health Care System*, ed. John Wilkerson, Kelly Devers, and Ruth Given (San Francisco: Jossey-Bass, 1997), pp. 136–161.

11. In our interviews, such informants as an official of the World Bank's delegation in Argentina and a high official of the Ministry of Health and Social Action of that country expressed this viewpoint about silent reform.

12. During the mid-1990s, examples of executive decrees or regulations in Argentina included *Decreto 578/93, Creación del Hospital Público de Autogestión; Decretos 9/93, 576/93, 492/95, 1141/96, 1615/96, 638/97, 1301/97,* and in Brazil included *Normas Operacionais Básicas NOB 91, NOB 93, NOB 96, Medida Provisória N· 1591.* These decrees and regulations targeted privatization and deregulation of social security trust funds that applied to retirement benefits and health services.

13. Médicos Municipales, "Entrevista al Dr. Visillac, Presidente de la Asociación de Médicos Municipales," *Salud Para Todos* (Argentina) 3, no. 23 (1995): 25–26; "III Jornadas de Economía de la Salud. Mercado y Estado," *Salud Para Todos* (Argentina) 5, no. 25 (1997): 15–19.

14. "Informe de Coyuntura. El Plan Brady. Economía y Política Tras el Acuerdo Acreedor," Buenos Aires: Instituto de Estudios Sobre Estado y Participación, 1992; "Informe de Coyuntura. La Era Posbrady. Balance de una Etapa 1990/92," Buenos Aires: Instituto de Estudios Sobre Estado y Participación, 1993.

15. Daniel R. García Delgado, *Estado y Sociedad: La Nueva Relación a Partir del Cambio Estructural* (Buenos Aires: Editora Tesis, Grupo Editorial Norma S.A., 1994); Celia Iriart, Francisco Leone, and Mario Testa, "Las Políticas de Salud en el Marco del Ajuste," *Cuadernos Médico Sociales* (Argentina) 71 (1995): 5–21.

16. Celia Iriart, et al., "Normas de Descentralización para Establecimientos de Salud," in *Normas de Descentralización para Establecimientos de Salud* (Buenos Aires: Editora Ministerio de Salud y Acción Social [MSAS]/Editora PRONATASS, 1993), pp. 23–34; Celia Iriart and Francisco

Leone, "Descentralización en Salud," in *Normas de Descentralización para Establecimientos de Salud* (Buenos Aires: Editora MSAS/ Editora PRONATASS, 1993), pp. 5–16; Ministeristerio de Salud y Acción Social, *Programa de Reconversión de las Obras Sociales* (Buenos Aires: Editora MSAS, 1996); Kent Buse and Catherine Gwin, "The World Bank and Global Cooperation in Health: The Case of Bangladesh," *Lancet* 351 (1998): 665–669; Howard Waitzkin, Rebeca Jasso-Aguilar, and Celia Iriart, "Privatization of Health Services in Less Developed Countries: An Empirical Response to the Proposals of the World Bank and Wharton School," *International Journal of Health Services* 37 (2007): 205–227.

17. Asa Cristina Laurell, "La Salud: De Derecho Social a Mercancía," in *Nuevas Tendencias y Alternativas en el Sector Salud,* ed. Asa Cristina Laurell (Mexico City: Editora Universidad Autónoma Metropolitana Unidad Xochimilco/Editora Representación en México de la Fundación Friedrich Ebert), pp. 9–31; Testa, *Saber en Salud.*

18. Miguel Benasayag and Edith Charlton, *Esta Dulce Certidumbre de lo Peor: Para una Teoría Crítica del Compromiso* (Buenos Aires: Ediciones Nueva Visión, 1993).

19. Celia Iriart and Hugo Spinelli, "La Cuestión Sanitaria en el Debate Modernidad-Posmodernidad," *Cadernos de Saúde Pública* (Argentina) 10 (1994): 491–496; Miguel Benasayag, *Pensar la Libertad* (Buenos Aires: Ediciones Nueva Visión, 1996).

20. Benasayag and Charlton, *Esta Dulce Certidumbre de lo Peor.*

Chapter II

1. Several sources influenced this formulation of the social constructions by which stakeholders interpreted their efforts in trying to affect policies connecting trade and health: Peter L. Berger and Thomas Luckmann, *The Social Construction of Reality* (New York: Anchor, 1966); Murray Edelman, *The Symbolic Uses of Politics* (Urbana: University of Illinois Press, 1985); Murray Edelman, *Constructing the Political Spectacle* (Chicago: University of Chicago Press, 1988).

2. To clarify stakeholders' constructions, several colleagues and I conducted interviews and examined publicly available records in the United States and Latin America. I acknowledge the important contributions of Rebeca Jasso-Aguilar, Angela Landwehr, and Carolyn Mountain to this work. Further details appear in Howard Waitzkin, Rebeca Jasso-Aguilar, Angela Landwehr, and Carolyn Mountain, "Global Trade, Public Health, and Health Services: Stakeholders' Constructions of the Key Issues," *Social Science & Medicine* 61 (2005): 893–906.

3. U.S. Department of Health and Human Services, "Global Health," www.globalhealth. gov, accessed December 13, 2003. Over time, the official construction of this agency's policies evolved subtly, for instance, in the mission statement offered by the Office of Global Health Affairs, a branch of the U.S. Department of Health and Human Services: "To promote the health of the world's population by advancing the Secretary's and the Department of Health and Human Services' global strategies and partnerships, thus serving the health of the people of the United States." www.globalhealth.gov/office/index.html, accessed November 13, 2010. Prioritization of U.S. interests, by enhancing the health of the world's peoples, persisted in this latter statement.

4. Henry Kissinger, "The Basic Challenge Is That What Is Called Globalization Is Really Another Name for the Dominant Role of the United States," Lecture at Trinity College, Dublin, Ireland, cited in Sam Gindlin, "Social Justice and Globalization: Are They Compatible?" *Monthly Review* 54, no. 2 (2002): 1–11.

5. For more information about the methods of selecting interviewees and analyzing their responses, see Waitzkin, et al., "Global Trade, Public Health, and Health Services."

6. World Trade Organization Secretariat and World Health Organization, *WTO Agreements and Public Health: A Joint Study by the WHO and the WTO Secretariat* (Geneva, Switzerland: World Trade Organization, 2002); Francisco Armada, Carles Muntaner, and Vicente Navarro, "Health

and Social Security Reforms in Latin America: The Convergence of the World Health Organization, the World Bank, and Transnational Corporations," *International Journal of Health Services* 31 (2001): 729–768.

7. Nick Drager and Carlos Vieira, *Trade in Health Services: Global, Regional, and Country Perspectives* (Washington, DC: Pan American Health Organization, 2002); World Trade Organization Secretariat and World Health Organization, *WTO Agreements and Public Health*.

8. Berger and Luckmann, *The Social Construction of Reality*.

9. For another slant on such beliefs, see James Davison Hunter and Joshua Yates, "In the Vanguard of Globalization: The World of American Globalizers," in *Many Globalizations: Cultural Diversity in the Contemporary World,* ed. Peter L. Berger and Samuel P. Huntington (New York: Oxford University Press, 2002).

10. Adam Smith, *An Inquiry into the Nature and Causes of the Wealth of Nations* (1776; Oxford: Oxford University Press, 1976); Max Weber, *The Protestant Ethic and the Spirit of Capitalism* (1905; New York: Routledge, 2001). See also Peter L. Berger, "The Cultural Dynamics of Globalization," in *Many Globalizations: Cultural Diversity in the Contemporary World,* ed. Peter L. Berger and Samuel P. Huntington (New York: Oxford University Press, 2002).

11. Pierre Bourdieu, *Acts of Resistance: Against the Tyranny of the Market* (New York: New Press, 1998); *The Weight of the World: Social Suffering in Contemporary Societies* (Stanford, CA: Stanford University Press, 1999); *Firing Back: Against the Tyranny of the Market* (New York: New Press, 2003).

12. Edelman, *The Symbolic Uses of Politics*.

Chapter 12

1. Naomi Klein, *The Shock Doctrine: The Rise of Disaster Capitalism* (New York: Metropolitan, 2007).

2. Among many expressions of this theme, the work of Noam Chomsky over several decades has clarified the scope and dimensions of the problem: Noam Chomsky, *The Culture of Terrorism* (Boston: South End Press, 1988); *Power and Terror: Post-9/11 Talks and Interviews* (New York: Seven Stories Press, 2003); *What We Say Goes: Conversations on U.S. Power in a Changing World* (New York: Metropolitan, 2005). See also Noam Chomsky, Lois Meyer, and Benjamin Maldonado, *New World of Indigenous Resistance* (San Francisco: City Lights Publishers, 2010).

3. William Winkenwerder and Robert Galvin, "The Complex World of Military Medicine," *Health Affairs* W5 (Supplemental Web Exclusives) (2005): 353–360.

4. President's Commission on Care for America's Returning Wounded Warriors, *Serve, Support, Simplify: Final Report* (Washington, DC: The Commission, 2007); Institute of Medicine, *PTSD Compensation and Military Service* (Washington, DC: National Academies Press, 2007); Charles W. Hoge, Carl A. Castro, Stephen C. Messer, et al., "Combat Duty in Iraq and Afghanistan, Mental Health Problems, and Barriers to Care," *New England Journal of Medicine* 351 (2004): 13–22; Charles W. Hoge, Artin Terhakopian, Carl A. Castro, et al., "Association of Posttraumatic Stress Disorder with Somatic Symptoms, Health Care Visits, and Absenteeism Among Iraq War Veterans," *American Journal of Psychiatry* 164 (2007): 150–153; Charles S. Milliken, Jennifer L. Auchterlonie, and Charles W. Hoge, "Longitudinal Assessment of Mental Health Problems Among Active and Reserve Component Soldiers Returning from the Iraq War," *JAMA* 298 (2007): 2141–2148; Charles W. Hoge, Dennis McGurk, Jeffrey L. Thomas, et al., "Mild Traumatic Brain Injury in U.S. Soldiers Returning from Iraq," *New England Journal of Medicine* 358 (2008): 453–463.

5. Joseph Lieberman and Barbara Boxer, "Make Mental Health a Priority: When Service Members Go Untreated, the Entire Military Suffers," *Army Times* 68, no. 3 (2007): 42; Matthew J. Friedman, "Veterans' Mental Health in the Wake of War," *New England Journal of Medicine* 352

(2005): 1287–1290; "Posttraumatic Stress Disorder Among Military Returnees from Afghanistan and Iraq," *American Journal of Psychiatry* 163 (2006): 586–593; "Prevention of Psychiatric Problems Among Military Personnel and Their Spouses," *New England Journal of Medicine* 362 (2010): 168–170. See also Alyssa J. Mansfield, Jay S. Kaufman, Stephen W. Marshall, et al., "Deployment and the Use of Mental Health Services Among U.S. Army Wives," *New England Journal of Medicine* 362 (2010): 101–109; Troy Lisa Holbrook, Michael R. Galarneau, Judy L. Dye, et al., "Morphine Use After Combat Injury in Iraq and Post-Traumatic Stress Disorder," *New England Journal of Medicine* 362 (2010): 110–117.

6. The term "GI" here refers to active-duty personnel of any U.S. military service and military reserves. This term historically referred to low-ranked members of the U.S. Army. "GI" originally derived from equipment issued to military personnel ("galvanized iron," later misinterpreted as "government issue" or "general issue").

7. Richard J. Westphal, "A Discourse Analysis of Navy Leaders' Attitudes About Mental Health Problems" (PhD diss., University of Virginia, 2004), http://stinet.dtic.mil/oai/oai?verb= getRecord&metadataPrefix=html&identifier=ADA429820, accessed November 13, 2010.

8. Steven H. Miles, *Oath Betrayed: Torture, Medical Complicity, and the War on Terror* (New York: Random House, 2006); "Hippocrates and Informed Consent," *Lancet* 374 (2009): 1322–1323; *The Hippocratic Oath and the Ethics of Medicine* (New York: Oxford University Press, 2004).

9. Victor W. Sidel and Barry S. Levy, "The Roles and Ethics of Military Medical Care Workers," in *War and Public Health,* ed. Barry S. Levy and Victor W. Sidel (New York: Oxford University Press, 2008).

10. In addition to the Civilian Medical Resources Network, described in the following paragraphs, the Soldiers Project organized a network of psychotherapists who tried to respond to GIs' mental health needs: www.thesoldiersproject.org, accessed November 13, 2010.

11. I acknowledge the important roles of Marylou Noble and Darrin Kowitz in this work. See also: Howard Waitzkin and Marylou Noble, "Caring for Active Duty Military Personnel in the Civilian Sector," *Social Medicine/Medicina Social* 4 (2009): 56–69; and http://www.civilianmedicalresources.net/, accessed November 13, 2010.

12. GI Rights Hotline, 2009, www.girightshotline.org, accessed November 13, 2010; Military Law Task Force, National Lawyers Guild, 2009, www.nlgmltf.org, accessed November 13, 2010.

13. Waitzkin and Noble, "Caring for Active Duty Military Personnel in the Civilian Sector." Coordinators of the Network collected anonymous data concerning 112 consecutive clients who recently received services. These data were collected during the intake process, through information provided by the GI Rights Hotline counselors, and/or an initial conversation between the GI and a network coordinator. For some clients, clinicians provided additional confidential information. The network implemented more than the usual measures to protect clients, including procedures pertaining to informed consent and protection of anonymity through the delinking of all identifying data. Because many of the clients were Absent Without Leave (AWOL) and therefore subject to military prosecution, the network did not maintain identifying data in hard copy or electronic form that could be subject to subpoena or similar attempts by the U.S. government or other entities to obtain information.

14. Military professionals made similar observations: Oscar A. Cabrera, Charles W. Hoge, Paul D. Bliese, et al., "Childhood Adversity and Combat as Predictors of Depression and Post-Traumatic Stress in Deployed Troops," *American Journal of Preventive Medicine* 33 (2007): 77–82; Rachel Kimerling, Kristian Gima, Mark W. Smith, et al., "The Veterans Health Administration and Military Sexual Trauma," *American Journal of Public Health* 97 (2007): 2160–2166; Tyler C. Smith, Deborah L. Wingard, Margaret A. K. Ryan, et al., "Prior Assault and Posttraumatic Stress Disorder After Combat Deployment," *Epidemiology* 19 (2008): 505–512.

15. Studies of combat personnel from the United Kingdom and Canada reached similar

findings, especially among reservists: Tess Browne, Lisa Hull, Oged Horn, et al., "Explanations for the Increase in Mental Health Problems in UK Reserve Forces Who Have Served in Iraq," *British Journal of Psychiatry* 190 (2007): 484–489; Roberto J. Rona, Nicola T. Fear, Lisa Hull, et al., "Mental Health Consequences of Overstretch in the UK Armed Forces: First Phase of a Cohort Study," *BMJ* 335 (2007): 603; Matthew Hotopf, Lisa Hull, Nicola T. Fear, et al., "The Health of UK Military Personnel Who Deployed to the 2003 Iraq War: A Cohort Study," *Lancet* 367 (2006): 1731–1741.

16. Miles, *Oath Betrayed*; Jonathan H. Marks and Mark G. Bloche, "The Ethics of Interrogation—The U.S. Military's Ongoing Use of Psychiatrists," *New England Journal of Medicine* 359 (2008): 1090–1092; George G. Annas, "Military Medical Ethics—Physician First, Last, Always," *New England Journal of Medicine* 359 (2008): 1087–1090.

17. Yochi J. Dreazen, "Suicide Toll Fuels Worry That Army Is Strained," *Wall Street Journal,* November 3, 2009, http://online.wsj.com/article/SB125720469173424023.html, accessed November 13, 2010; Ann Scott Tyson, "Soldiers' Suicide Rate on Pace to Set Record," *Washington Post,* September 5, 2008, www.washingtonpost.com/wp-dyn/content/article/2008/09/04/AR2008090403333.html, accessed November 13, 2010.

18. Sarah Anderson, John Cavanagh, Chuck Collins, and Eric Benjamin, *Executive Excess 2006: 13th Annual CEO Compensation Survey* (Washington, DC, and Boston: Institute for Policy Studies and United for a Fair Economy, 2007), pp. 8–9, www.ips-dc.org/getfile.php?id=155, accessed November 13, 2010.

19. Joshua Kors, "How Specialist Town Lost His Benefits," *The Nation,* April 9, 2007, pp. 11–21; "Disposable Soldiers," *The Nation,* April 26, 2010), http://www.thenation.com/article/disposable-soldiers, accessed November 13, 2010.

20. Military researchers documented the limitations of screening for mental disorders before entry into military service: Charles W. Hoge, Holly E. Toboni, Stephen C. Messer, et al., "The Occupational Burden of Mental Disorders in the U.S. Military: Psychiatric Hospitalizations, Involuntary Separations, and Disability," *American Journal of Psychiatry* 162 (2005): 585–591; Hans Pols and Stephanie Oak, "War and Military Mental Health: The US Psychiatric Response in the Twentieth Century," *American Journal of Public Health* 97 (2007): 2132–2142.

21. Winter Soldier, *Iraq and Afghanistan,* http://ivaw.org/wintersoldier, accessed November 13, 2010.

Chapter 13

1. This chapter developed from a long-term study of Latin American social medicine and an attempt to bring this field to the attention of health workers, activists, and the general public outside Latin America. The study's methods included a review of books, journals, unpublished documents, and archives in Argentina, Brazil, Chile, Colombia, Cuba, Ecuador, and Mexico, as well as in-depth interviews with leaders of the field in those countries. I am indebted to many colleagues and friends who offered advice, participated in interviews, and provided examples of courage in pursuing social medicine despite threats to their safety for doing so. For more details, see: Howard Waitzkin, Celia Iriart, Alfredo Estrada, and Silvia Lamadrid, "Social Medicine in Latin America: Productivity and Dangers Facing the Major National Groups," *Lancet* 358 (2001): 315–323; and "Social Medicine Then and Now: Lessons from Latin America," *American Journal of Public Health* 91 (2001): 1592–1601; Howard Waitzkin, Celia Iriart, Holly Buchanan, Francisco Mercado, Jonathan Tregear, and Jonathan Eldredge, "The Latin American Social Medicine Database: A Resource for Epidemiology," *International Journal of Epidemiology* 37 (2008): 724–728. See also Debora Tajer, "Latin American Social Medicine: Roots, Development During the 1990s, and Current Challenges," *American Journal of Public Health* 93 (2003): 2023–2027.

2. Howard Waitzkin, "Is Our Work Dangerous? Should It Be?" *Journal of Health and Social Behavior* 39 (1998): 7–17. The following accounts came from respondents' narratives during in-depth interviews in the above research on Latin American social medicine. These interviews took place during the mid-1990s.

3. Max Weber, *Max Weber on Capitalism, Bureaucracy, and Religion*, ed. Stanislav Andreski (Boston: Allen & Unwin, 1983).

4. George Rosen, *De la Política Médica a la Medicina Social* (Mexico City: Siglo XXI, 1985); Michel Foucault, "El Nacimiento de la Medicina Social," *Revista Centroamericana de Ciencias de la Salud* (San José, Costa Rica) 3, no. 6 (1977): 89–108; Saúl Franco and Everardo D. Nunes, "Presentación," in Saúl Franco, Everardo Nunes, Jaime Breilh, and Cristina Laurell, eds., *Debates en Medicina Social* (Quito, Ecuador: Organización Panamericana de la Salud, 1991).

5. Rudolf Virchow, *Gesammelte Abhandlungen aus dem Gebiet der Oeffentlichen Medicin und der Seuchenlehre* (Berlin: Hirschwald, 1879), and *Letters to His Parents, 1839 to 1864* (Canton, MA: Science History Publications, 1990). See also Chapter 2.

6. María Angélica Illanes,"*En el Nombre del Pueblo, del Estado y de la Ciencia, … ": Historia Social de la Salud Pública, Chile 1880–1973* (Santiago, Chile: Colectivo de Atención Primaria, 1993).

7. Elizabeth Fee and Theodore M. Brown, *Making Medical History: The Life and Times of Henry E. Sigerist* (Baltimore: Johns Hopkins University Press, 1997); Dorothy Porter, *Health, Civilization, and the State: A History of Public Health from Ancient to Modern Times* (London: Routledge, 1999), and "How Did Social Medicine Evolve, and Where Is It Heading?" *PLoS Medicine* 3 (2006): e399.

8. Salvador Allende, *La Realidad Médico-Social Chilena* (Santiago, Chile: Ministerio de Salubridad, 1939).

9. Mirta Z. Lobato and Adriana Álvarez, *Política, Médicos y Enfermedades: Lecturas de la Historia de la Salud en la Argentina* (Buenos Aires, Argentina: Editorial Biblos, 1996); Marcos Cueto, ed., *Salud, Cultura y Sociedad en América Latina* (Washington, DC: Organización Panamericana de la Salud–Instituto de Estudios Peruanos, 1996); Gilberto Hochman, *Aprendizado e Difusão na Constituição de Políticas: A Previdência Social e seus Técnicos* (Rio de Janeiro, Brazil: Instituto Universitário de Pesquisas do Rio de Janeiro, 1987); Eduardo Estrella, Antonio Crespo, and Doris Herrera, *Desarrollo Histórico de las Políticas de Salud en el Ecuador, 1967–1995* (Quito, Ecuador: Proyecto Análisis y Promoción de Políticas de Salud, 1997); Marcos Cueto, *El Regreso de las Epidémias: Salud y Sociedad en el Perú del Siglo XX* (Lima, Peru: Instituto de Estudios Peruanos, 1997); Anne-Emanuelle Birn, "Skirting the Issue: Women and International Health in Historical Perspective," *American Journal of Public Health* 89 (1999): 399–407; Anne-Emanuelle Birn and Armando Solórzano, "Public Health Policy Paradoxes: Science and Politics in the Rockefeller Foundation's Hookworm Campaign in Mexico in the 1920s," *Social Science & Medicine* 49 (1999): 1197–1213.

10. E. Richard Brown, *Rockefeller Medicine Men* (Berkeley: University of California Press, 1979); Marcos Cueto, ed., *Missionaries of Science: The Rockefeller Foundation and Latin America* (Bloomington: Indiana University Press, 1994); Saúl Franco-Agudelo, "The Rockefeller Foundation's Antimalarial Program in Latin America: Donating or Dominating?" *International Journal of Health Services* 13 (1983): 51–67.

11. Franco and Nunes, "Presentación"; Debora Tajer, "La Medicina Social Latinoamericana en los Años Noventa: Hechos y Desafíos," in *ALAMES en la Memoria: Selección de Lecturas*, ed. Franciso Rojas Ochoa and Miguel Márquez (Havana, Cuba: Editorial Caminos, 2009).

12. Wim Dierckxsens, *Capitalismo y Población: La Reproducción de la Fuerza de Trabajo Bajo el Capital* (San José, Costa Rica: Editorial Universitaria Centroamericana, 1979); Raúl Rojas Soriano, *Capitalismo y Enfermedad* (Mexico City: Folios Ediciones,1982), and *Sociología Médica* (Mexico City: Folios Ediciones, 1983).

13. Friedrich Engels, *Dialectics of Nature* (New York: International, 1940); Richard Levins and Richard Lewontin, *The Dialectical Biologist* (Cambridge, MA: Harvard University Press, 1985).

14. Jaime Breilh, "Componente de Metodología: La Construcción del Pensamiento en Medicina Social," in Franco, Nunes, Breilh, and Laurell, eds., *Debates en Medicina Social*.

15. Marcos Buchbinder, "Rol de lo Social en la Interpretación de los Fenómenos de Salud y Enfermedad en la Argentina," *Salud, Problema y Debate* (Buenos Aires, Argentina) 2, no. 4 (1990): 37–50.

16. Juan B. Justo, *Teoría y Práctica de la Historia* (Buenos Aires, Argentina: La Vanguardia, 1933).

17. Che Guevara, "The Dilemma of What to Dedicate Myself To," in *Venceremos! The Speeches and Writings of Ernesto Che Guevara*, ed. John Gerassi (London: Weidenfeld & Nicholson, 1968).

18. Che Guevara, "The Revolutionary Doctor," in Gerassi, ed., *Venceremos!*; Gordon Harper, "Ernesto Guevara, M.D.: Physician-Revolutionary Physician-Revolutionary," *New England Journal of Medicine* 281 (1969): 1285–1289.

19. Francisco Lynch Guevara, personal communication, Buenos Aires, Argentina, 1995.

20. Eugenio Espejo, *Voto de un Ministro Togado de la Audiencia de Quito* (Quito, Ecuador: Comisión Nacional de Conmemoraciones Cívicas, 1994).

21. Pablo Arturo Suárez, *Contribución al Estudio de las Realidades entre las Clases Obreras y Campesinas* (Quito, Ecuador: Imprenta Fernández, 1934).

22. Ricardo Paredes, *Oro y Sangre en Portocavelo* (Quito, Ecuador: Editorial Artes Gráficas, 1938).

23. Julie M. Feinsilver, *Healing the Masses: Cuban Health Politics at Home and Abroad* (Berkeley: University of California Press, 1993); Howard Waitzkin, Karen Wald, Romina Kee, Ross Danielson, and Lisa Robinson, "Primary Care in Cuba: Low- and High-Technology Developments Pertinent to Family Medicine," *Journal of Family Practice* 45 (1997): 250–258. See also Chapter 3.

24. Howard Waitzkin and Hilary Modell, "Medicine, Socialism, and Totalitarianism: Lessons from Chile," *New England Journal of Medicine* 291 (1974): 171–177; Paul B. Cornely, et al., "Report of the APHA Task Force on Chile," *American Journal of Public Health* 67 (1977): 71–73. See also Chapter 3.

25. Richard Garfield, *Health Care in Nicaragua: Primary Care Under Changing Regimes* (New York: Oxford University Press, 1992); Richard M. Garfield, Thomas Frieden, and Sten H. Vermund, "Health-Related Outcomes of War in Nicaragua," *American Journal of Public Health* 77 (1987): 615–618.

26. Frei Betto and Fidel Castro, *Fidel and Religion: Castro Talks on Revolution and Religion with Frei Betto* (New York: Simon & Schuster, 1987).

27. Camilo Torres, *Revolutionary Priest: The Complete Writings and Messages* (New York: Random House, 1971).

28. Paulo Freire, *Pedagogy of the Oppressed* (New York: Herder and Herder, 1970).

29. Nilson do Rosario Costa, "Transición y Movimientos Sociales: Contribuciones al Debate de la Reforma Sanitaria," *Cuadernos Médico Sociales* (Rosario, Argentina) 44 (1988): 51–61.

30. Paulo Freire, *Pedagogy of Freedom: Ethics, Democracy, and Civic Courage* (Lanham, MD: Rowman & Littlefield, 1998).

31. Nina Wallerstein and Edward Bernstein, "Empowerment Education: Freire's Ideas Adapted to Health Education," *Health Education Quarterly* 15 (1988): 379–394; Raúl Magaña, et al., "Una Pedagogia de Concientización para la Prevención del VIH/SIDA," *Revista Latino Americana de Psicología* 24, no. 1–2 (1992): 97–108.

32. Juan César García, *La Educación Médica en la América* (Washington, DC: Organización Panamericana de la Salud, 1972); *La Investigación en el Campo de la Salud en Once Países de*

la América Latina (Washington, DC: Organización Panamericana de la Salud, 1982); *La Mortalidad de la Niñez Temprana Según Clases Sociales* (Medellín, Colombia: Universidad Pontífica Bolivariana, 1979); "The Laziness Disease," *History and Philosophy of the Life Sciences* 3, no. 1 (1981): 31–59.

33. A. Mier, *La Nacionalización de los Servicios de Salud: La Organización Sanitaria en los Países Latinoamericanos, 1880–1930* (Washington, DC: private distribution, 1975).

34. Franco, Nunes, Breilh, and Laurell, *Debates en Medicina Social.*

35. Jaime Breilh, "Componente de Metodología: La Construcción del Pensamiento en Medicina Social," in Franco, Nunes, Breilh, and Laurell, *Debates en Medicina Social*; Asa Cristina Laurell, "Social Analysis of Collective Health in Latin America," *Social Science & Medicine* 28 (1989): 1183–1191.

36. Antonio Gramsci, *The Prison Notebooks* (1929–1935; New York: Columbia University Press, 2007).

37. Costa, "Transición y Movimientos Sociales"; Saúl Franco, "Tendencias de la Medicina Social en América Latina," in *Actualización en Medicina Social*, ed. Jaime Sepúlveda et al. (Santiago, Chile: GICAMS, 1989).

38. Asa Cristina Laurell, "Trabajo y Salud: Estado del Conocimiento," in Franco, Nunes, Breilh, and Laurell, eds., *Debates en Medicina Social*; Márquez & Ochoa, eds., *ALAMES en la Memoria.*

39. Jaime Breilh, *Epidemiología: Economía, Medicina y Política* (Mexico City: Fontamara, 1989).

40. Jaime Breilh, *Género, Poder y Salud* (Quito, Ecuador: Centro de Estudios y Asesoría en Salud, 1993); Doris Acevedo, "Mujer, Trabajo y Salud: Una Orientación" in Ochoa and Marquéz, eds., *ALAMES en la Memoria* (1994 [2009]); Yolanda Arango Panesso, "La Promoción de Salud y el Autocuidado: Qué Dicen las Mujeres desde sus Propios Saberes," in Ochoa and Márquez, eds., *ALAMES en la Memoria* (1994 [2009]).

41. As in Chapter 10, by "ideology" I refer to the distinct ideas and ideals that characterize a specific social group and that become the basis of key political and economic policies. For sources, see note 1 of that chapter.

42. Mabel Grimberg, "Programas, Actores y Prácticas Sociales: Encuentros y Desencuentros entre Antropología y Políticas de Salud," *Salud y Cambio* (Santiago, Chile) 3, no. 9 (1992): 6–18.

43. Jaime Breilh and Edmundo Granda, "La Epidemiología en la Forja de una Contrahegemonía," *Salud Problema* (Mexico City) 11 (1986): 25–40; and "Epidemiología y Contrahegemonía," *Social Science & Medicine* 28 (1989): 1121–1127.

44. Asa Cristina Laurell, "Mortality and Working Conditions in Agriculture in Underdeveloped Countries," *International Journal of Health Services* 11 (1981): 3–20.

45. Asa Cristina Laurell and Oliva López Arellano, "Market Commodities and Poor Relief: The World Bank Proposal for Health," *International Journal of Health Services* 26 (1996): 1–18; Karen Stocker, Howard Waitzkin, and Celia Iriart, "The Exportation of Managed Care to Latin America," *New England Journal of Medicine* 340 (1999): 1131–1136; Celia Iriart, Emerson Merhy, and Howard Waitzkin, "Managed Care in Latin America: The New Common Sense in Health Policy Reform," *Social Science & Medicine* 52 (2001): 1243–1253.

46. Asa Cristina Laurell, "La Salud-Enfermedad como Proceso Social," *Revista Latinoamericana de Salud* (Mexico City) 2 (1982): 7–25; Saúl Franco, "La Cuestión de la Causalidad en Medicina," in Grupo de Trabajo, *Desarrollo de la Medicina Social en America Latina* (Mexico City: Organización Panamericana de la Salud, 1989).

47. Juan Samaja, "La Triangulación Metodólogca: Pasos para una Comprensión Dialéctica de la Combinación de Métodos," in Ochoa and Marquéz, eds., *ALAMES en la Memoria* (1992 [2009]).

48. Asa Cristina Laurell, et al., "Disease and Rural Development: A Sociological Analysis of

Morbidity in Two Mexican Villages," *International Journal of Health Services* 7 (1977): 401–423; Jaime Breilh, Edmundo Granda, Arturo Campaña, and Oscar Betancourt, *Ciudad y Muerte Infantil* (Quito, Ecuador: Ediciones CEAS, 1983).

49. Jaime Breilh, *Nuevos Conceptos y Técnicas de Investigación* (Quito, Ecuador: Centro de Estudios y Asesoría en Salud, 1995); Alexis J Handal, et al., "Occupational Exposure to Pesticides During Pregnancy and Neurobehavioral Development of Infants and Toddlers," *Epidemiology* 19 (2008): 851–859.

50. Stocker, Waitzkin, and Iriart, "The Exportation of Managed Care to Latin America"; Iriart, Merhy, and Waitzkin, "Managed Care in Latin America"; Celia Iriart, "La Reforma del Sector Salud en Argentina: De la Salud como Derecho Social a Bien Público a Responsabilidad Individual y Bien de Mercado," in Centro de Estudios y Asesoría en Salud, *Reforma en Salud: Lo Privado o lo Solidario* (Quito, Ecuador: CEAS, 1997); Jaime Breilh, "Reforma: Democracia Profunda, No Retroceso Neoliberal," in Centro de Estudios y Asesoría en Salud, *Reforma en Salud*; Emerson Merhy, Celia Iriart, and Howard Waitzkin, "Atenção Gerenciada: Da Micro-Decisão Corporativa à Micro-Decisão Administrativa, um Caminho Igualmente Privatizante?" in *Managed Care: Alternativas de Gestão em Saúde* (São Paulo, Brazil: Editora PROAHSA/Editora Fundação Getulio Vargas, 1998).

51. Mario Testa, *Saber en Salud: La Construcción del Conocimiento* (Buenos Aires, Argentina: Lugar Editorial, 1997); Leticia Artiles Visbal, "Marco Antropológico 'Generalizado' como Herramienta de Aplicación de las Determinantes Sociales en la Práctica Social," in Ochoa and Marquéz, eds., *ALAMES en la Memoria* (2007 [2009]).

52. Colectivo CEAS, *Mujer, Trabajo y Salud* (Quito, Ecuador: Ediciones CEAS, 1994); Oscar Betancourt, *La Salud y el Trabajo* (Quito, Ecuador: Centro de Estudios y Asesoría en Salud y Organización Panamericana de la Salud, 1995); Handal, "Occupational Exposure to Pesticides During Pregnancy and Neurobehavioral Development of Infants and Toddlers."

53. Breilh, "Componente de Metodología"; *Nuevos Conceptos y Técnicas de Investigación*.

54. Naomar de Almeida Filho, *Epidemiología sin Números* (Washington, DC: Organización Panamericana de la Salud, 1992).

55. Asa Cristina Laurell, "The Role of Union Democracy in the Struggle for Workers' Health in Mexico," *International Journal of Health Services* 19 (1989): 279–293; Laurell, et al., "Disease and Rural Development: A Sociological Analysis of Morbidity in Two Mexican Villages."

56. Colectivo CEAS, *Mujer, Trabajo y Salud*; Betancourt, *La Salud y el Trabajo*.

57. Sonia Montecino, "Madres Niñas, Madresolas, Continuidad o Cambio Cultural?" *Salud y Cambio* (Santiago, Chile) 4, no. 11 (1993): 6–8.

58. Túlio Franco, Wanderlei Silva Bueno, and Emerson Merhy, "O Acolhimento e os Processos de Trabalho em Saúde: O Caso de Betim, Minas Gerais, Brasil," *Cadernos de Saúde Pública* (Rio de Janeiro) 15, no. 2 (1999): 345–353.

59. Saúl Franco, "International Dimensions of Colombian Violence," *International Journal of Health Services* 30 (2000): 163–185; "A Social-Medical Approach to Violence in Colombia," *American Journal of Public Health* 93 (2003): 2032–2036.

60. Alfredo Estrada, Mónica Hering, and Andrés Donoso, *Familia, Género y Terapia: Una Experiencia de Terapia Familiar Sistémica* (Santiago, Chile: Ediciones CODEPU, 1997).

61. Ignacio Martín-Baró, *Writings for a Liberation Psychology* (Cambridge, MA: Harvard University Press, 1994); "La Violencia en Centroamérica: Una Visión Psicosocial," *Salud, Problema y Debate* (Buenos Aires, Argentina) 2, no. 4 (1990): 53–66; Alicia Stolkiner, "Tiempos "Posmodernos": Ajuste y Salud Mental," in *Políticas en Salud Mental*, ed. Hugo Cohen, et al. (Buenos Aires, Argentina: Lugar Editorial, 1994); Alicia Stolkiner, "Human Rights and the Right to Health in Latin America: The Two Faces of One Powerful Idea," *Social Medicine* 5 (2010): 58–63.

Chapter 14

1. In this chapter, as in Chapter 5, Rebeca Jasso-Aguilar participates as a co-author, reflecting our long-term collaboration.

2. Observations in the sections on El Salvador, Bolivia, and Mexico derive from the participatory field work of Rebeca Jasso-Aguilar and the sources cited below.

3. Union of Workers of the Salvadoran Institute of Social Security (*Sindicato de Trabajadores del Instituto Salvadoreño del Seguro Social*, STISSS), "Chronology of the Movement," San Salvador, El Salvador, 2002; Leslie Schuld, "El Salvador: Who Will Have the Hospitals?" *NACLA Report on the Americas* 36, no. 3 (2003): 42–45.

4. Schuld, "El Salvador: Who Will Have the Hospitals?"

5. Sindicato Médico de Trabajadores del Instituto Salvadoreño del Seguro Social (SIMETRISSS), "Historical Agreement for the Betterment of the National Health System," San Salvador, El Salvador, 2002.

6. STISSS, "Chronology of the Movement."

7. Ibid.

8. SIMETRISSS, "Historical Agreement for the Betterment of the National Health System."

9. STISSS, "Chronology of the Movement"; SIMETRISSS, "Historical Agreement for the Betterment of the National Health System."

10. Leslie Schuld, "El Salvador: Anti-Privatization Victory," *NACLA Report on the Americas* 37, no. 1 (2003): 1.

11. Maude Barlow, *Blue Covenant: The Global Water Crisis and the Coming Battle for the Right to Water* (Toronto: McClelland & Stewart, 2009).

12. Carmen Peredo, Carlos Crespo, and Omar Fernández, *Los Regantes de Cochabamba en la Guerra del Agua* (Cochabamba, Bolivia: Centro de Estudios Superiores Universitarios de la Universidad Mayor de San Simón, 2004); William Assies, "David vs. Goliath in Cochabamba: Los Derechos del Agua, el Neoliberalismo, y la Renovación de la Protesta Social en Bolivia," *Revista Tinkazos* 4, no. 8 (2001): 106–131.

13. Alberto García Orellana, Fernando García Yapur, and Herbas Luz Quiton, *La Guerra del Agua, Abril de 2000: La Crisis de la Política en Bolivia* (La Paz, Bolivia: Fundación PIEB, 2003).

14. Peredo et al., *Los Regantes de Cochabamba en la Guerra del Agua*; García et al., *La Guerra del Agua, Abril de 2000*.

15. García et al., *La Guerra del Agua, Abril de 2000*; Oscar Olivera, *Cochabamba! Water War in Bolivia* (Cambridge, MA: South End Press, 2004).

16. *Monitor* archival television footage. *Monitor* is a news monitoring organization in Cochabamba that keeps archival television news for public consultation.

17. Assies, "David vs. Goliath in Cochabamba"; Roberto Cardozo, "A Donde Vas Democrácia?" *Cuarto Intermedio* (Cochabamba) 55 (May 2000): 64–89.

18. Cardozo, "A Donde Vas Democrácia?"

19. Ibid.; Assies, "David vs. Goliath in Cochabamba."

20. Raquel Gutiérrez Aguilar, *Los Ritmos del Pachakuti: Levantamiento y Movilización en Bolivia (2000–2005)* (Mexico City: Bajo Tierra Ediciones, Sísifo Ediciones, 2009).

21. Howard Waitzkin, Celia Iriart, Alfredo Estrada, and Silvia Lamadrid, "Social Medicine in Latin America: Productivity and Dangers Facing the Major National Groups," *Lancet* 358 (2001): 315–323; Howard Waitzkin, Celia Iriart, Alfredo Estrada, and Silvia Lamadrid, "Social Medicine Then and Now: Lessons from Latin America," *American Journal of Public Health* 91 (2001): 1592–1601; Asa Cristina Laurell, "What Does Latin American Social Medicine Do When

It Governs? The Case of the Mexico City Government," *American Journal of Public Health* 93 (2003): 2028–2031. For more on Latin American social medicine, see Chapter 13.

22. Constitución Política de los Estados Unidos Mexicanos, www.constitucion.gob.mx, accessed November 13, 2010.

23. Laurell, "What Does Latin American Social Medicine Do When It Governs?"; Asa Cristina Laurell, "Interview with Dr. Asa Cristina Laurell," *Social Medicine* 2, no. 1 (2007): 46–55; Asa Cristina Laurell, "Health Reform in Mexico City, 2000–2006," *Social Medicine* 3, no. 2 (2008): 145–157.

24. Laurell, "Health Reform in Mexico City."

25. Laurell, "What Does Latin American Social Medicine Do When It Governs?"

26. Ibid.

27. Ibid.

28. Laurell, "Health Reform in Mexico City."

29. Ibid.

30. Laurell, "Interview with Dr. Asa Cristina Laurell."

31. Laurell, "Health Reform in Mexico City"; Julio Frenk et al., "Comprehensive Reform to Improve Health System Performance in Mexico," *Lancet* 368 (2006): 1524–1534.

32. Laurell, "Interview with Dr. Asa Cristina Laurell."

33. Carles Muntaner, et al., "Venezuela's Barrio Adentro: Participatory Democracy, South-South Cooperation and Health Care for All," *Social Medicine* 3 (2008): 232–246; Charles Briggs and Clara Mantini-Briggs, "Confronting Health Disparities: Latin American Social Medicine in Venezuela," *American Journal of Public Health* 99 (2009): 549–555.

34. For a helpful comparative overview of national health programs in Europe and elsewhere, see T. R. Reid, *The Healing of America: A Global Quest for Better, Cheaper and Fairer Health Care* (New York: Penguin, 2009).

35. A summary and major components of the U.S. health reform legislation appear in "Understanding the Patient Protection and Affordable Care Act," www.healthcare.gov/law/introduction/index.html, accessed November 13, 2010. For information about Obama's switch from single-payer to market-oriented principles and the campaign contributions that supported this conversion, see: "Barack Obama on Single Payer in 2003," www.pnhp.org/news/2008/june/barack_obama_on_sing.php, accessed November 13, 2010; Brad Jacobson, "Obama Received $20 Million from Healthcare Industry in 2008 Campaign," *The Raw Story*, http://mlyon01.wordpress.com/2010/01/13/obama-received-20-million-from-healthcare-industry-in-2008-campaign/, accessed November 13, 2010.

36. Steffie Woolhandler, Terry Campbell, and David U. Himmelstein, "Costs of Health Care Administration in the United States and Canada," *New England Journal of Medicine* 349 (2003): 768–775.

37. Physicians for a National Health Program, "Single-Payer National Health Insurance," www.pnhp.org/facts/single_payer_resources.php, accessed November 13, 2010.

38. Western Pennsylvania Coalition for Single-Payer Healthcare, "Single-Payer Poll, Survey, and Initiative Results," www.wpasinglepayer.org/PollResults.html, accessed November 13, 2010; Healthcare-Now, "Another Poll Shows Majority Support for Single-Payer," www.healthcare-now.org/another-poll-shows-majority-support-for-single-payer, accessed November 13, 2010.

39. White House, "The Obama Plan: Stability and Security for All Americans," www.whitehouse.gov/issues/health-care, accessed November 17, 2009.

40. "Health Bill Leaves 23 Million Uninsured," http://pnhp.org/news/2010/march/pro-single-payer-doctors-health-bill-leaves-23-million-uninsured, accessed November 13, 2010.

41. Steffie Woolhandler, Benjamin Day, and David U. Himmelstein, "State Health Reform Flatlines," *International Journal of Health Services* 38 (2008): 585–592.

42. Reid, *The Healing of America*; Thomas S. Bodenheimer and Kevin Grumbach, *Understanding Health Policy: A Critical Approach* (Stamford, CT: Appleton & Lange, 2009).

43. Howard Waitzkin, Rebeca Jasso-Aguilar, and Celia Iriart, "Privatization of Health Services in Less Developed Countries: An Empirical Response to the Proposals of the World Bank and Wharton School," *International Journal of Health Services* 37 (2007): 205–227.

44. Physicians for a National Health Program, "Single-Payer National Health Insurance"; Healthcare-Now, "Organizing for a National Single-Payer Healthcare System," www.healthcare-now.org, accessed November 13, 2010; Howard Waitzkin, "Clarifying What a Single-Payer National Health Program Is and Is Not—and How It Differs from a 'Public Option': Selling the Obama Plan: Mistakes, Misunderstandings, and Other Misdemeanors," *American Journal of Public Health* 100 (2010): 398–400.

45. http://en.wikiquote.org/wiki/Winston_Churchill, accessed November 13, 2010; http://refspace.com/quotes/america, accessed November 13, 2010; http://www.nytimes.com/1998/04/17/world/clinton-urges-latin-america-to-be-patient-on-free-trade.html; http://www.businessinsider.com/steve-keen-crisis-deflation-2010-11, accessed November 13, 2010.

46. Membership in the alternative trade agreements was current as of November 2010.

47. These electoral victories were current as of November 2010. In Chile, a conservative candidate, Sebastián Piñera, gained the presidency in March 2010 by a narrow margin, after progressive President Michelle Bachelet, whose popular support was 84 percent at the end of her term, according to polls, could not run due to a constitutional two-term limit. Bachelet did not rule out a presidential candidacy in 2014. www.nasdaq.com/aspx/stock-market-news-story.aspx?storyid=201003090924dowjonesdjonline000277&title=chile-president-bachelet-maintains-84-approval-after-earthquake—poll, accessed November 13, 2010.

48. Naomi Klein, *The Shock Doctrine: The Rise of Disaster Capitalism* (New York: Metropolitan, 2007).

49. Vladimir Ilyich Lenin, *Imperialism, the Highest Stage of Capitalism: A Popular Outline* (1917; Moscow: Progress Publishers, 1963). The following quotations come from chapters 1, 3, 7, and 10. More recent, highly nuanced sources that recall many of Lenin's predictions include: Immanuel Wallerstein, *Decline of American Power: The U.S. in a Chaotic World* (New York: New Press, 2003) and *Alternatives: The U.S. Confronts the World* (Boulder, CO: Paradigm, 2004); Chalmers Johnson, *Blowback: The Costs and Consequences of American Empire* (New York: Henry Holt, 2004); *The Sorrows of Empire: Militarism, Secrecy, and the End of the Republic* (New York: Metropolitan Books, 2004); *Nemesis: The Last Days of the American Republic* (New York: Metropolitan Books, 2006); and Johan Galtung, *The Fall of the US Empire—And Then What?* (Basel, Switzerland: Transcend University Press, 2009).

50. John Bellamy Foster, "The Financialization of Capital and the Crisis," *Monthly Review* 59, no. 4 (April 2008): 1–19; John Bellamy Foster and Fred Magdoff, *The Great Financial Crisis: Causes and Consequences* (New York: Monthly Review Press, 2009).

51. Pierre Bourdieu, *Against the Tyranny of the Market* (London: Verso, 2003).

52. William Robinson, *A Theory of Global Capitalism: Production, Class, and State in a Transnational World* (Baltimore: John Hopkins University Press, 2004).

Index

academic medical centers, 33–35, 37
activism, and public health, 15–16, 111. *See also* advocacy groups
addiction, drug, 19
advocacy groups, 140–142, 143, 144. *See also* activism, and public health
Aetna, 101, 103, 106, 108, 109, 117
Afghanistan, troops in, 146–154
Agency for International Development, U.S., 99
Agreement on Application of Sanitary and Phyto-Sanitary Standards (SPS), 74, 75*t*
Agreement on Technical Barriers to Trade (TBT), 74, 75*t*, 84*t*
Agreement on Trade-Related Aspects of Intellectual Property Rights (TRIPS), 74, 75*t*, 83*t*, 137–138; advocacy groups on, 140–142; and pharmaceuticals, 80–81, 96
Aguas del Tunari, 175, 175–177, 177
AIDS (acquired immune deficiency syndrome): International Fund for AIDS, 97; medications, 75*t*, 81, 83*t*, 96, 140
alcoholism, 11, 19
Alianza Bolivariana para los Pueblos de Nuestra

América (Bolivarian Alliance for the Peoples of Our America, ALBA), 186–189
Alianza Republicana Nacionalista (ARENA, Republican Nationalist Alliance), 172, 173
Allende, Salvador, 9–10, 21–22, 43–44, 44, 46–47, 159–160, 163, xi–xii; *La Realidad,* 16–21, 23–24, 160, xii–xiii; suicide, 157
Alma-Ata declaration, 92
Althusser, Louis, 166
American Association of Health Plans (AAHP), 99, 101
American College of Cardiology, 36, 41–42
American Heart Association, 36, 37
American International Group (AIG), 107
American Optical Company, 30, 31, 32, 34; links to academic centers, 34
Amil company, 108
Antigua and Barbuda, 186
Argentina, 66, 99, 104, 105, 106, 109, 109–110, 186, xiii; consultation reports, 195*t*, 123; debt burden, 126; under dictatorship, 158; health research, 169; ideology, of privatization, 128; privatization of healthcare, 185; social

medicine, history of, 161–162
Armada, Francisco, 180
Association of Latin American Pre-Paid Health Plans, 100
Australia, 99
Autonomous Metropolitan University, Xochimilco, Mexico City, 164

Bachelet, Michelle, 219n. 47
Balanced Budget Act of 1997, 101
Balmaceda, José Manuel, 157
banana republics, 6
bank bailouts, of 2008, 65
Bay of Pigs, 54–55
Bechtel Corporation, 175
Benasayag, Miguel, 129–130
Berlin, cholera outbreak, 14–15
Bernal, Freddy, 181
Betto, Frei, 163
Bismarck, Otto von, 182
black lung, 13
Bolivia, 187, xiii; resistance to privatization of water in, 174–177
Bourdieu, Pierre, 144, 188–189
Brazil, 99, 106, 109, 116–117, xiii; 1998 Health Plans Law, 120; adult literacy, 164; health research, 169; liberation theology, 163; privatization of healthcare, 120–121, 121; resistance, to managed care, 111,

ABOUT THE AUTHOR

Howard Waitzkin is Distinguished Professor at the University of New Mexico. He also practices medicine as a primary care practitioner in rural northern New Mexico. His work focuses on social conditions that lead to illness, unnecessary suffering, and early death. Dr. Waitzkin's previous books include *The Second Sickness: Contradictions of Capitalist Health Care*; *The Politics of Medical Encounters: How Patients and Doctors Deal With Social Problems*; and *At the Front Lines of Medicine: How the Health Care System Alienates Doctors and Mistreats Patients . . . And What We Can Do About It.*